MW00656934

LITSCAPES
COLLECTED US WRITINGS 2015

LITSCAPES

COLLECTED US WRITINGS 2015

EDITED BY CAITLIN M. ALVAREZ & KASS FLEISHER

STEERAGE PRESS

See Page 455 for additional copyright and permissions information

Production Manager: Jane L. Carman, Codirector, Publications Unit
Department of English, Illinois State University
Guest Editors: Marion Sakaluk, Mike Shier, Julie Tran
Editorial and Production Consultant: Joe Amato

Cover design by Marion Sakaluk and Mike Shier

This project was completed with the generous support
of the Publications Unit, Department of English
at Illinois State University

Paperback edition:
ISBN-10: 0983632685
ISBN-13: 978-0-9836326-8-9

Kindle edition:
ISBN-10: 0983632693
ISBN-13: 978-0-9836326-9-6

~ STEERAGE PRESS ~
steeragepress.com
Normal, Illinois

As long as mixed grills and combination salads are popular, anthologies will undoubtedly continue in favor.

Elizabeth Janeway

CONTENTS

COLLECTED US WRITINGS 2015

WILLIAM ALLEGREZZA

if the disbelieving eyes could see

or be stable,
then action would necessarily
dissipate under the spell
of decision,
for we are collecting
a scattered people without
selves who search for
anything that can really
happen visually (we can
trick our imagined spaces
into being). ourselves—the
design of what
we can handle understood through
water eyes in motion
by those who value use
though the beautiful is
enough on its own—our collection
read below
our own filters,
seen as boxed without
the borders.

consider our direction misdirection

i have replaced the old words
with what can be, can be:
 old with sold. sold with bold--
 a replaying of a substitution game,
 like a switching of shells so that
 we forget which path was chosen
 for us.

and yes, i understand the sorting of layers,
the tides to be parted and assume we'll
have difficulty in stepping away.

still, our construction is a variation
 as light in words opening,
 a hand expanding beyond the view.
 (we must read beneath the goal
 for action.)

conform

any
deviation from
listening is temporary

 our
 participation was
 quite widely engaged

concern
is doubtful
at any rate

 we
 attempted to
 reject the cyclone

the
institution has
a popular history

we
wanted to
break the language

i
heard the
sounds at dawn.

the dance

the
dance. broken
the dance. we

laugh
though we
know the dance.

broken.
the dance
and me; listen,

we
know no
forward, but we

are
content with
the dance as

we
dance just
now so slowly.

from *STILL. WALK.*

am self here◌ voice◌
catalogue◌ i to chance◌ the
regular motion◌ thing not un-
derstandable as usual◌ am
re seeing◌ unavoidable◌ to
explore what is only memory
now◌ still walk ing◌ only
still◌ the repeat◌ i could◌
but now, no change◌ just mo-
tion◌ am self here◌ to explore
what is not◌ just move◌ keep
motion◌ thing not
understandable then, now
typical◌ am syntax◌ to
reverse◌ for myself◌ if i
remember◌ only memory◌ un-
avoid able◌ no change◌ just
motion◌ the re peat◌ i am re-
seeding◌ a room in light◌ no
light now◌ the warm food, the
feel of touch◌ just voice◌ self◌
what is not is memory◌
streets◌ trees◌ without
change or growth, still life◌
unavoidable memory◌ the
sun◌ a guide◌ in that, the
only same◌ to continue
unrecognizable◌ not spirit in
triumph◌ just motion◌ but
now, no change◌ thing not typ-
ical◌ to reverse◌ the feel of
touch◌ the bird, oh happy bird,
on a limb◌ the journey, just
footprints◌ following the
roads for food◌ with map◌ al-
ways somewhere to stop◌

a list◌ gathered
into a pack◌ a bicycle◌ my
continuation◌ this, my nation◌

as stillness◌ have become◌ this motion◌ without response◌ voice◌ i will leave these words wherever i go in case i return◌ if this continues◌ i cannot run out of that which will sustain◌ if i have been here before◌ i have not taken all◌ still◌ no change◌ and what am i to say to myself◌ here◌ i scratched this here◌ i hid this paper, but i only mark us as having been in the no time◌ present◌

undenying am this place below i◌ walk through i◌ transit◌ belief in sign◌ nation am distinctly i driven nothing to find again◌ myself with conversation◌ this a place◌ alone◌ circle this◌ words◌ to parts◌ cohesion need no i◌ whom for?

no history now◌ in each place, i can explore what was◌ why? to people stillness◌

in time, i'll replace the words just to play◌ numbers perhaps first (2 nation◌ 1 2 5 7 words◌ 1◌ 6 relapse◌ 1 2 just still◌ 6 sadness◌ just here◌ 8◌ 1 walk◌ nothing all◌) then other languages◌ then mixed languages◌ syntax◌ with no other, no difference◌ all will be left for me to puzzle out in some distant place◌

and you—even if a you were here—would not understand◌̲

such frustration in not having to do◌̲ no do, no be◌̲ situation mark, though i am still—i move and speak◌̲

will the words change with time for me alone?

ROBERT ARCHAMBEAU

THE POEM THAT DOES NOT EXIST

The poem that does not exist walks into a bar.
"Knock knock," it says, to get to the other side.
The poem that does not exist is all you can eat
driving through the drive thru.

The poem that does not exist "falls upon the thorns of life,"
it reads.
The poem that does not exist as distiches
shops for its organic form at the organic farm.

The poem that does not exist exits,
but it's the wrong exit. Fucking GPS.
Anxious that it has missed its audience,
the poem that does not exist loops back to line one to start again,

but, finding a volta in a cup holder just when it needs one,
hurls the coin at the toll basket & turns away.

CHARLES BERNSTEIN

HIGH TIDE AT RACE POINT

for Norman Fischer

A commercial with no pitch.
A beach without sand.
A lover without a love.
A surface without an exterior.
A touch without a hand.
A protest without a cause.
A well without a bottom.
A sting without a bite.
A scream without a mouth.
A fist without a fight.
A day without an hour.
A park with no benches.
A poem without a text.
A singer with no voice.
A computer without memory.
A cabana without a beach.
A bump with no road.
A sorrow without a loss.
A goal without a purpose.
A noise without sound.
A story without a plot.
A sail without a boat.
A plane without wings.
A pen without ink.
A murder without a victim.
A sin without a sinner.
An agreement without terms.
A spice with no taste.
A gesture without motion.
A spectator without view.

A slope without a curve.
A craving without a desire.
A volume without dimension.
A Nazi without a Jew.
A comic without a joke.
A promise without a hope.
A comforter without the comfort.
The certainty without being sure.
Stealing with nothing stolen.
The might have beens without the was.
Mishnah without Torah.
The two without the one.
The silken without the silk.
The inevitable without necessity.
Logic without inference.
Suddenness without change.
A canyon without depth.
Fume without smell.
Determination with no objective.
Gel without cohesion.
A cure without a disease.
A disease without a trace.
A mineral without a shape.
A line without extension.
Persistence without intention.
Blank without emptiness.
Border without division.
A puppet without strings.
Compliance without criteria.
A disappointment without an expectation.
Color without hue.
An idea without content.
Grief with no end.

THE LIE OF ART

I don't want innovative art.
I don't want experimental art.
I don't want conceptual art.
I don't want abstract art.
I don't want figurative art.

I don't want original art.
I don't want formal art.
I don't want emotional art.
I don't want nostalgic art.
I don't want sentimental art.
I don't want complacent art.
I don't want erotic art.
I don't want boring art.
I don't want mediocre art.
I don't want political art.
I don't want empty art.
I don't want baroque art.
I don't want mannered art.
I don't want minimal art.
I don't want plain art.
I don't want vernacular art.
I don't want artificial art.
I don't want pretentious art.
I don't want idea art.
I don't want thing art.
I don't want naturalistic art.
I don't want rhetorical art.
I don't want dull art.
I don't want rhapsodic art.
I don't want rigid art.
I don't want informal art.
I don't want celebratory art.
I don't want cerebral art.
I don't want formulaic art.
I don't want sardonic art.
I don't want sadistic art.
I don't want masochistic art.
I don't want trendy art.
I don't want adolescent art.
I don't want senescent art.
I don't want grumpy art.
I don't want happy art.
I don't want severe art.
I don't want demanding art.
I don't want tempestuous art.
I don't want incendiary art.

I don't want commercial art.
I don't want moralizing art.
I don't want transgressive art.
I don't want violent art.
I don't want exemplary art.
I don't want uplifting art.
I don't want degrading art.
I don't want melancholy art.
I don't want chaotic art.
I don't want provocative art.
I don't want self-satisfied art.
I don't want nurturing art.
I don't want genuine art.
I don't want derivative art.
I don't want religious art.
I don't want authentic art.
I don't want sincere art.
I don't want sacred art.
I don't want profane art.
I don't want mystical art.
I don't want voyeuristic art.
I don't want traditional art.
I don't want expectable art.
I don't want hopeful art.
I don't want irreverent art.
I don't want process art.
I don't want static art.
I don't want urban art.
I don't want pure art.
I don't want ideological art.
I don't want spontaneous art.
I don't want pious art.
I don't want comprehensible art.
I don't want enigmatic art.
I don't want epic art.
I don't want lyric art.
I don't want familiar art.
I don't want alien art.
I don't want human art.

R. M. BERRY

3. EVENT

When I recall my separation, I don't think I knew what happened to me at the time. After all, I suffered the event; I didn't watch. Still, suffering feels like knowledge, too, I mean afterwards, though not any you could claim or, if others doubted, show. There are scars, I suppose. Every division leaves marks, even long since grown over, but that's the part of me it happened to, a bond with my old surroundings, and so exactly what, if I know at all, I'm still trying to discover. As I said, there was this glare, a flatness unrelieved, and then on the surface droplets. My picture's stark, each time the same, all barrenness and washed out color, and although beyond me, its recurrence is how I'm sure. Projecting particulars, trying to see there taking place, never gets me any closer. I reimagine my descent, come to a full stop, and then approaching the highpoint, almost on the level, everything dissolves. Before, which meant nothing before, the within I for lack of other call myself seemed boundless, an outpouring into all without, or so I reconstruct it, and the point where, had I reflected, I would've located my object, felt indescribably close. However, the arc of downfall makes a circle, and only its near side is lighted, so when I write *boundless* or *without* or *point,* I don't mean as now, am yielding to just what obscure plot I can never tell. No, what's constant is this resonance, the echo in my box. My object eludes me. Still, a picture hardly amounts to nothing, and even if I couldn't have watched in the first place, merely suffered the event belatedly, from wherever this glare, flatness, moisture come back, well, that's where my knowledge must be.

Divided now, I picture all that follows clear as day, the baked tints and harsh refraction, each whitening shade. Not that any aftermath's essential. Its pieces come trailing God's own mayhem, aren't parts. Even boxed, my past's incomplete, but only recollected does what happened ever occur to me, and by then, the whole's in thirds: an it, the surroundings, my picture. A fourth and fifth will come later, but they represent further decline. Assuming the accustomed stance, I revisit my first meanderings, the randomness, confusion, each of my former being's turns, but nearing the full stop, there at my banishment's outset, I inevitably reverse direction and, repeating what once came so naturally, look ahead. At my back must stretch an immeasurable distance. More than that, I can't say. I haven't started narrating yet, try not to reflect, but peering down the arc, I see all my future mishaps and feel sure the event's behind me. This access of color, my outline's disturbance, each uprearing angle, edges racing away, it's a kind of memory, not just in myself, but there without me, as though my separation had been violent, even if unfelt, a brutal casting out. None of which seems puzzling. No, the wonder's slower to come home. I picture my surface, the pale folds I've named flesh, these salts forming, water, and amid brilliance, austere blanching, a limb. But then, I ask, where's my predicament, where's the heat? Suffering's no enigma, not even unforeseen. The puzzle's what's missing, the point of past violence, my suffering's place. I don't need to add that seeing's not everything. Strictly speaking, I'm struck dumb, breathless, and can recall an uproar, oppressive odor, jolt, all without projecting per se. But heat allows no distance, which is its peculiar terror, and despite the long decline since, after everything's hard and lined, when I try to envision before before, well, the glare seems unavoidable. If I knew what I mean, I'd call my picture scalding. It melts. Is that the scar? Whenever I say *there was*, a picture's what was. The event's the there.

I watch it now, my abandoned part lurching off, its body upright, free-standing. Under the light, an outcrop appears, some opacity or earthen mass, and this detachment, this bare it, navigates around. Vapors seep, entanglements loom. Whatever can move of itself, I'm persuaded, is the past's animation, my former holding sway. It assigns toward and back, alongside and retreating. This whole surrounding gets parsed. Water becomes its water, salt its salt. I watch, and whatever's manifest, whatever's outjutting, first belongs, though at an instant I feel beside myself again, can hardly tell one thing from another. For no mistaking, when heat comes, it doesn't accumulate, doesn't amass, scarcely stirs. It consumes, and that's the enigma, or perhaps an engima's what this arc has made of it, for heat's entire, as though it were my beginning, my former plenitude all over. I don't picture heat. I succumb. At the full stop, imagining what's behind me, I sense the event's recurrence, a violence my origin perpetuated. Every wound comes back, either time-healed or decomposing. Before myself again, caught in the act, where's the point of recounting? But heat dissolves all questions. I pass into forgetfulness.

4. YOU

But enough about beginnings. My immediate object remains, just as always, with you. *Life* lies, they said, or some such, right here. To dream, despite this box, that more's still to come, that one day my odds could even. I know anticipating's futile, but how does a body stop? I mean, if the soul were unfettered, so to speak, wants boundless and differences no matter, would this meandering now, my so-called subject, would even its echo reach you? I've tried. Never think I haven't tried. I've imagined you nearby, an abundance of musk, forehead as cool as clay, the pinking of one nipple. And if I no longer dilate on your eyes, it's merely that, even within, self-possession has its limits, but how to believe, miserably provisioned as I am—a voice, this box, some pictures—that another being could feel touched? Of course, the possibility isn't lost on me that you're no longer you, and I'm, to acknowledge the obvious, abstracted. I don't mean inside, it goes without saying, but as all would have it, transparently, so that, if I could rise above my adversity, transcend this present situation, I might see how I'm circumstanced in truth. Here within, of course, I could never tell or stop trying, but overlooking myself there without, perhaps I'd know peace.

Does that sound like rationalizing? Anyway, I recall no moment when I wasn't trying to recount, either for you or some approximation, the story of my enclosure, how being without—*life*, they said, or life*like*—became this now. Of course, if you were only you in the first place after a fashion, growing by intervals more detached, as much from our past as me, then my story, as though the margin possessed your lips, were composed as slenderly, with that same gaze, square shoulders, your amber hair...I will go mad, mad. To imagine this lack, everything's upstart, the darkness, violence, to imagine it unimagined, your absence absent, as though I'd simply been deposited here by mistake. No, dream that no one's without, that your semblance doesn't hear, that beyond these sides lies rubble, mayhem, purest devastation, well, nightmares have been tolerated before and will be tolerated much longer, but, please, never say this absence wasn't you, that your silence hasn't been pronounced. How to explain further? Even nothing comes to an end somewhere.

As I began, I was trying to account for my limitations, hoping for who knows how long to renew contact, to feel you inside, all despite the vagaries of minutes, measures, intervals, when the stillness grew discouraging. Between resonating into space and keeping everything bottled, what was the difference? I started to waver between interminable periods, those infernal outpourings hopeless of punctuation, and mutterings so bland that pandemonium sounded richer. Unless I could locate you, if nowhere I knew, then past calculation, I felt I must establish some distance. This far, I tried to tell myself, or this, remarking each withdrawal with a line. One disturbance, of course, no matter how slight, would've brought me back. The relief of still experiencing your hold on me! But all to no account. I felt like a child who, given its way, finds no way its own. If I could never feel you there, if I couldn't tell I wasn't just reverberating, then I feared I would never tell anything again.

Well, I came to myself in time. Who knows how? For longer than I care to think I remained inert, the captive of longings, when one morning—or, if morning in a box sounds fanciful, then whenever it dawned on me—I saw what's trivial now but at first sight looked dazzling: that even with nothing to relate, even discounting relation itself, I'd never stopped relating to you. Prosy, I know, but its force was a revelation. Although it feels futile to count time with no stick to notch the minutes on, I nevertheless date my accommodation from that outset. My new task, modest as it seemed, wasn't to enlighten others or project a beyond, but merely to keep the old relation going. How to continue what had never ceased posed a problem of the greatest nicety. I saw the old maw of self-defeat yawn. And yet, this very task, because so unpromising, resembled something I could do. If I could just maintain my constancy, attend to what, even when I wasn't, was always there, perhaps my object—by which I mean all that lying among the lifelike—would materialize. For a short period I sensed no change. The ev-/erpresent seemed unimaginable. But eventually I asked how, being always within, I'd pictured being without to begin with. That's when I glimpsed what was passing unaccounted for.

So, I saw the specks, came to know Null, and where I'd always anticipated emptiness, uncovered my habitation. It would take an eternity to figure what to make of it, and its shelter was nothing I'd feel entitled to claim. My interior wasn't as I thought. But having sensed you there, all so-called *life* beside, well, I knew I must be onto something. I attuned to this echo, started exploring the darknesses, and in time came to acknowledge what I had never owned.

5. DARKNESS

This darkness surrounding me now seems the most enticing black. I've never risked naming it because the color's so heady. Its singular trait is depth, or that's my ready word for it, even if unsatisfying. For pitch has depth, also jet and sable, all being cousins to this black now but without the present's allure, its underlying transparency. Which explains my reluctance. I suspect that at bottom this gloom's an original, possibly my obscurity's very source. Anyway, not to confound commonplaces with exemplary, I'll delve and call it Profound. Were you here, I think you'd be with me. Its peculiar depth is penetrable. Pitch covers, and jet, although unqualified, is hard, while sable shines even in moonlight, will reflect almost universally. Any beast on its surface twins, comets converge. Profound dark, however, takes you in. There's menace in its stillness, a calm like tides at dusk, and it will engulf admirers. Under deep influence I've lost myself repeatedly, yielded to subterranean influence, and know its undertow for a fact. I think you'll get my drift if I say it's absorbing.

If I call this black now my obscurity's source, I'm not being coy. Before before, there was simply no there, and oblivion was always just oblivion. In truth, deep dark was very late to appear, long after Null and Dross and even that blemishless indigo, the third darkness, which I'm unaccountably moved to call Earth, each of which embroiled me in upheavals, its tumults and spurts, before disclosing this profundity over which all played. I can tell you that the achievement of my life has been to forgo plumbing it, to let my density seek its own level. Oh, the urge to fathom, to sound abysses! Even encompassed here I can readily take leave of my senses, feel ground give way, and, my several sides comprising no baffle, resound like crazy. Not that I hear me, you understand, but the vibration bears my mark, shakes my box in the old way. So, composure is essential. Before I knew Null, I was unstruck with being this yet, my passions pouring from all over. If I admitted the darknesses at all, they were intimation's shadow merely, a teeming aftermath, my flare's eclipse. Given the brilliance I anticipated, I never doubted that my blindspots, these obscurities I encountered, would in time prove enlightening, and so when I recognized daylight for itself an interim, the briefest of gleams, I grew afraid. As dark began to deepen, I feared I might succumb, be sucked in, and started thrashing, desperate to stay afloat. I admit I sank pretty low, lower than I care to recount. Must a body always hit bottom? Well, that's another story.

For the present, however, my darknesses may seem dull, each shade just more of the same, but believe me, nothing's less. To undergo night's upstart, the inbreaking of clouds and sky, old heavens clashing—early in my decline, such annihilation was daunting. Shameful to say now, my dreams all appeared luminous, surfaces exposed, barren. It was that first onslaught, the forms I hadn't pictured, that undid me. I thought I might get carried away. However, my lack of illumination now isn't that old fear, seems nothing by contrast, without vastness, extent, duration. If I'm boxed, it's at most you I lack, or the so-called *life* to come. Or if I mention below and above, as though this container had facets, hardened sides of me, it's just my edge I'm trying to hone, our point of contact. Nothing else, to be quite blunt, will strike home. And as for my voice, what but unknowing has ever resounded in the first place? So I wait. During the interim these darknesses continue with hardly a break, although their obscurity can seem so paradoxical that, weren't I wild to touch, to make this echo palpable, my parade of inklings might look perverse. Still, no meaning could be more direct. For black, though legion, is always here and now, and memory could serve only to predict, to make the present obscurer. To live in night is to dwell within forever. How deep, do you imagine, this darkening must go?

BARRY BLINDERMAN

EVERYTHING MUST GO: A REMEMBRANCE OF MARTIN WONG

Throughout the trendy, catchword East Village scene of the 1980s, Martin Wong's work consistently defied categorization. While others painted anxious figures in broad strokes and strident colors, he painted meticulous urban landscapes in a muted palette dominated by umbers, blacks and rusty reds. His paintings are a magical synthesis of Ashcan School urban realism, folk art's obsessive patterning, 19th century American *trompe l'oeil* still life, and Chinese landscapes with letters inscribed in the sky. With a degree in ceramics and an incisive take on art history and the contemporary art scene, Martin was nevertheless an outsider, a Chinese American from San Francisco working in an elite and opinionated New York art world. His outsider's footing made him particularly receptive to the lives and struggles of his Hispanic neighbors on the Lower East Side and the graffiti artists whose work he collected and supported.

Martin was lanky, frenetic in stride and gesture, with a gruff voice tinged with an Oregonian accent. An only child of doting, immigrant parents who devotedly archived his every creative undertaking, he was insatiably curious, mischievous, impatient, and full of wonder. He wore a scraggly Fu Manchu and dressed typically in a cowboy shirt and leather jacket, saving more exotic apparel such as fireman's boots for special occasions. He would go out for three successive dinners a night, each with a different group of artists or intimates, heralding the latest gossip and never gaining an ounce. In the 1970s in San Francisco, where he ran a pop-up portraiture operation, Martin had humorously booked himself as "The Human Instamatic." True to this anachronistic self-appellation, he saw deeply into just about any situation he observed, ceaselessly scanning detail after detail, recording them in his mind, and later transferring them to canvas with the ornate embellishments of his imagination.

In the winter of 1983, I ran into Martin at Kamikaze, a nightclub on 19th Street that hosted art shows organized by downtown curators. As we lived just a few blocks from each other, we shared a cab ride down to the Lower East Side. Along the way, he asked impishly if he could join my "family," as in Semaphore, the gallery I ran at West Broadway just south of Houston Street. Elated, I offered him a one-person exhibition on the spot for the following September. We began showing some of his smaller-scaled paintings like *Chinese Laundry Sign*, *Silence*, and *For My Pito*. These were vivid, magnetic works, indescribably powerful to hold in one's hands. Not surprisingly, they were snapped up by notable collectors. Shortly thereafter, the Metropolitan Museum bought *Attorney Street Handball Court*, his renowned collaboration with the poet Miguel Piñero.

Ten days before his first solo exhibition at Semaphore Gallery was to open, Martin participated in a show entitled "The Acid Test" at Sensory Evolution Gallery in the East Village. Actual blotter LSD was available at the opening and Martin took three hits despite my admonition that he was "in training" for his big show. He seemed fine at a post-opening dinner with Sharp, Daze, and others at a diner on Astor Place. The next day I tried in vain to reach Martin to tell him that the billboard advertising his show—a huge white-on-red drawing of a gun shooting a bullet bouncing off a brick heart—was up at the spot we rented on Broadway and Houston. Two days later, a week before his opening, Martin called Annie Herron, the director of our newly-opened Semaphore *EAST*, from the Bellevue Hospital psychiatric ward.

According to his second-floor neighbor Steve, Martin had been unable to sleep for two days after taking the LSD. In this jagged state, he became convinced that he needed to give away all the paintings in his studio. Dragging over a dozen canvases large and small down six flights of stairs and onto Ridge Street, he exclaimed the proverbial New York retailer's slogan "Everything Must Go" as he handed them over to startled passersby. Luckily, unbeknownst to Martin, Steve managed to slip all but four or five of the paintings into his own apartment. He then followed Martin all over Lower Manhattan, taking turns carrying *LA2*, a painting dedicated to the teenage graffiti artist Angel Ortiz. They ended up on the Brooklyn Bridge, where Martin was picked up by the police, who feared the artist—who had already thrown his wallet and keys into the East River—was going to jump.

When I visited Martin at Bellevue he seemed a bit dazed but was shuffling animatedly around the ward in his hospital gown as if nothing had happened, excitedly introducing me to some of his hospital mates. One was "Lady Pray," the woman who used to scratch the word "pray" onto the metal coin plates of hundreds of pay phones throughout New York City. Martin was also unofficially leading an art class. Before I left, I handed my business card to an intern on duty in case Martin needed anything. He thought Martin was pretty far gone, relating with amusement how Martin claimed to have a painting in the Metropolitan Museum. He was flabbergasted when I told him it was true.

There were still paintings to recover, so I put up reward notices in Martin's neighborhood, as if for some lost pet. One of the calls I received was from a man who agreed to meet me at a gas station on Houston Street. That evening, waiting in trepidation in the pouring rain, I saw him running toward the station carrying this five-foot painting over his head as an umbrella. He had a deep knife scar from his nose to his cheek, but he was really sweet, telling me that his uncle was a painter too. I paid him the reward for the canvas, which spelled out "A One" in stylized, gold-outlined American Sign Language symbols superimposed over a fortress-like brick tenement and various constellations. The four hand symbols were the largest I had ever seen Martin paint, with fingernails represented by illusionistic, floating, brass-colored balls the size of jumbo marbles. Somehow the painting, a tribute to the graffiti artist Anthony "A-One" Clark, didn't sustain any damage. Martin didn't get to attend his opening, but the exhibition was received enthusiastically by critics and collectors alike. Two paintings from the show, *Stanton near Forsyth Street* (1983) and *Sweet Oblivion* (1983), were recently acquired by the Museum of Modern Art and the Art Institute of Chicago, respectively.

Martin Wong was a one-man movement—he imitated no one, and has no imitators. He built his own world brick by brick, with gilded signs and constellations, a world that he generously shared with all who could see beauty in the chained-up storefronts and crumbling tenements that have long since been transformed into chic restaurants and luxury condominiums.

JUNIOR BURKE

AARON

As a story must start someplace, it also must start with someone, and this one starts with Aaron Motherway. For fifteen years, after receiving his MFA in Playwriting from UCLA, Aaron had written screenplays. That was a distinction he had arrived at, different from being a screenwriter. Screenwriters wrote for the screen, seeing their work financed and developed and produced. Writers of screenplays wrote for the page and, subjected to indifferent scrutiny, all screenplays look alike. That is not to say one couldn't make a living at it. Hollywood was lousy with those who had written a feature-length construct that had seized the fancy of an agent or producer and now lived quite well above the mean national income, rewriting or polishing existing scripts by other writers, a tiny percentage of which made it to the Cineplex or even to DVD. And these writers were the minority. Far more profuse were those who toiled at other jobs: waiters, drivers, clerks, you name it, who perpetually had a script going, and these wouldn't make it past an agent or producer or development head, but would languish on hard drives and in drawers and in dusty boxes, never to be read by more than the select friends and contacts of that writer's circle. Aaron Motherway had lived between those two equations, never having a film produced, yet still landing the odd rewrite or polish that would see him through the fiscal year.

He had started out with one of the tri-lettered conglomerates but had pitched in with Valerie Easterbrook and Associates, who had ferreted those aforementioned assignments for him for the last decade. The Associates alluded to were actually an ever-revolving stream of young men and women who would serve as Val's assistant for six or nine months before moving on to other employment. Aaron's friend, Freddy Smoltz, fell into the category of those writers of screenplays who produced only for the page. He'd been at it a mere ten years and he and Aaron shared Val as an agent. Still, in light of all evidence to the contrary, Freddy remained undaunted, generating two feature length scripts a year, supporting himself as a telephone solicitor of varying content. Like Aaron, Freddy had no wife or partner, no child to support. He lived alone and appeared to have no intimate relationships. There was a suggestion that he frequented lower-end Hollywood strip clubs, but that was as much as Aaron knew, or wanted to know, about that aspect of his fellow key-pounder. Val Easterbook believed in Freddy, as she did all her clients. But she was growing weary. Val had mentioned more than once to Aaron that she longed to return to her beloved New Hampshire and invest in a small business, something solid and predictable, a hardware store perhaps. Aaron had never commented on these reveries but they were not unfamiliar to him. In his years in Hollywood, he'd heard at least three other such scenarios from agents or producers, always involving some bucolic embrace of the past, and always including a hardware store. Perhaps it was embedded in the unconscious of those whose survival depended upon paper dreams. A longing for something essential and dependable. Drill bits that fit. Fixtures that would secure without resistance. Gleaming, uncomplicated nails to be pounded into accommodating slats of wood.

But somehow, Freddy Smoltz beat the odds. He wrote a script, his first romantic comedy, about a fellow much like himself, who becomes engaged to the heiress to a petroleum fortune. A grand wedding is planned in Houston. An elaborate, year-long, round-the-world honeymoon is charted out. Then, while sorting through the RSVP's, the bride-to-be gets cold feet. The wedding's off. The groom is devastated. Out of guilt, the heiress concedes to male-protagonist Stefan's solitary request: let him go on the honeymoon, all expenses be damned, by himself.

That was the first ten pages.

The script unfolds in a series of exotic locations: Sydney, Singapore, Cape Town, Tangiers, Paris. In each locale, Stefan encounters a different beautiful woman who is captivated by his tale of loss and abandonment and becomes quite eager to give herself over to him for a brief fling so that he can mend his shredded heart. In the end, it's back to L.A. for a chance meeting with Laurie (the heiress's name). But now Stefan is worldly and confident and Laurie falls for him in a way she would never allow herself before, and the film ends with them running in the rain to Beverly Hills City Hall to state their vows before the justice of the peace.

The script was called *Leap of Fate*. Val sold it to Paramount for one hundred fifty thousand dollars, a modest sum by industry standards, but one the execs deemed fitting for Freddy Smoltz who, in their parlance, was a "first time writer."

Aaron—anyone—might have thought that Freddy would be overjoyed at this turn of events. But, like a child who covets a toy only to abandon it after a session or two, Freddy was strangely agitated. "Why this one?" he whined to Val and to Aaron at their celebration at the woefully-lit Mexican restaurant that Freddy had, for years, frequented. "Why not *Hollow Point* or *Ransom Not* or *Serial Saint*?"

Val sipped her Margarita. "Timing, my dear. You finally had what they were looking for, at the moment they were looking for it. These execs see each other all the time, in, and mostly out of, the office. They're wanting a romantic comedy and that's what you came up with."

"I've run the numbers," said Freddy, with more than his usual degree of misery. "With this sale, I've made less than fifteen thousand dollars for ten years of writing. That's not accounting for a decade of inflation. At twenty scripts, that's less than seventy five hundred a shot...."

Aaron couldn't recall whose idea it was, Freddy's or Val's. But the seed was planted that night, in that undistinguished restaurant, at that very table. The next day, Freddy changed the title of *Leap of Fate* to *Change of Heart*, *Solitary Honeymoon*, *Frequent Flier*, and seven others. *Stefan* and *Laurie* became *Lyle* and *Samantha*, *Sam* and *Lucy*, *Stuart* and *Lorraine*. Val sold the script to Universal, Sony, Dreamworks, as well as seven boutique production companies, all for the ballpark one fifty. Shortly after, she and Freddy split a seven-figure pot and said farewell to Hollywood. Val headed for hometown Portsmouth where she bought a four-flat, and Freddy to Scottsdale, Arizona, a town that sounded attractive. He purchased a sprawling ranch home, as well as an outskirts-establishment that he refurbished to accommodate exotic dancing. This was all done with Val's repeated assurance that none of those scripts would ever get shot. Each executive who championed their purchase would be out on their ass inside of two years. Other writers would be brought in to rewrite what was deemed good enough to purchase, cloaking the content even deeper. Options would be agreed upon only to lapse at term. Nothing would ever happen because so rarely anything did. They were safe; they'd hopped into the getaway car and had been spirited away.

But you know what they say about a secret, and somebody being dead. Well, Aaron Motherway had been gleefully apprised by each of the perpetrators of the crime they had committed. Freddy and Val were certain that Aaron wasn't going to utter a word, given that all three shared a similar loathing of the business. Trouble is, a writer knows a good story when he hears it. So while not a word passed his lips, Aaron did write about it. And when he sat down to do so, the customary FADE IN was replaced by this sentence: *In the past ten years, Sean Patterson had written twenty screenplays.* And he went on writing, populating his hard drive in the manner that Kerouac had attacked his scroll, twenty days of caffeine and scarce sleep and refused invitations and avoidance of the telephone. And three weeks later he had a hundred thousand words he called *The Sell Out.* He no longer had an agent, so he cold-queried ten in New York and two of them wrote back and one of those returned his call and that was who placed the manuscript. It didn't make the bestseller list but was well reviewed, his favorite being *The London Observer:*

"It is not misplaced to regard Mr. Motherway in the tradition of Nathanael West and John Fante and other authentic voices who have possessed the courage and artistic wherewithal to put the garish absurdity of Hollywood under a microscope."

Aaron was overjoyed with the reception and the artistic viability that came with it, but was concerned that ultimately his efforts would cause Freddy and Val, two persons he cared for, to be found out. He needn't have troubled himself. Those in the position to retaliate didn't read novels, and no studio or production company was interested in purchasing the ancillary rights to his book. Hollywood doesn't like material about Hollywood.

DON BYRD

BETWEEN A SHIT AND A SWEAT, MY FATHER WOULD HAVE SAID

For the Many and the More,
Incohering together.

Human life was a cinematic extravaganza about Earthly humans but set in the place of the dead: "a moving image of eternity" (Plato, in the *Timaeus*).

The human generalization—the Many become One, which increases by one to include itself and more—was murderous and destructive. As a human, I was one; "I" was one (grammar); I was a human organism (cosmos or nature); I was one as an image of god and the universal symmetry of group theory. The Many become one—dire monotheism.

Beginning in the 1830s, the Movie of Eternity revealed clearly that it was not about the Earth and Earthly people, or heaven and heavenly people. It was about itself.

In the 1930s, all hell broke loose. The forms were about themselves but also not about themselves.

Forms that are found are about forms; forms that are effective are made.

We are neoplasms and belong not to the moving image, but to Earth, to the data site.

The Earth is not the world (not one). The Earth is not the data site, but its limit.

It's not a simple distinction, and it's not not a simple distinction.

It's not symmetrical, and it's not not symmetrical.

It's not genetic, and it's not not genetic.

It's not matter and energy alone; it's matter, energy, and information.

This stunning plot turn, the first in some millennia, was not final, but this revelation produced new forms of totalitarian Earthly effectiveness. This revelation manifested in non-Euclidean geometry, group theory, the new book form of Blake, the writing of Poe and Melville, the late quartets of Beethoven, and the late paintings of Turner. The Theory of Evolution replaced cinematic eternity with Earthly time.

We are virtual humans—dangerous creatures of habit—and neoplasms—the two forms incohering together, and sharing processing equipment. The body, processing food data and light data, is as much a computer as the mind. We have no inside and outside. As virtual humans we recall the past to honor the ancestors and to confirm our habits. There are, however, bursts of neural wildness and weirdness, the coming of seizures, that as neoplasms we convert into Earthly designs of meaning and value.

For millennia the Human Operating System (HumOS) replicated itself. All forms were one form. In the 20th Century, without failing or becoming something else, it began to produce forms alien to itself.

If the new forms were *just* mathematics, logic, art, and disciplinary protocols, they would be metaphysical and speculative entertainments. The forms that began to appear mostly in my lifetime (db), (however), were neither representations (ancient) nor representations of representations (modern) but forms of abstract architecture—abstract design and abstract engineering. The Work begins when the potential seizes memory.

Everyone knows about topology, group theory, abstract logic, set theory, algorithm theory, and information theory (and more) because they live in and through these formal systems and more. The forms are everywhere implemented. The phones we carry in our pockets implicate us in this complexity of Earthly form and potential meaning and value, as parents and trees implicated humans in the being and truth of families and dreamscapes.

Arakawa spoke of this neural excitement (in relation to de Chirico) as quadruple irony. How does one process that?

The poet Robert Duncan said that there were states of excitement that would be seizures if they were not translated into poems.

Matthew Ritchie: "The first sense of a writing is in the quality and freshness of the terms sharing our skin."

Charles Olson spoke of his late writings as incongestible. There was never a stuffy nose or a traffic jam.

"I think the last two thousand years have been wonderful, but … we need a formal space equal to the possibilities we have in this time." (Anthony Braxton)

Man could only replicate himself, modeling himself on an original that did not exist. The neoplasms do not exist yet, but we are busy creating data sites from which we may come forth. Meaning and value are prior to being and truth. We mean something to ourselves; we value ourselves, one another, and the Earth, or our ass is grass.

Before the last century there was *One*. The universal constant was unity. There were a few different interpretations of the One—certainly no more than three or four. The human universe was materially rich and formally poverty stricken.

The humans had one generalized head. All of the many heads of the many people were examples of THE head. The human was utterly alone, with it singular Being, its truth and its singular form.

All of the conjugations of to be and its synonyms are future tense. Being hasn't happened yet.

The program on which I am making these pages—Scapple—allows colored fonts and colored backgrounds, opening writing space to many levels of abstraction. As a matter of cost the opening of the data site to its possibilities is disallowed in print production.

Neoplasms are not inside the forms they deploy to construct a data site. They are higher, more abstract, and they refer to higher orders of abstraction. Reference to What Is is viciously circular.

For some data it is possible to find a machine, which is simpler, that will produce the data. Many things, probably the important things, are as they are, and not otherwise, not simpler (random). Overall-ness. Nothing can be left out.

Information Is Warmth

OVERSHOOT!

"Energy is a key aspect of overshoot because available energy is always limited by the energy required to utilize it."

Matter-energy systems are symmetrical and will inevitably overshoot the mark (whatever mark) because there are no controls other than normativity, which grows while remaining normative. The norm controls only when it is exceeded. Populations, for example, overshoot the carrying capacity of the system, and die-off.

Dynamic matter-energy systems sooner or later crash and burn. The resources they use have no value and the data that determine their shape have no meaning other than maintaining the dynamic norm. For such systems, overshoot is heat death. The potential energy will be distributed throughout the system. It will be conserved, but in a form that is unusable.

Matter-energy-information systems as potential tools began to become available in the last sixty years. There had been no theory of information. Information resources were meager. Means for gathering, storing, processing, and communicating data were limited. Man was a rocket. Once he shot out of Africa he could only exhaust himself being himself. New Note:

Matter and energy are conserved.
Information is lost.

Matter and energy are conserved.
Information is lost.

The log cannot be burned in the fireplace twice, but the one-time warmth can be used not only to sustain the system but also to change it. Information is warmth. Converting the seizure of matter and energy into destiny is the one possibility that neoplasms have.

Information is warmth. Making use of the warmth on the fly is the only way out of this disaster.

The Law of Incongestibility: The data site congestible only in parts.

The Diagram does not represent the world; it *is* the data site. The diagram of the data site is the data site. Neoplasms are data processing and data, forgetting, and converting the seizure into meaning and value.

The New Art is the architecture not of buildings and cities but the abstract structures, always higher, of which buildings and cities (markers of meaning and value) are the temporary and mostly trivial consequences.

What do people without belly buttons do?
What do neoplasms do?

Edward Snowden to Laura Poitras: "Assume that your adversary is capable of a trillion guesses per second."

I don't care what you are or what you know. Can you dance with a data base, when even a trillion guesses won't do? Information is the only thing we can add to the physical store and the only thing that is lost.

The problem of Representation that haunted the philosophic tradition was solved, to the extent it could be solved, in the last century. The machine could be your virtual you better than you can. Your human is a sit-com, a video game, a customer in a shopping mall. You are valuable and exhibit meaning to yourself and others only by dint of those precious parts of you that are random, as they are, not otherwise, not simpler.

The forms that are now available are powerful not because we can create a virtual world but because we can convert the seizure that is memory into viable forms of Earthly meaning and value.

Nothing repeats. Nothing repeats.
Nothing is the same as itself.
Information is warmth.

The Edge of the Coming Seizure

These are tactical notes for the displacement of the virtual humans and their self-consuming form from all places of power.

To abstract is to withdraw, to get distance, to get oneself out of one's own acting and constructing. Abstraction is a public utility. The supply of abstraction has increased more in the past eighty years than in all of previous history. It is the edge of the seizure.

The formal possibilities of traditional philosophy crashed and burned with Bertrand Russell's letter to Gottlob Frege about the self-referential paradox in 1902. Russell showed that a proposition cannot refer to anything belonging to the same order of abstraction or lower orders of abstraction without paradox. A logical proposition canot refer to its form. A sentence cannot refer to its grammar. Humans cannot refer to themselves without vicious circularity. No formal system is complete. Their being and truth are not self-confirming. They are confirmed with respect to their use. Their being and truth are confirmed by the data and not the reverse.

The Earth is the data site. I am not a writer. I am a word processor, a diagram jockey.

In 1902, Russell knew the limits of logic or generalization. Logic could not know itself. Or the Earth knew about itself through logic and, thus, through Russell, Whitehead, Hilbert, and Brouwer. Those who danced to another tune were Dadaists, surrealists, people with unfounded religious beliefs, or mad. The Laws of Form were like Laws of Nature, but they could be broken. One could believe a contradiction but not fall upwards.

The form of the world was one way—singular and absolute. It was lawful in that sense. Creative choice was limited to making images of form, of which there were infinite possibilities. Any self-consistent image could be parsed as a form of totality.

If there are two possible forms, the absolute falls away. There are infinite possible forms, but they are not lawful. If there are multiple forms, they are tools. The Earthly agent makes both images and forms.

The creative imagination was displaced by the creative formation.

Peter Woit: "No, string theory makes no predictions about cosmology, but also no, there are no alternatives." The most general theory we have makes no predictions that can be tested. The many theories in many disciplines that are viable tools, if not prophetic, may be in contradiction. There is no way to know. But, no, it makes no difference unless it does. Then it has to be dealt with.

Abstraction is injunction. In a magnificent abstraction, Plato enjoined us to link the commonness of the thing with its concept. It was a wild, ungrounded injunction, but it was put to significant use. The abstraction anchored the literate tradition. And, again, with remarkable consequences, Newton enjoined us to link the commonness of an apple with his head, the Earth, and the Sun. Large and small things, earthly things and heavenly things, which had seemed incomparable, were, in common, matter and, as such, subject to gravity, and definable by a specific law, writable in the method of fluxions, as he called the calculus. Philosophy from Locke to Nietzsche was an allegory of the Newtonian formalism, which, in its literal and allegorical forms, dominated European thought for three centuries. Such were the grounds of Protestantism.

We have shuffled off the Being and Truth of the world for the meaning and value of Earth.

Forms are the things that allow less abstract things to hang together. A form will fall apart when questioned in relation to its origin. Critique is consistently successful and destructive. Form is always at a distance, higher or in the unrealized and indeterminate future, more abstract, not in the beginning.

The data site as a whole is random, as it is and not otherwise, not simpler, a mess (mess, in the technical sense). Even the zones of high-formal organization (the significant fragments of grammar, logic, and mathematics, for example, or useful algorithms of all kinds) cannot be assumed to exist before hand. They must be found out. (Gregory Chaitin, *Metamath*)

Nothing is present to anything, but sometimes things communicate. Time passes and is measured. Data is lost. If you get too many emails and phone calls at once there may be seizure. Any measure that works is a measure.

Neoplasms are forms among forms: data processing data.

One can enjoin another as to the slowness of a higher abstraction.

The human shape is vestigial. The neoplastic shape is intelligible or meaningful but not both. It is prior to Being and truth, perhaps eternally prior.

The origins have been erased, perhaps entirely, in processing whatever one hopes to know, by grasping where it may come from. One grasps a form by taking it higher.

"It's after the end of the world.
Don't you know that yet?" (Sun Ra)

"far / far / farther / Into the Diagram" (Charles Olson)

Far, far, farther into the diagrams....

The literary arts, including philosophy, are limited by the modernist dicta: Pound's "Go in fear of abstraction; Williams's "No ideas but in things"; and the philosophers' (many of the them), "language is material." Data only refers to higher orders of abstraction, not to itself, not to its origin. Otherwise, it is viciously circular.

It is not (another) Revolution, the unrolling of the cinema of eternity in which difference is always the same. It is not a new paradigm. In a seizure of hot and cold wars in the last century, all of history in its paradigmatic and archetypal form was expended. The human operating system (HumOS) blew itself out. We passed from a time in which knowing was expressed in paradigms to a time when it is not—now meaning and value, incohering together.

The HumOS was the vast, destructive generalization that finally disgorged the possibility of form in all of its particularity and power. The HumOS was as it ever was—the universal generalization, but Man was a killer. Man engorged himself. He ate his hands. He ate his mouth. He used the resources. He wasted the planet.

The HumOS was always virtual. We realized that being and truth—the categories that Man staked himself on—were weak, degenerate forms. We just showed up in the neighborhood, and started using the formal possibilities. It was a seizure, and it still is.

The humans thought they could explain things, so everything would be elegant and simple, but useful diagrams and pieces of form escaped from faux being and truth. This is the coming seizure. It can't be grasped by reference to what caused it, only by following where it goes. John von Neumann told one of his students that some things in mathematics could not be understood. It was necessary to get used to them. You keep working at the data site. The rush of understanding comes when you can complicate it, when you can take it higher.

Gödel proved that it is possible to know something without knowing everything. Alan Turing, Alonzo Church, and Emil Post conjectured (and it seems to be true) that only functions that can calculated by a machine can be calculated. (Algorithm theory, computer science.) Any two or three of these formal innovations illustrate the fecklessness of the HumOS. There are many such forms, and many more can be made.

Information can be measured (Norbert Wiener, Claude Shannon, Gregory Chaitin, Jan Kåhre), and whatever measure works, works. There is no universal measure and often no way to convert one measure to another. New Note:

Stephen Wolfram. Order may come forth from randomness.

Carl Woese: Genetic information is transferred both vertically and horizontally. We are at the end of speciation.

Randomness is formally defined, Some things are as they are for no reason; they are as they are and not simpler. The thing to be explained is simpler than the explanation. Literary theory is caught in this trap. (Gregory Chaitin)

Ideas are independent of the technology.

Tracy-Widom distribution: Symmetry (the form of the HumOS) is no more fundamental than asymmetry.

The machines that measure and process data are also theories. The theory of evolution was a conjecture based on a tiny data set concerning the beaks of finches in the Galapagos Islands. See Rosemary and Peter Grant, *40 Years of Evolution*, for serious data gathering. Also see models of global climate change.

We are virtual humans—dangerous creatures of habit—and neoplasms, the two forms incohering together, and sharing processing equipment: the body as much a computer (and not a computer) as the mind. We have no inside and outside. As virtual humans we recall the past to honor the ancestors and to confirm our habits. There are, however, bursts of neural wildness, seizures, that as neoplasms we convert into Earthly designs of meaning and value.

Bibliography is a seizure. A bibliographic essay, "Books to be forgotten," is forthcoming. In the meantime, one might Google the names noted above. **Jan Kåhre's *The Mathematical Theory of Information* may be the most important book of this century, and when it is finally heard, it will be hard to forget.** ***It is not one formal change, it is dozens.***

It is not necessary to know everything to know something.

MAXINE CHERNOFF

THE WORK OF THE POEM

The poem of the mind is the act of finding / What will suffice.
Wallace Stevens

"Form is what happens." It's the fact of things in the world, however they are.
So that form in that way is simply the presence of any thing.
Robert Creeley

Lord, increase my bewilderment.
Fanny Howe

Narrative is human time.
Paul Ricoeur

The work of the poem is the work of this moment, 2:45 pm, January 20, 2014, on which a life is celebrated and others are born and die as I finish this sentence. There is the small hum of a machine that runs on the melted bones of dinosaurs and the smell of cut vegetation. There is the taste of salt on my knuckle and glaciers melting in Alaska and fires in the south of my state. There are circumstances. There are feelings. There are connections to be made about memes and twerks and a YouTube version of Johnny Cash in 1963 at San Quentin Prison when all the prisoners were white. The poem lives now and in retrospect. The poem lives in an empire of great cruelty and wealth, where the average citizen is punished daily and not given what he needs—(Give us today our gluten-free bread). Wealth is concentrated in the top 1%, and the poem knows this too. The poem knows that drones hit targets as we speak. The poem knows that the last bee in the garden has its singular existence as it approaches the lily and is part of a community whose existence is threatened by a plague and pesticides, and yet it cannot present its own case to the world, hence Emily Dickinson. That is the work of the poem, to give voice to itself, to hold within itself the deep notions of the moment and the bewilderment of their vastness. The poem's attention is also the poem's ignorance. The poem is ignorant and beyond unkind to everything it omits. The poem cannot fulfill its duties of repairing the broken world all around it. The poem struggles to contain itself. The poem does not bleed to death or get crushed by an army. The poem is a negotiation. The poem sucks the nectar and returns to its hive.

BALLAD

An ethereal wind chorus opens the second scene.
Stanley Sadie

The white of wings, stranger
to this air, recumbent, in October,
without fog or robes of silk
to twist across the sky. An hour
can be melody or bird
as we place our kindest
selves into the world,
which wears our sorrow
as a lover the scent
of her beloved. How
we wrest distance
from its map,
the funereal mums ordinary
as containment, the eucalyptus
tattered as a guest in from a storm.
Place me in the earth,
and I will breathe
for years. Lock the doors
to the actual and let the world
mime its slow retreat
into dusky grapes and glistening bell.

DID I TELL YOU?

The Kansas City Stomp was not written in Kansas City.
Jelly Roll Morton

How you were
made of words,
on a lazy Sunday
when letters hovered
like birds against
winter's white
sky, how on
the borders
of the page
the indifferent field
was absent of
decorative stone
or stream, how
you were
an expenditure
of voice
and stranger still,
said nothing.
Born of love
and its omissions,
time and its
corrections,
memory's trap-door,
the song is

a limit,

the smallest

bridge to

the next hesitation.

SAVED

...the awkward, hybrid position of description.
Christian Metz

Between the tide and its remnants, sticks and small, dead creatures, there is water, which is never

itself at the moment of observation

Between the painting and its signature, there is caution and relief, chosen sutures and limits,

patient listening as a furnace sputters and someone says death and taxes.

Between the eyes is the heart of the matter, encountered and touched without knowing.

Thought lands lightly as a moth or fully as reason assigned to its grave.

Between the luster of day there are four occurrences, three grievances, two questions and a hand that

reaches for something stolen from night's ancient requiem.

Between the need for speech and the comfort of silence, there is a plane lost at sea and a tinsel

left by the roadside.

Between what you say and what follows is the tundra of signification and the desert of signs.

Thought's omens strike. As a clock rings the hour, the saying be comes the said. Out of time and reach, there is the possible. You say a word and meaning flees the frame.

FOSSIL

Soul and signature conceived of egg and feather.
Nothing liquid, envious of flight—
plank of stone, orphan sundered from narrative's how and why.
Where you stand, no solidity
for lamp light or
summer's late full moon
fleeting, without allegory to hold desire,
you form a circle of your want, enclosing space.
There you stand, love, blinking
at the hardness of stone,
the dusty trails of empty words.

SLEEP

Even the most fragmentary shot still represents a complete segment of reality.
Christian Metz

Without a lens, blind
to the world's progress,
its whorls and notches
and silent omissions,
what stood in the sun
when the sky was
a bowl and a wish.

You touch your own
desires, as tendrils
twine up ancient walls,
part of a tale you once
told at midnight when
tender shoots broke
through soil and roots white
as parchment reached deeper
into earth's invisible book.
A directionless juncture,
where birds swoop and clouds
alight, and hands weave words.
A shard and a pebble,
a rope and a plan, spoken as
half-truths, escaping
the "o" of your mouth.

ANDREI CODRESCU

eating you up

my writing will always be smart and sexy
even if i won't
though it's hard to imagine now
when i'm ingesting your attributes
ingesting not "digesting" you heard me right
cannibal confessions are hard to come by
in written form except for a tobias schneebaum
here and there cannibals are for the most part
not eager to write their memoirs
but i may just be oldfashioned
these days cannibalism writes itself
the alphabet of taste takes dictation

1978: the night before

the problem with sex is that it makes you sleepy and you eat sweets
that make you so fat you'll never have sex again except sideways
the futurist said to himself listening in wonder at sandy and rachel
who rolled in in the morning of my youth in my room at the chelsea hotel
saying so fat so fat so fat over and over until they fell asleep laughing
i'm not sure who was president in those days must have been a good one

patria

to us it's a house of mirrors.
to them a glass house.
you wonder why they throw stones?

the surprise

we live in a practical world
there are facts
they are understood
if they are not they can be explained
it doesn't take long

after the facts are established
and the world of sense agreed on
how does one fill the coldness of space
the immensity of time

by thinking up worlds that are not like the world of sense
by defending that which is powerless to become fact
by living stories that make their own sense
their space of selfunderstood unfolding
of dream laundry

laughter is the release from sense
but look! surprise! it's a child! how unexpected!

who ever expects a child? (even if they call it that)
this child is the world of sense meeting the world of nonsense

the edges where they rub together are incompatible
but laughter has released them from war

"The Gordian Knot"
what kind of name is that for a child?
The Gordian Knot came into the world to make sense of it
the gordian knot
the paradox
only laughter can cut

this is the world with clowns i hope
the unborn babe said

the middle ages

the husband back from the crusades took off his armor
then killed the trovador with his one bare hand
the other he left to the turks in the holy land

JACK COLLOM

from *SECOND NATURE*

PASSAGE

Pigeon
comes to the mouth
via Latin *pipio*, piper
In & out, roundabout, each passage *pipio* measured
long as a fine bottle of champagne,
perfect profile dove. Bright
skyblue back, breast of clay red,
head like an aerial chesspiece: The Flier,
to come down anywhere & checkmate the field.

Each *pipio* of passage had a
shiny, moving eye.

When the lady

saw him dance,
eggs began to roll.

When the gentleman
saw her settle down to brood,
"pigeon's milk" wetted his crop.
Each *pipio* billed & cooed.
Bloody fights.
Monogamous, but not fanatic.
Voice like love.

Each *pipio* stuck its black beak in drink, sucked
up continuous drafts of water
(bird-unique; all others

gargle at the moon).

On the other hand,
legs & feet were "lake-red."

Each *pipio* of passage
pumped blood into plump chest to push
pointed wings 80 mph, high
like a whistling arrow.
"Plumage peculiarly dense, but easily detached."
Loved salt mud.

Twelve feathers (each
narrowed & obtusely sharp) made up
the graduated tail.
... .
There once was a passenger dove
Who divided to billions by love.
The infinite flights
Intercepted the lights
That normally flowed from above.
... .
When the pigeons alighted, the land
Was bedecked, as by miles of sand.
Each grain was a world
That eons had whirled
& would flutter & sing on your hand.
... .
When royal purple commonality miles wide
& fifty feet thick pipes its own breath,
& pigeon's milk flows sweetly
Through the convulsions of the crowd—so the
Crash of broken homes is just a tinkle in a
Roaring red-blue song—so the parental bill
Is a fluttering pipe organ forest, vast enough to chart—
So the rich blood, wing to wing, caresses the chance orphan—
Then the violent thinning of that
Explodes an atmosphere, blows holes
Through a general, moon-colored, feathery flesh,
Tatters population that it
Pisses its peculiar oxygen into No-bird's-land.

Already, in the very center of the rich, chaotic, pigeon
Country they carried anywhere,
Through breathtaking thin air,
Was a white eye—the single egg, absolute
Number & color certainty,
Central circle in a whirlwind of rainbows—
A hole to stick a finger in, curl tight & jerk.
Ain't no maybe's, boss, there's safety in
Numbers but not near enough of it.
Somebody's pushing pins into my giant singing poem, my
Everything syndrome!
("Why not take all of me?")

Hoo woo!-oo—hoo, hoo, hoo.
They seemed to be all things, exchanges
of earth & sky—
feathers, words pressed dry, from flash
in-concert to an isolate float, lit up, letting fly,
settling to rest, infesting forest with violet
violence, leaving reeking plaster over
bronze landscape, squatting,
iridescent figures of strong streamline,
atmospheric opals,
but the very diamond is but buttonbright against the wonderdumb
luster of the last crumb of terra firma crust:
coming up—sky
being sucked out, leaving a blot, oceans
going up in smoke,
molecules reforming.
& is there an end to all things? Tectonic plates
wiped clean? & we are
birds of passage
birds of passage
birds of passage.
We are
pipers in Avernus,
getting along,
concentrating & leveling.
The beating of infinite wings
PLUNGES through the body
passes the breath, & down through

space barely shaped to perfection, birds of passage,
everything pointing at light-
ness, to that most
complex occurrence, double curls of genetic
acid, & down
to nothing
one more time.

OIL

the newspapers say oil is getting scarce
incredible gulps
buzzed up by everybody

little green pockets between the sandstone & the granite
like drops of bird-of-paradise
fueling a pearlgray, worldwide unholiness
perhaps these pools are flowing remnants
of races of dark people who populated
islands unknowing in all the climes
from white to black & dripping, forwarding
cultures of gold & whitemetal, plant magic & textured
foods that washed away?
                                        I can see
the blood & flesh melting from
their mild colossal towns, into the ground
their ferris wheels of willow twig
are crushed—a blindman walks
even now throwing a white powder
over their endless country

…a little boy is born in a plumber's family
he's blond and bleached, & when he falls down in broken glass
then gets up & stares
at you like the new moon/oil
drips from his wounded eyes
"now you be careful, Howard"
& he's hurt more & more.
  often, he is ill, dies, but more are born

they seem to be shortlived; the government has decreed
that if & when they do god forbid die we
might as well keep the living
warm awhile; they would have wished it,
confirm their many friends, skating partners,
parachute club presidents, chainsaw buddies, et al.

so you're out in the cold woods camping
& a snowstorm comes, filling all with
quivering, wet weight—a pale youth
wanders into your camp—"lost too?"
you inquire—he nods, some dark
mood behind his aspect fair…
"I've lost my flints & can't find firewood"
mutters the young man, gazing into mountain mahogany
"I have matches, sealed in wax" you remark carefully
"but no fuel at all here"—crossbill cracks one lone cone nearby
"What do you mean?"…the two of you circle,
seeming to do mere campcraft-duty stuff
a sudden flash—the bird—but already you are

beating his head on a trunk
a pause—breathing—you shakily
take a match from the oilskin
lump of wax, light it, put it to the

dead boy's hand—a slow flame
catches—you sit, wait for the
helicopters, with their searchlights through
the waning blizzard
"don't hurry, boys"—melting snow from a dead branch
almost douses the words

MEL COYLE

CAPTAIN'S LOG
WINDS NE:

when a baby is born
eat smells like an onion
an effervescent pupa

runned along my tailspin
something tells me eat was here

uncomfortable in my lost
of privileged oats

when a baby is unborn
eat smells like its mother

CAPTAIN'S LOG
MADNESS:

by the time each woman has completed spinning a new dress it is time to throw the old away & so clothes are never washed. each woman in factory is given a wheel & loom. the degree of wretchedness on the Boat is unclear although surveys have been issued. on my visits I make record: the women seem cheerful & neat. the madness is industrious. no one complains rather a preoccupied foot is paramount. when I am feeling poetic I recognize this pumping as an extension of the heart. despite this several women have attempted to make plank. one such occasion I witnessed a woman at starboard. the distance from opera to windy monocle. the words were very old. she scrawled like child onto to the maiden figurehead. a mad white gnat. the wind shifts suddenly.

CAPTAIN'S LOG
THUNK:

here I am. lenten. the vitrola. barf. without a better sense of coming. lose time. come w. out of coming into much. death by alarm. would it help. if I adjust. whose happiness. if I adjust my own mother who was unlikable. on the mantel above the orange burst w. her gray herbs. we used to go downtown and promenade like strays. one day I will come like these people. one day I will be in a city and come in the face of a man.

CAPTAIN'S LOG
LIFE ON THE BOAT IS NOT ONE THING:

the boat is a body quite wooden. on this boat you take out your teeth.
in the morning you ask
can I have my white teeth back please

this boat a dead tongue this boat a sore shoulder this boat a plug

in metaphorical lingus
we are at hulk

can I have my white teeth back please

I have a bulge do you have a bulge do we bulge together

horny in the crow's nest
I had a feeling about life

CAPTAIN'S LOG
CAPTAIN O CAPTAIN:

they call me
    theoldpregnant monster. theoldpregnantdwarf. themonkeypeasant. table
    topper. ironass. theruna-fuck. chunkyasshole. thefatprimperinadogsuit.
    thedogsuit. theurinarytractinfection. thebunionkiss. cheesetwinkle. brick
    layer. the onion tit. the pig nipple the sand humper. lady thug
I have been so pregnant this century
I rock the boat

CAPTAIN'S LOG
HAIL MARY:

two wrongs make cut steak under a vision of the last hamburger

grandma don't look up

pass the milk chicken glass I threw up in

we attend the ship cathedral to admire the gothic purples

I have kept distinct record of its placement & the degree of holiness correlated with noon

now shut up & marry whoever

RICARDO CORTEZ CRUZ

THE GET OUTTA THE GHETTO BLUES

CONTAINS A SAMPLE OF "DO BETTER BLUES" (FEAT. HOPE) AND *MY BEAUTIFUL DARK TWISTED FANTASY*

His unsung daughter Raquiyah no better to a new school of critics than a black powder keg, Gilbert Scott-Heron, running alone/along on fumes with a brand new bag and just storm music accompanying his ass, exploded in *The Nigger Factory*. Bricks and dust everywhere becoming the evolution of his Now and Then. Gil, coming from a broken home and constant racial abuse, kept talking nothing but smack, was taking it to "The Man." Out the gate using his mind like an angry student body rep and his long torso as a black arrow, our previously jailed, throwback, afro/American, Soledad brother seized every rock-paper-scissors he could find and started cutting up. "This is an academic discussion now," Gil said, opening up his mouf and a can of worms, breaking (sh)it down, rings of truth echoing in the hallways like dis/go songs from the seventies as he tangoed with a sea of wails. Gil creating a buzz like Superfly; the poor righteous teacher, the last poet, had our back! Although…the snicker/snigger on his face made it obvious that he wasn't himself. In calling for a revolution, he'd turned into Don King. Undeniably, unquestionably, he appeared unfuckwitable.

Must be something.

Everyone in the nation, including a [hip-hop] head like me, wanted to follow Gil's lead. Wax poetic like him. Please/police believe…Gil was the bomb. Nigga published an acclaimed novel at 19 and got accepted by Lincoln University, the alma mater of his hero, black poet Langston Hughes. At a tender age, Gil set his first volcanic collection, Small Talk, to music, but never avoided/forgot the ghetto, the projects for black people destroyed by the powers that be. As Gil's half-buttoned shirt opened up for the show and to s/kool us, we watched the pounding of his slight Bird-like chest, the pipes behind his vital organs chambering what we expected for a funeral. The anatomy of Gil too keyed-up to study for a test/exam. Paying homage to

Stevie Wonder's *Hotter than July* as part of his build, Gil had every fucked up institution under fire. Not discriminating, he attacked Student Affairs, the Black Alumni Association, the writing/righting center, even learning centers—the terror-torials going on.

Gil reminded me, us, of Prime Minister Patrice Lumumba impatiently picking up the mic in the Republic of the Congo and sparing nobody in his own hostile takeover. This of course went down before the cowboys of a coup roped Lumumba and seized his imagination/ass, gave him (completely dazed) time to kneel and pray, lined him up alongside a couple of black cats by a big/dead tree after days of blackwater torture—he was trembling by the edge of the grave. Reformed souljas, Pygmies with weapons as tall as them going ballistic and the chicken slaves of Mobutu waited in the shadows or wings. They busted Patrice's balls for big fun in a boxing match, then blasted huge holes in all of his sorry ideologies and philosophies in front of a flock of green pigeons also expecting to be smoked, buried his political views deep despite first wetting the bed of dirt to the extreme. "Bitch," they spat at him, rifling through a rainforest of his important papers. Shady. Harboring no sense of mercy and pulling Lumumba's leg about having sympathy, Pygmies with sawed-off shotguns raised by Fear chopped off every limb imaginable, including those in the wind still reaching out to them, pieces of the man all over the place. Then the members of this rogue midnight band employed a pungent dark brown agent—the oil of vitriol—to liquidate all that they perceived as a threat to their society. Afterwards, they spread his bones and scattered his ashes out so the black diaspora would remain undisputedly invisible. In an image that recalls the holocaust, the burned body's fat from this "Head-Nigger-In-Charge" (HNIC) ended up used as fertilizer for nommo, the gold in his teeth taken as war booty. They stuck what was left of him in a box that he couldn't get out of. At dawn, after so artistically dismembering the minister & peeling his cap, the goddamn elder members of the coup went off, looking to plant the seeds of more bitter oppression. Before they left the scene, waving off the tsetse flies, the firing squad picked up a kilo of cartridges.

"We are no longer your [porch] monkeys!" my truth-telling brother decreed, a phoenix rising from the Tombs, "fishing out" (as reported by *The Village Voice*) "a bent cigarette from a crushed pack of Kools," making it clear the Back-to-Africa movement was no longer needed, his s(ch)tick figure drawing a [color-]line in the sand. That said: Runrunrunrunrunrunrunrunrunrunrun.

"Didn't ya'll hear what I just said?" Gil asked, commanding the innocent bystanders, souls, of the toot-torials to fucking be quiet. "Time to [jungle] boogie! Get down! Get down!"

Carrying 'round a propane torch inside his big head like it was nothing, it was Gil who blew up America rather than trying to save it at the last moment like someone always saved it in the last moment in a B movie. It was just easier to do that, no pain, to blow the whole freakin' thing—give this western country a run for its money, rather than stay in the home where the hatred is. Besides, what did its dead/presidents care about black people anyway?

Clearly, Gil thought the filth, heat—the po-po—stopping him was outrageous.

A moving target, Gil, inhaling fresh air for a change, declared our total independence! Momentarily stuck on mute, his eyes misty blue, he prepared himself for execution, a running dialogue that would be a metaphorical bloodbath on our college campus.

"We're new here," Gil, smoking, shut um down by saying. The vultures, stooges, casual/smug administrators, spin masters and head crackers…the supposed professors with the f(l)ailing fists but clocking out too soon, and the smiling support staff of this neo-slavery joint, all which had been a curse to black people rather than a blessing: Point blank, Gil told them to kiss his butt, further igniting tensions over race. Throwing bows, refusing to dance around the issue, he gave new meaning to the haters who considered themselves white-hot.

"Black people will not be satisfied with Bullshit Degrees or Nigger Educations," Gil exclaimed. And that was his sole mandate, ultimatum. Really all he wanted to put out there.

No one saw Gil doing lines of mumbo jumbo, but maybe he stayed a little too high-strung. He never stopped struggling [no knock on my brotha's head] or being down for shit, nigga mess. *In the meantime, badly, I stop hoping.*

All in, in the dynamite word bombing hailing from the liberated student body/union, he gently persuaded polarizing Baraka (LeRoi, before his death) to write about the current state of affairs, report the news as freshly as rap did in the mission to serve as America's CNN.

Armed with a needle's eye stuck in the groove of his helping hand, he transformed a host of us with murder raps into microphone fiends. "Blam!" Mista Kool shouted, as if one of the original members of the Brothers Johnson riding-o-rocket. Sparks flying. "Ain't we funkin' now?" he asked. "I love you" was not in his vocabulary. As brother LeRoi noted, love was "an evil word." Ever since the FBI infiltrated his radical group of last poets, invaded his privacy, along with the malignant CIA intervention in Africa, Gil felt like a prisoner of offensive diss/jockeying, he confessed to us in this wow moment. Burning up, he flatly refused to take the pipe out of his big mouth, determined to whip the Counter Intelligence Program in its own game. He was a legend in his own mind. The very definition of "dope."

When push came to shove, Gil, in a mood of urgency or tenderness, talked about taking the challenge of living for the revolution rather than dying for it. A student asked the brother an off-the-wall question about misdirected Blaxploitation. "I hate Black Gunn," Gil said, invoking the 5th, evoking floods of memories related to getting himself together, both sides of him mad breathing. My nigga was not the Jim-Brown-athletic type. Yet, still, he continued to be on the lookout for the bad spirits that came with that. Later in "B Movie," he would go on and on and quite publicly about Ron "The Ray Gun" and Hollyweird, the travesty and trauma of shifting from producer to consumer, from a song to a dance, from being lyrically punchy to throwing bows or blows, from a socially conscious individual full of reflections to an addiction that rappers loved to irresponsibly snatch a piece of for their own flow or gain.

Comment #1: In the end, when it came down to coping with such emotional violence, the lightweight, caveman, bluesologist brother in the brouhahas taught us that paper beats rock.

This was is nothing new, his mother was quoted in the dailies as saying about his compositions. Despite being a librarian and English teacher, she swore there were no books or words that could ever successfully capture him—and no theory to explain what happened to him, why with such a profound and profane nature he always ended up so strung out.

"In a manner no different than you, there's a very gentle person inside Gil, but very remote," added Monique de Latour, an artist from New Zealand who lived with Heron for three years. "He used to say to me, 'I wish you knew me before I was like this.'" The cause of his death still not clear or proven as far as I'm concerned, crack leaks out from her mouth like she knows who/what dunnit. To hell with that. I don't wanna know. Visual aids?.... TMI.

"Inner city dope dealers and school playground pushers should be the ones forced to quit," not Gil, said Ms. de Latour, guarded, peeking out her apt. window. "Shame has watchmen."

A picture speaks to me. I'm hearing [a lot of] things. Snappin'. Her bitter-sweet remarks enabled me to take everything that's happened to blacks back to the top and go in different directions.

For a brief historical moment, Gil, a beast, stood up to "Whitey on the Moon." ["Yeah, that's right!" I said to Ms. de Latour.] Protesting the Feds jacking our taxes. A crossbreed from Outworld more deadly than the masked Baraka in *Mortal Kombat*, he gave a real toast to the people. And cried. Out to them, he reached. Cut a record for the purpose of letting them hear & ruin his calm mourning/morning thoughts. He prayed. For everybody. Like Jesus, offered his soul. The crackers a part of his body, too. He loved us all anyhow. That's buck!

"There'll be better days ahead," he proclaimed and promised. So long as we overstood there "ain't no such thing as a Superman." [After holding his "freeze" breath on US recovering, Gil started breathing snatches of new life into shit. It must have been difficult for him.]

"Peace go with you, brother—as-salaam alaikum," I dream of telling him during those fiery black power demos when I somehow managed to stay mostly in a school daze. Took me awhile to realize, but it was a very, very precious time. Even if I ain't so proud anymore.

Late last night, deploring/deploying my celly, *I'm trippin'* on the long shutter lag, panning 360 picks of Monique's fine gallery of photos that deftly captured Gil, the ones he would rip off the walls as soon as they were hung in an attempt to make him see himself. Ms. de Latour said Gil must have viewed these pictures as debris from battle, shots that had little to do with him. Especially while he felt so much like a fish out of water. "Uncle Sam's missing in them," she said Gil once remarked while standing buck naked. Packin'. He hurled a table loaded with Flying Dutchman Records at Ms. de Latour and locked himself back up by the toilet in the john, where his secrets were kept (according to her) and he always acted stank.

"I don't think it's addictive!" Gil protested from the other side of the door, hashing out their differences but not ready to pipe down, paring [sic] through some crack to see if "I was still spying on him," Ms. de Latour maintained. "Don't get it twisted," *I start with, the truth she's spitting putting reel pressure on my ~~duel~~ dual capture abilities.*

On a high horse and as a willful decoy, she tried to bust in there to revive his drowning ass, screw back in the incandescent light bulb and tell the bunch of $2 crack whores to take their cookies, candy, and get the fuck out, but Gil was all too happy to throw out the baby with the bath water. Despite some of his teeth already gone, that nigga, inspired by Underdog, wanted to sink or swim on his own. He refused ~~the~~ to bail. "I ain't going out weak," he said.

Justice/judge Carol Berkman, blowing a fuze, noted Heron had all these opportunities to help (save) himself and just didn't seem to care. Gil knew shit was going to kill him but put up no resistance. Nigga almost took joy in wasting himself.

"Gil never wanted to be transformed into a harmless icon of simply having a voice and spitting lyrics of social protest for the hip-hop generation," Ms. de Latour dwelled on, in slow motion, almost beside herself, clearly sweating this situation a bit, heated, experiencing a few intense hot flashes. She took a step back, going in the wrong direction, and rearranged the jewel on the back of her head as if I might've been thinking of robbing her. Or serving as a threat to her like a brother from *Normandie.*

I have no idea how to deal, cop(e). She was a trickster figure, clever 'nuff to speak wit convictim [sic] about her estranged boo, strong enough to survive anything a motherfucker could throw at her.

"Sometimes rap's just wrong," she added, owning the conversation. "Messy. Full of misanthropy. More fucked up than flippin' funky. Really, realistically. There's nothing going on but posturing there. Like my baby said, he shouldn't be taking the blame for that."

I shoot Ms. de Latour several times to evidence the fact she remains a lover of the brother—that he's still/alive, threw her. It's more than a broken record. "Comment Faire" from Vitaa is in my ear. How?

"Enough," she said, as if her voice had been put on tape delay. So as to not jawn on me.

Neither one of us (Ms. de Latour being a professional/photographer) outwardly expressed concern about the potential of our pictures to steal his soul. After all, we were not interested in focusing on afro-eccentric, grim fairy tales or snapping for the sake of some sort of frame story. This would not be the second coming of *Things Fall Apart.* Although Ms. de Latour did have visions of creating a slide show, I never dreamed she'd go "through" with it.

I shoot a selfie, too. Able to look at myself straight in the guerrilla glass, fleetingly enjoying a freedom that hero(n) attempting to fly high, without the n— in him, could not.

"Later," I said to Ms. de Latour, noticing Charlie's Angel (or, a sizzling mama) hanging outside, blacks on tv's *America's Got Talent* show totally off the chain, acting satisfied. Having spent an entire life saying what I had to say, I'm thinking, now I gotta go where I gotta go.

BRENT CUNNINGHAM

from *BACK TO EARTH*

9

these poems
are poems
they have ideas
affixed in-
to simple cry-
stals
welcome, dear
aquarium
to the former
future
unprepared
unseasoned
not what but
who
the Ma-
sters working
in a circle
lit by tapers,
word-people,
they eat, drink
sleep
in a little
cocoon: wine & meat,
cloth & glazes,
forerunner
of Peter
Thiel's is-
land, wrapt
in the very
first predicate
back on Earth

10

inside this
earth-
en shield
is space, limited
telling it-
self
an unhappy
tale: of s-
carcity, w-
omen as prizes
stay in
your tent
letting death
do its work—
who really
acts? who
sees? why
would a Ruler
give up
their things?
a heart
in the un-
derworld,
purple rug-
s
back on earth

11

o tireless,
tiresome com-
plaints
& reme-
dies for extinct
disease
embalmed, o
the com-
plaints of Men—
gnarrrrr!
why not be

what
you were
in Oaxaca
enthused, taking
notes
the idea of
the idea
of thought—
remember?
anything
you wrote
real because
of poetry
oran-
ge, bison-head-
ed creatures
eating, shitting,
crying
& especially
thinking
back on earth

12

again
the idea
to look out
blot out
from the train
my boredom
not special
at the pass-
sing things
stars, moons
seeming
to glimpse
an importance
greater
than money
well, forget it
your con-

cerns,
to carry
the fight
into num-
erical
space, O
Ruler, O great
tables, what-
ever was thought
first for
when time
was young &
speech a dis-
stant dream
back on earth

GARIN CYCHOLL

from *PRAIRIED*

Prairie

my body)

is a

journey four

strings
plucked

from *here*

I is the poet of the plain;
the poet of standing waters,
of lungs gone to seed, of
ancient seepage

but as the song gets
closer to me, it
loses its place

prairie
collapses under the eye's
weight into a fistful of
smokestacks, a waterless
tower, five drums tagged
Simple Hazard—
grasses' flat momen-
tum against me

all this hear
lost in the horizon,
I's a shrinking map

a played out land "a
place that threatens
to become no place"
the sq. ft. of the black
prairie soil beneath me

"that's the thing
about turf—it ain't what
it used to be"

whole country,
no longer demarcated by
rivers, but fallow and
gridded, barbed and razor-
wired "Kansas City,"
Wilbert Harrison screaming
into all-night radio about
those "crazy little women"
a voice sunk in soil (not a-
cross it) territory lost in Sun-
day drives and half-assed
oblivion

some prophet yammering
about the "photosynthesis of the
heart"
the prairie gods
laugh him down—they prefer the
reptile's cold hiss, slime mold
slipping current, the stream,
the shallow well, the spring,
the crick, the water-
hole—
"the begin of the end of things"

against the cartographer's dream—
every water in its place, the Atlantic

shelved and every blues in its delta
—but the Lakes, the nation's work
bench or the empire's slop sink? the
canal, the seaway, and "international
waters"

to recover the ponds
to recover the streams
to recover the aquifers
to recover myself

*   *   *

(when Douglas Ewart invented the prairie

like Gwen in wild weed,
Ewart blows westward,
his ax pointed square
south; he reinvents the
compass, spits it from
his mouth; downbeat
and long tones mixing
in & out of new harmony

there are those who'd
say the prairie dreams
us perhaps

Duriel's laughter
strikes out across that
sound like some boy a-
mong the Dan   like
some Dan Diss caught
between the blood &
the gospel,

I is dis-
solved in their songs

*   *   *

no prophet is

ever born far
from the sound
of seeping waters—

but in this
corner, this Zeke,
this scroll-eater, his
vision of flesh
made grass, of
corn growing
from the corpse's
mouth:
                "an end
has come; the rod
has blossomed.
tune your dobro
to the flood; it
will arrive with
the sound of
1000 dobros,
the sound of a
leaf skidding
across asphalt"

he'll find his
voice there
and "there was
nothing startling
in the weather"

or *to leave the
gods out of all
this*, this Ty,
this prairied Ti-
resias, croaking
canary stung w/
Testicular Dis-
genesis:
                "the
reptile is an
oracle; the salt

science of fish
kills and en-
docrine dis-
ruptors, true
BLACK WATER.
the frogs inter-
sexed

what crank
what atrazine
what shallow well

between them,
a taunt, a
warning, and
a horror

*   *   *

Ty's song

so much of me is hooked to a rumor—
if Hera'd not struck me, two-tongued
and memory in my fingertips, nearly fifty
and quick as fuck

quick as sea water
quick to catch my body's own murmurs
quick to cast a shadow

or some other Zeus,
my tongue, stress-
fractured and
mythy

astream
abed
with you,
a stranger

my mouth is always

working at the world;
cock and cunt and
you, Wm Blake

the great frog on
which the world
rides

gigged 'n battered
cooked 'n et
cooked 'n et

* * *

Zeke's song

hear the word I've overheard:

"They had the form of men and
the sound of their wings like
the sound of many waters, the
appearance of the brightness
round about as they go forth
into the plain, where they shall
drink water by measure and in
dismay—
rumor follows rumor;
knees weak as water, every man
in his room of pictures, walls
drawn with all kinds of creeping
things and loathsome beasts. The city
is the caldron and we are the flesh."

* * *

the organic
or the chemical
prairie—is
there really a
difference? a-
sog w/ runoff

aflame in memory

or the eye
abuzz with
bee or gun-
fire?

(flowers lit to some forgotten lady

is water ever not
peculiar to its mud
and rock, its soup
boiling
down from
the Iron
Range

the prairie's insides
are more of the same—
roots and bone

DEBRA DI BLASI

from *ANYTHING NOW GONE*

SONG OF THE MONKEY KING

I turned two too fast. Terrible twos: language waterlogged by my fluid vision: fluent Right Eye. I couldn't speak words for all the visuals to interpret, translate to a voice that only sang strange noise tied to ribbons of light strung patterned from other to other, one to two, here to there, everywhere colors and colors on colors and colors in colors. Squeak-squawked crow caws until the mother stomped her feet until the father bought me a used Hohner harmonica I sucked on at night to sleep, see-sawing a single chord. During the day I held the harp to my left ear and listened to Little Walter blow "Juke" over and over on black vinyl spinning under an old needle on a record player somewhere downstairs, master music maker rising like a bear on its hinds: bitchin beast blues, sweet as goat's teat. And the father dancing in his suit, strip teasing the mother—neck tie and white starch and gray gabardine landing in her lap growing wet with want. Those were the days when, they were. Then.

Lower math: Three plus one equals misery. Especially if the one is a fat-ass mother-fucking car-dealing money-laundering pornmonger.

Big Bad Wolf knew the depraved cravings of men. Knew his own sewn from the want of big cock more than of little women. Knew he'd never have the big to get the little, thus never get *the whole balla wax*. Never be *the cat's pajamas, cat's meow*—not even the cat, for that matter, fat cat though he was, with dough rising high in that Los Angeles sky like exhaust fumes from tailpipes of the thousand-plus of automobiles he sold each year at the Sale-O-Rama, yeah, sooner or later they'd all want to buy the shiny gorp and paint, sooner than later they'd find a way to get no matter how low their credit or how high their debt.

Hindsight: Truth is, he could've had the power but for his own fear. Fear of climbing the tree, ape/man afraid not of heights, no, but of falling, getting knocked down, *pulled* down a limb or two by every big-cock ape below who could see Big Bad Wolf's hiney and tiny testicles and peter petered out before its time. See, fear has a scent: acrid like piss and musky like skunk; it has a look: blue-black convolution like squid ink shat in a stormy ocean. And Big Bad Wolf must've stunk, must've waddled darkly through his glass showroom and tinseltown, tripping over his trepidation, leaking low esteem and chagrin down his triple chin. Because he was no different than most: The more he got the more he realized he lacked, the more he lacked the more he wanted, the more he wanted the more he found any goddamn way to get more. And he did. And he didn't.

Showed his nudie photos of beauty to his rich suck-ass pals who drooled and har-dee-har-har'd, growing hard in their tailor-mades while the maid came and went in the Wolf's den, serving hors d'oeuvres and cocktails to cocksuckers of L.A. who'd pay, they said, for photos like those, or knew someone who would. And oh by the way: A whole new movie industry was opening up as wide as beauty's thighs, and it was gonna make some bastard fucking rich, selling moving crotch shots to movie big shots for private screenings and who-knows-who. After all, the rich had been paying to finger erotica from time immemorial—Kama Sutra to Carmina Burana, Venus of Willendorf to Venus de Milo—and the more forbidden the more they'd pay.

So Big Bad Wolf sucked on his big fat cigar and nodded his big fat head and grinned his big fat mouth. Said nothing. Thought: *I'm way aheada ya boys.* Beauty's beautiful cunt already gracing thousands of bathrooms and backrooms of mechanics and autoworkers and electricians and plumbers and oil riggers and carpenters, ad nauseam, spread legs spreading across the nation, inviting every pecker to take the plunge, her sleepy bedroom eyes wanting, it seemed, *them!* Of course it was the fatherlover she imagined behind the camera lens, imagined him probing so deep inside her that every John, Dick and Harry felt he was handsome and hung. *One helluva woman who could make you feel that much a man just by lookin at ya, and from a glossy, no less!* And they all wanted beauty. And they all needed beauty. And they all couldn't have beauty. And so they struggled and strived toward the top of the tree, dangling in the lower branches as pencil-thin limbs overhead snapped in their greasy fists. Still they tried to ascend, spurring the nation's vast economic growth of the 1950s, goaded in part by beauty's juicy pink lips parted here and there. What's more, Big Bad Wolf'd already bought a movie camera. Already hired a cameraman fired from a Hollywood studio for not sucking a producer. And Wolfman knew in his ice-blue heart that if he could capture beauty and handsome on film—fucking and sucking and bucking…plucking each other's groin feathers—he'd be the luckiest fucker in the whole corn-shucking country. And maybe then then then he'd get his little head up and thus hold his big head up and taste that savorysweet monkey meat from the leafy green canopy of life.

Imagine four strands of packing string. Pristine, uncorrupted white cotton twisted thin. Imagine each strand converging on one point: • Then dirty fingers, imagine, caked in cum and spit and shit and blood, twisting a knot so tight there's no way to undo what's been done. Braiding now sullied skeins into a rope, tying the rope into a noose, saying, *Hang yourself.* And there's simply no other way out but swinging from the long high branch of a tree.

String theory.

There's no such thing as empty space, see. It's all soup. Even the soup bowl's soup. Oh sure, maybe a bubble here and there where time expands, then pops, then sucks in its belly. But inside that bubble there's something, which ain't nothing. And when objects or people or thoughts expand, moving away from each other, they're still linked by the thread of what was. And what is. And what will be. Sum: One fine mid-afternoon scientists with their better-all-the-time machines will discover the broth and finally see what I see: strings of light and dark all tangled pretty—or pretty ugly when there's a big fat dirty knot growing fatter as the strands converge toward chaos. Toward the rope, the noose, the hanging tree.

Big Bad Wolf insisted: "Get yer hubby to fuck ya on film."

Beauty blanched. "But he doesn't know!"

"Bout the nudies?"

Shook her pretty head no.

Big Bad laughed Wolflike and sneered. "He's *gonna* know. Either you tell or me. Which?"

"Give me a week," said she, weak-kneed. Knowing she'd need more time. Without end.

The sacred monkeys of India live on human rooftops, eating human food, drinking human water, excreting monkey shit and piss. Indians worship and revere them as hairy scuttling gods and goddesses. Not a care in the world, those lucky lucky primates. Except:

Old patriarch monkey gets older, slower. Gets fat, indolent and complacent. He reclines between the crenels, propped up on one elbow like a potentate of antiquity, overseeing his dusty domain, his harem, his progeny. Every now and then he fornicates, lazily, as if bored with boring. Every now and then he gazes into the distance as if knowing, by means of a scenario extant in this DNA, there's trouble just over the horizon. And whaddya know! Somewhere over the horizon outside the city gates a young monkey general grooms his soldiers for battle. They subsist on next to nothing. Train amongst the scraggy trees and craggy soil. Forego wet heterofuck for a dry homohump now and then. And then the general, the despot, the hairy Attila with this hairy hordes invade the placid monkey city. They sweep and swarm. They stalk offspring of old eminence and mortally wound, exterminating his lineage. The young general chases the patriarch. Young soldiers surround and bite. Old blue-blood's bleeding in a distant treetop now. The king is dead—or at least routed from his kingdom—long live the king! And the females tremble. They know what's coming: Rape of the simian Sabines. See them quiver not out of ecstasy but terror as the new patriarch ravages them from behind. Rape after rape after rape after rape. Until his firstborn spills writhing from a wounded womb. Then all is calm. For a while. All is paradise. For a while. For a while, all is right with the helter-skelter world. Depending, of course, on whose perspective.

Whose: My Right Eye's.

One week later at the Sale-O-Rama the handsome father took a break and took a piss alongside Big Bad Wolf. Said nothing, neither one. Not the father. Not Big Bad Wolf who had a hard time peeing, especially next to the mighty matey. Couldn't relax, no. Shut his eyes and thought of water…oceans…fish swimming…dolphins leaping…whales spouting…that made him think of the father's gleaming orca. And his little minnow knew damn well the pecker pecking order and fled dry. The father however foundain'd nicely. Finished up, zipped up, washed up. As he passed Big Bad Wolf on the way out, his eye caught the other's. And he winked. Oops. The father would've taken it back if he'd known. Would've said, "Just a friendly gesture, buddy. Nothing implied." But he hadn't known. Couldn't've. No one knew what evil lurked in the clogged arteries of Big Bad Wolf. Not even Big Bad Wolf himself knew how green his envy grew like mold on old meat. How his hunger for revenge sat bitter on his tongue, lump of phlegm, clot of blood, turd of shit. How his want to whatever he couldn't have drove him to drink. Too much. Not enough.

In a drunken rage Big Bad Wolf raped the mother. Not with his cock but his fist. All that teeny-weenie small-balls flaccid fertility-flask curled-tight knuckles he shoved into the mother's cunt, pumping violently in and out, growling, *Ya owe me this, ya stupid bitch, anna whole lot more.* And however she screamed nobody heard. Not in that bleak backroom office of the cavernous car dealership locked tight after hours and no one around for miles, seemed to her. Not the father her husband her lover her friend at home stirring a pot of Campbell's tomato soup color of blood for he and Lucy-me, singing *Here I got one pretty kitten. There one pretty cat. I'm a lucky ol' Tom everywhere. Now whada ya think a that?* while the mother was forced-bent painful over a desk, her face pushed nose-flat against sweaty mahogany, her pretty pink lips sliced against her pretty white teeth, pretty pink pussy bruised blood blue.

"I gotta a huge fuckin dick," shouted Big Bad Wolf, pump-pump-pumping, "a big whale's dick!" (The mother wailed.) "Sperm whale!" he screamed. (The mother wailed.) "Great blue fuckin whale!" he shrieked. "Orca! Orca! Orca!" (The mother spewed vomit.) Came in his drawers, Wolf did. Black silk tailor-made boxers smegma'd sticky and hot. Then cold. Chill clear down his spine to his asshole. The body's hint—*uh-oh omen*—he ignored. Only farted to warm his sphincter. Smelled his fist. Admired the glisten. Lit a cigar. Sat.

He watched beauty fumble with her pink panties caught on the heel of her pink shoe, trying to pull her silkies up, hands and knees trembling so badly, *Looks like a fuckin spazz*, he thought she did, and briefly felt empathy no more than a fleeting flicker at the fringe of his suet-filled soul. Remorse come-n-gone. Then a huge swelling-looming: *Fear.* That she'd tell the cops. That they'd come for him. That there'd be scandal and momentary disgrace. And it would be so goddamn much work effort time energy sweat to make it all go away quick, clean it up, shrug and forget. And his wife, *Christ! how she'd bitch and nag and shop!* Made him tired already thinking about it so fast. So he opened his safe and counted out five twenties. Beauty stared at the handout in the outstretched hand. Stared into the open safe. And though really not smart at all, she calculated all real quick and figured there wasn't enough money in the whole damn-bitter world to pay for what he'd done to her. But the plenty stacks of Jacksons still inside the safe might be a sufficient start.

She took his puny handout. Promised not to tell.

Big Bad Wolf thought he heard the click-clack of an engine shift to high gear as beauty walked out of his office in her high bloody heels.

Who deserves to die? Where do you draw the line between abiding life and causing death? Which crime's that Nth worse, that breath too much wind against the tightrope walker? The monkey governor puts to death the retarded killer, then kills half a village of children sleeping in their beds. The fundamentalist fanatic threatens us with eternal damnation for our body's desire then fucks the skanky whores along the airport road. The redneck mouthbreathing preacher condones the shooting of homosexuals during the day while at night shoots his wad onto pics of little boys. *Who's to say who's to die?* Well, I've wanted death for plenty in my life. Prayed for a *deus ex machina* to drop rocks from the rafters and land heavy on the head of some fucker so bad *fucker*'s a commendation. I've imagined twisting a knife in twisted hearts. Imagined shooting, pummeling, eviscerating the vile. Imagined banishing the bad to a parallel universe where they're prey to themselves as predator, times a thousand. Imagined a handheld weapon set to *vaporize*, erasing evil's name and number from history forever, his story gone forever good. I've seen my onyx need to destroy bead like sweat on my furrowed brow. Watched it evaporate from the backs of my hands hairy with nullifying vengeance and swirl through the world. I've tasted pleasure in another's pain. Spit schadenfreude at Icarus descending. Each reprisal's the scree underfoot that sends me backward down the slippery slope. Two steps forward, three steps back. Sisyphus with a monkey on his back chewing the fat. *Eee eee eee!*

Forgive me, you whom I've forsaken with my fury. Even you, Wolf/man/chimpanzee/ass who set the ball rolling, the boulder tumbling, the mountain crumbling beneath all our feet. Even now.

JOHN DOMINI

CLOSING CREDITS FUN & COUNTERFORCE

So you've seen what there is to see, start to finish, but you're still in your seat. Wasn't a great flick, no, that's not what brought you out—and anyway, didn't some smart guy sometime say that the movies were an artform based on how long a person could go without having to pee? Smart guy, and you can vouch for him, after, what's it been, here? Ninety minutes, a hundred? The movie had its limits and so does the old flesh and bones. Still, now that they're rolling the credits, you'll take a minute more. There was that recurring snatch of music, theme and descant, playful. Could've been Monteverdi, and let's nail that down, composer and title. Also, let's watch the fantasy die. Come the credits, everyone dies, even the assassin with half a dozen passports and a dusting of anthrax in each. Everyone collapses into a set of phonemes, white on black. The trickbag turns inside out: physical trainers and Personal Assistants and the crew in Wardrobe and Makeup. As for the zombies, these days there's a boutique operation out in the Valley. The fantasy falls into cemetery rows, names and brand names. Except, not this time.

This time you see the credits turn cannibal. They turn on each other, pieces tearing out pieces.

Is this a trick cooked up by the tech people? A joke? A joke would mean you've been watching a comedy. The comedies throw in a last gag as the screen goes black. They show the outtakes, interrupting the credits with the failures, like when the cameras caught some pretty boy in his Dodgers cap, though the scene was set in gladiatorial Rome. The outtakes, that trick, that's a risk, come to think. It can look as if the better laughs took place over in the real world.

Anyway, tonight, this might not've been a great flick, but it wasn't for laughs. That's not why you laid down eight or ten bucks. If all you'd wanted was a bit of diversion, you've got that at home, the smaller screens, the handy remotes. Hey, don't they call it a "joystick"?

Tonight, you came out for something bigger and more mindless. The full in-the-round. And look where you wound up, with credits that turn cannibal. Big letters that go all Godzilla on the little ones. You never realized the letter F posed such a threat, you never noticed its Tyrannosaur overbite, but here the F has erupted out of some perfectly well-behaved word, some tidy and justified line of print. Somehow the dinosaur DNA got in and the F has 'shroomed and gone carnivore. It's chomping out chunks of the rest and gobbling them down. It's not just tearing into the stuff up-screen, the information you might've gotten through already, if you gave two hoots, it's taking the attack down-screen. Ripping away the recognition that's yet to come! Imagine the crushed hopes, for some fringe player in the industry. Some guy listed as Octopus Wrangler, maybe Tattoo Finagler, he's sitting in the theater waiting for just one name to scroll into view, and he glimpses its penumbra, the glow that peeks above the screen floor, the rising of the dream. His own immortal name. But then out of the black'n'white above, in a ruckus too fast to follow, this mass-murdering blind raptor of an F rears and snaps and tears it away.

Imagine the crush and bewilderment. Except, wow, you don't have to imagine. You're there. Shrinking in your seat, wondering about the people in tech, wondering about 3D. Hullaballoo-cination.

There's the F run amok, and okay, F as in freak and fierce and fuck-all. But what's this one, an R? That letter's always seemed a peaceable galoot, the better half of purr. Look at it now, though, R as in fuck-arr, a capital that towers over the rest, galumphing around and using that long front strut like a tentacle with a claw. The letter yanks smaller ones out in clusters and scoops them up into its belly-bulge. It's complicated. First the names and name-fragments get plucked up and shoveled into a black belly, then inside that white outline the white nubbins cook down, in enzymes or something, and then as those crumbs of captured chalk evaporate the chalk outline around them grows denser. The breakdown of one seems to buttress the other. It's complicated, it's not uninteresting—and it's not even the weirdest thing. You've got the shreds of former signifiers frittering away inside the R's parabolic gut, and you've got an F ripping out dreams before they happen, and it looks as if the party's just beginning.

Also there's a kind of vacuum U, just look, a U wildly overgrown and schlupping down chunks of credits. Wherever the U rumbles into place, above it the rows of print start to tremble, for a while they resist, but soon there's some slippage, a little a, or is that an @, part of a logo or website. Once that piece drops into the maw beneath, into the rattling U, as in fuck U, other rivets start to give, the lines crumble, and there's that chalk circle-of-life again. The fallen frags evaporate, their cook-pot waxes stronger, and from there things only get crazier. In a couple of spots where the white flotsam and jetsam have been sucked away, the letters and what-have-you sucked into the big vowel's gape, whoosh, in a couple spots the black doesn't hold out either. Not only the credits themselves get vacuumed from the screen. Also the credits' backdrop, the black, rips loose and tumbles into the vacuum. The very earth beneath our feet rips loose!

Or something like that, if you can picture our eyeballs having feet. It leaves you wondering: what's underneath? Behind the black, the border of our universe, insofar as eight or ten bucks buys you the universe—what?

Not much of the backdrop tears away, a scrap here and there, and beneath it the most you can make out is more scraps, fragments again, this time composed of color and jitter. Fire ants and Daisy Dukes? What are you watching? The movie, it could be, under there, where the black's been torn away. The flick you thought you came out to see. It could be, as you sort out a detail or two more, Kalashnikovs and synchronized swimming. It's something familiar, these tatters, these flashes where the black used to be. Granted, the edit is à la nutso. That slam-dunk for the championship, it's so far out of synch, no way it could be the work of the people in tech. Still, whoever did this, they couldn't take everything down to smithereens. They left a few stretches of aqueduct above the ruins. And isn't that what you came out to see? A story with staying power? It's as if one of the monsters threw a wrench into the works and then the spit-out gears and bolts and sprockets came together as a better mechanism. Wrench-aissance.

Though you'd swear that no machinery could function long among these Zilla-Letters, these Destructo-Glyphs. They've got friends, more trouble. They've got three Ns running interference, when did that happen, one N pitching in with the F and the U, helping to pry loose a recalcitrant white bit here and there, and the other two running interference around the lumbering tentacled R. Not quite so large, this auxiliary three. Not so monstrous, but no less of a menace to the lingering credits, the huddled names and brand names. Brand logos, websites, stubborn traces of a former reality—though stubborn, yes. They do appear to be hanging in, now that you've hung in, now as you get the larger picture.

They do appear, these bits and symbols here and there, to have banded together into a barricade. Or they've made themselves over as, what, a spiderweb? Lines of white print, or what used to be print, have wound themselves into thread and stitched back and forth across a patch of the confounding emergent movie.

When did that happen? How could it happen?

Wherever the backdrop came off, wherever the black split open and erupted in color and drama (isn't that drama, in those torn spaces?), the white bricabrac must've first been stripped. You couldn't tear out chunks of black, or the U couldn't, without first cleaning off the white. Yet there's some kind of comeback afoot. Some kind of resistance, that's the larger picture. The credits have mustered a counterforce. Those huddles are deliberate, that barricade is holding, and dinosaur DNA alone isn't enough to turn a few random letters into Masters of the Universe. They may have the size, but the others have the numbers. The others can shake loose of their rank and file, the torpor of reading left to right. A setup like that, left-right-left-right across the colorless flats, wasn't it ripe for plucking? Wasn't it bound to shred and crack and flinder? In the end, turn cannibal?

Now that the smaller critters have been set free, they can find ways around the marauding jumbos. Where the fabric of the former universe burst open, where there's an outbreak of story, no matter how bizarre and pyrotechnic, they can sling lines of containment.

Is the monster R in trouble? Is that what you're seeing, a brave squad of lower-case w's and h's, maybe a t or two, wrapping their arms around each other to create a kind of lasso? You never noticed that about letters before, how they've got arms, most of them, loving arms apparently, and extensible too. The way this squad links up, they might be taking that Sistine ceiling touch-of-God to the next level. They're a rope, a group-grope-rope, and they pitch their loop past the hench-Ns and around the fixed foot of the R. They yoke the big roughhouse and set him flailing and tottering. As it wobbles, wow, look, a few of the bits in its belly tumble out. You never thought of that, how the bastard may be huge but he's still two-dimensional, he's got his limits. He spills undigested nubbins of credit.

Elsewhere some of the advertising trademarks have woven a kind of barbed wire around the F. A cage for a Tyrannosaur? A mad experiment, homespun white wire, but then again, why not? If the credits birthed the Destroyer, can't they build a box to hold it? Some of those advertising trademarks were bristly to begin with, the people in Design wanted tension in the graphics, and meantime, over in another quadrant, other leftovers have come up with a tactic for the omnivorous vacuum U. A trick out of Machiavelli, bait and switch. First, a couple-three broken lines of phonemes will gather and compose themselves, as if they still added up to something comprehensible. Of course they don't—what you're seeing would never be mistaken for words in sequence—but nonetheless those few chameleonic lines will attract the U, eager as ever to schlup. It's not as if the big upright can read, after all. But no sooner is the urn in place than, above its hungry mouth, the ruse breaks and scatters. The signifier was only signifyin'.

The idea is, each time, you leave the freak vowel more run down. Doesn't even the Devourer get run down? Doesn't an anomaly, too, hit the Wall? Anyway what you're seeing is all a mad experiment. A counterforce of the blind, unsure of its end, it scrabbles on feeling its way.

It's a good thing you got out! Back home you'd have fallen into that stalling tactic, that channel-surfer's tactic, blipping from scene to scene in search of just the right shock on which to end. That notion that the right scene would set up your destiny. Good thing you came out instead, you risked a doddering and fusty entertainment, based on how long a person can go without having to pee. The flicks themselves have long since run out of surprises. The assassin falls in love; the bookish girl in black whoops it up in a candy-colored romper room. There never was much opportunity for surprise, in ninety minutes or a hundred, and there's even less these days, when you need a multi-million-dollar urban-renewal package just to save the downtown moviehouse. The big star-studded shebang, winding up through the coming attractions and down through the credits in their grave-rows, that's long since been squeezed dry and shoehorned into smaller screens. Yet here you sit, putting off the bathroom. It feels like a stone in your belly, but that's nothing compared with what's going on in the belly of the R. It's mostly empty now, that upper-storey belly, now that the rebels have lasso'd its back foot. As the flabby consonant struggled against its leash, most of its half-digested bits and pieces tumbled out. The remains, gnawed and pitted and no way legible. But, look, wow, the monster's stomach acids had a side effect. Look, a few of these nubbins have been infected. We're talking zombie nubbins, and they're sprouting up, too, muscling up. The alien spawn flex their dorsi, they spread their talons, and one of them's going after the rope that holds the mother-letter's legs. The resistance needs to regroup, and if they had any last semblance of jot and tittle, of names or logos, they've lost it now. Next thing you know, anything's possible, it's fresh dynamics altogether, here a Visigoth or a chimera, there a warrior saint or a comely stranger with a quick sword and a reflecting shield. Now when did that happen?

JOHANNA DRUCKER

EcoLaLia: UnNatural Selection: Procedurally Driven

START

Automata replicate. Antic cannibals appear. Morpho-zooic memes divide and rule the earth.

Restart. Cannibal antics rule the earth. Proto-memes replicate in the primordial state. Initial conditions divide the earth. The automata have their way.

Everywhere is chaos and primordial combinations. Cellular memes automate the start conditions. The entropy field generates the earth. First generation organisms are fallen and rise again. All through the night their cries are heard.

A red cellular storm comes from the west and automata fill the sky. Cannibals replicate and divide their cries. Memes have their combinations and generate again. The darkening clouds shelter the antic herds beneath the initial threat of destruction. Placing a mark before them they are safe, but not from the species of their discontent, which breeds remarkably, prolifically, and with admirable invention of initial detail. The combinations divide to rule the earth. The more the automata struggle, the more they roam through primordial chaos where zoo-morphs eat the blood of memes and suck dry the hot stones which lie on the earth at midday. The true replicants are swathed in automated rags and lie like primordial bundles on the backs of entropic wagons, hauled into the night marketplace to be sold as fallen organisms.

Machinations eat the antic creatures and chaos rules our waking lives with or without the earth. Cannibal cries shelter the threat of strangers in the animate world. Replicate the start conditions.

PAST TENSION

The mad alpha entity caused them all to dance before him, keeping the night from the rooms he filled with feasting. Mad alpha: A plague took its toll on the peoples of the south, who came begging at the gates for the means to understand their plight. The plague: reptile locked into the primeval garden came straight through the walls and gave his prophecy. A reptile and: No one wanted to hear the rest, but settled into the soft cushions and watched the lithe movements of the spectacle projected from the belly of the beast. No one wanted: Horror spread across the eardrums of the listeners as they made the signals of the dance into a tune. Horror: In the west were projects, being made, and executed, with the labor of many loves and skin of the lost. Projects: The effort of the sounds echoed across the plains, carrying with it the threat of physical forces. Effort: News travelled through the network coolly and threw itself with material urgency before the outliers of the distribution. News: They snuffed out the flame of rebellion by burying it in their own actions, but never before had such misery played out in the collective tone of their communication networks. Flame: Repressed by desire for a better way, the night beasts took their revenge in dreams of dark and unmentionable dimension. Desire: Hot milk came to scald the lining of their pouches and had its way with the hatchlings who had been left outside the walls to appease the ravaging hordes. Heat: The earth trembled and the tracks left in the sands were deep. Tremblings: But the jaws of the ruthless soldier drones had been sewn shut, and their legs were bound before them with the rough stuff of their collective undoing. Ruthlessness: In the heavens the storms rose with bombast and whirring, making good the foretold history. Rising: But in the north more rumors and uprising sent chills back into the body politic. Uprisings: The heartfelt urge to propagate the earth was shunted off into a ditch where the furrows ran deeper than wide and the seasons proved unfruitful across a rapid cycle of generations. Urges: Nothing begat nothing and the population withered on the vine as well as their hopes, which hung in the wind and were signs to all to stay away. Withered: Nothing could be done to coax the crops from the barren face of the land which dried into a grimace and refused to be subjected to the law. Coaxed: The hardships were inherited and passed into reinforced memory as the stories told to justify the shape of time and earth. Dried: And the offspring went forth into the world to try and find wives with names already on them. Find: A strong instinct drew them to the mild east, the cardinal point associated with the constant replenishment of fountains and food supplies. Drew: Kissing their mothers on the blind cheeks and keeping aloof from the vale of tears, the many set out to find the scarce resources, sniffing blind along the pheromone trails. Kept: Small rodents crept from their holes to view with disbelief the new preview of a fertile world without rupture and the minor flora bloomed in anticipation of a fervent spring. Without: The beasts of the field gave up their earlier addictions and rose to the occasion on the sprightly wings of hope and charity. To the occasion: The darkened moon returned to its former place against the breast of the sky while dangling its feet in the fields of time, waiting for the new seed to burst from its room and be welcomed. The wings of: Foodstuffs long wrapped up and stored beneath the wings of night were brought out again, and the ruling minds held their energy aloft just long enough to permit the genetic mergers to take place. In the fields of: The harsh judgment of the ages was suspended as the selection process melted the bitter frost with regret. Beneath the wings of: A moment in time broke free from the rest and threw itself into the primordial heavens and all the creatures stopped their heavy hearts with rejoicing. With: It became an age of wonder and slipped on the patterned movements of ambiguous renewal. Away: Nothing *was the same.*

PRESENT PERFECTION

Now is the moment like the rest made to order and delivered through the window into our hands before we even manage to put up the means of payment. A landscape under construction throws itself into the action. A scaffolded canyon absorbs the traffic and the old trails near downtown. Taking a signal from the monitor, the brilliant blush of a manufactured dawn breaks into an eager smile for a bank of cameras tucked up under concrete beams where they find their way into everybody's file, sooner or later, according to the system of networks by which the analogue bits engage freely with each other. Moment *throws the traffic into the system.*

The newspaper is inclined to treat the human spill as a toxic interest piece but the committee on images is fighting internally to have the whole case suppressed. A minor dignitary still entitled to protection is pulled from the headlines and put into the silo while the media shoot their feed into an underground storage unit whose seal is timed to last for seventeen statute years. Released from a long confining sentence another not so minor figure registers a shift in magnetic fields as the crowd gathers to contest his conviction or celebrate his captured progress from obscurity back into the bright light of continual reinvention. News*paper entitled a long shift of reinvention.*

The election cycle leaves no space to breathe and so the climate managers put their automatic filter mechanisms back to the zero point and wait while the public theater plays itself into an augmented off-screen version of the story. Major *vehicles are being moved around the circulation system and the ways into the center nodes are being paved with protest.* No *choice of blood is offered and no control of supply except by the monolithic forces of justification lying its way into the hearts of millions where it festers in tabloid poses.*

Anything that can be asked of them is, first by virtue of pollution, etching its way through the minds and hard finish of their cars, then leaking through the plumbing as if by accident and washing up on beaches just beyond the limits of vacation time in order to stain the hands of baby animals with tag markers. The traffic elements outweigh the comic in the blast of poison clouds, but the willingness of the corrupt to document their ways with energetic chic remains a major tool of distraction. Funneled into housing too short for their long legs and raised up on the hydraulic lift of high resolution video, they march out into the marketplace full of expectation. The reduced menu is barely interactive, so the need for drugs is balanced against the desire to be in the colorfast track of this year's theme song. Anything else outweighs the hydraulic drugs of the world.

Pollsters announce their own inquiries by forcing a foot through the questions and the mail comes later as if surprised to find that material objects still need to be moved through small spaces and beg to be held in the light while being read. A scanner makes it possible to leave the planet briefly but in order to sustain life a few more drawers of instructions manufactured in a breach of contracts wait to be decoded. The vines entwine and viable commodities swear they have been here before, but the noise from the machine is no longer heard above ground. We wait for winter to regain its former seasonal complaints. The melting core of fears lets off steam and the glare of my brother's other new technology passes itself off as a part of another marriage. The unknown kidnapped to prove a point, the newsstand hours fill with days and the story blinks back at us as if to fool us into believing it is really here. Inquiries make commodities regain the glare as if to fool us.

Familiar insights, carved in the arc of history, remain long with us. Machinations are the stuff of our waking lives with or without the theory language to describe them. Insect forms revive the animate world, their passion for collective action able to sustain the impulse towards renovation in the face of an equal and opposite disinterest. Waste not want is the poison of choice. The rising sun made a promise of heat it was unable to keep. Haze muffled the air, taking an edge off the rays. The grey green sludge lightened and structured patterns emerged from the woolly atmosphere. Arc of waking choice unable to take note.

Then the bees appear. Shimmering in their bright titanium waistcoats, robot whiskers alive to the least amount of sun, they are under a new command; brilliant as raindrops in another time they refract wave motions while they move. The headline patterns of their well regulated dance just miss the verve of the original, but the whole hive shudders at an occasional disturbance when a stochastic re-org resets the system. Parables in a radically altered universe of relations, particles, that is, they appear swift as upstream ions making their way against ever increasing odds of collapse. Bees alive just miss parables swift as odds.

We have lost our horizon. The view dampens spirits but the devastation continues, plundering the remnants of the natural risk management. The derivatives of exploitation are resold on an open market even as spring songbirds make their way back into the neighborhood looking for lumber, twigs, building materials. How to court the wind? Put out bowls and watch the surface ripple. Impossible to hold the forces that move us. Mechanical pendulums find their way into synchronous motion without any overt control. Proximity relations determine outcomes as surely as isolation enervates. Horizon continues as an open wind, wound. Watch the forces without isolation.

New and ever more fragile ecologies of language iterate, never confusing mere complexity for adaptation. System dependence is not just a start condition, but an ongoing one. Tongues abound, unbound, free wheeling their capacity for blending unhindered by mores. Once apparently entropic, the situation reorganizes, surprising itself as well as the us who are its collective ancestral soup. Method? No, just media and mediation, the relational forces of a gratefully unstable situation. Generative irritants foster transformation.

FUTURE TONGUE

Language will shrink fit demands rapidly emerging universe.

The big horizon is constructed according to nostalgically figured tropes holographed projection stale map heavens repeating its constellations over over again.

Nothing gained. Sum total equilibrium is preserved certain stochastic permission within everything appears aloud.

Whose inheritance is this anyway, asks small black instrument panel soft place making time disappear again again according well known intimate cycles.

Plague was long ago wiped out association though scars remain not every animal can recall full encyclopedia activities appropriate every occasion, which is why streets are posted
instructions, reminders decorum.

Power migrates St. Elmo's fire touching heads with shimmering aura instantaneous notice striking beating heart a virgin broadcast her hands plunge searching rapid stream of images.

But accumulation material has been banned use influence remains residual instrument control must be deployed rapidly rapidly swift kiss placed machine brow figure forming itself public sphere mind.

Takeover bid considered bad action all urgency concentrates exchanges.

Whole generation robotic entrepreneurs polish bright suns and sky with their vervet enthusiasm, opening opportunity window.

No scheme will have been more complete and less orderly than this one, everything spoken is spoken already, accident, according, proliferating combinatoric poetics.

Prevailing polluted forces may either rob imagination wisdom or eliminate controls.

All speaking software may fill air, thickening sky, while record shall rewrite their activities receptive site of earth, continually erasing, changing transcription across contingent layers relations.

No permanence dialogue, only endless invention, struggling remains long enough air be meant. The self-observing system may suffer own dependencies.

MARK DUCHARME

from *ALCHEMICAL NOD*

I.
Sleep! I court you like a fickle
Lover, like a cloud of vapor
Which melts into a flicker
Of light—&, like a lover,
The more unsure I am of Sleep's
Return, the more she fills me
With unease. I lie in wait for Sleep's
Embrace, while scraps of dailiness
Swirl my head. Breath steadies, &
                    I slip halfway
       Into that gauzy corridor
Which leads toward dreams & vivifying loss

Of thoughts & cares & dim awareness—
The threshold between self & night—
The interior of the typical
Where we interrogate this retinal energy
That makes me dizzy. Is dreaming vertiginous?
Is breath, which slows us down?

          I am not, nor have I ever been
A somnambulist, but have I written in
My sleep? Whom have I interrogated
While dreaming? What flights &
                              Memories stir
In sleep's overpowering embrace, her dark
Recesses, her apocryphal texts?
                                   Shall I grow
Fat, because the fat sleep better? Dreams figure
       In narratives, or the other
Way round? I'll never forget the dream scene in

Bergman's *Wild Strawberries*,
Whereas the Salvador Dali-directed dream
In Hitchcock's *Spellbound* is great but too
Stylized to seem 'real.'

What is a 'fake' dream?
Do you remember one?

I do. After hitting my head
Clumsily on a brick wall, as a very small
Boy,
My memory is of a blue-lit room
With three or four faces in surgical
Masks
Round my head,
Round my bed, like a Greek chorus, or
The witches in *Macbeth.*

Very like a dream, yet 'real.'

What was I dreaming
What, remembering
& What, recovering?

Mayer
Writes of sleep, as Homer
Writes of the Trojan War, except
Without all the heroes & bloodshed.

Who needs heroes?
We need sleep!

Proust writes of sleep, as does O'Hara,
But where are we now, in the tethers
Of wakefulness, with all of daylight
Gnashing at our hoped-for calm, our
Gushing dream-gluttonies
Filled with sleep's horizon. Rivers of sleep.
Filled, against enchantment, with oceans—
Oceans & oceans of sleep!
Filled with rest against all ruin,

Filled with love, or else its doomed,
 Orgasmic, futile hope.
Filled with the diminished, wicked loves of every waking dream.
Filled with drowned lovers' eyes (as a man, I sometimes wake
   Engorged, with a vitality I have no
  Present use for
Even if a lover might wake next to me)—
Filled with shots of memory, trickles of blood
& All our restless becoming—
Or else everything which is lost, becoming
  Breath[1] (our bodies still escaping)—

IV.
It is finally raining; rain is
Rushing down my eyelids
Like swift sweat; the night is
A lion, content in his power, yet capable
Of pouncing; I am neither bloated, nor
Content, though less deprived, lately
Of sleep's vast rivers,
The pulse & richness of them.
      Mayer writes

Of her fear that there will not be time
To complete her writing, & that fear
Hangs over me, too.
(Did I write *The Unfinished* in part to assuage
    It?)

---

[1]Sleep's an "epic
 Novel" (as Ted Berrigan
Noted)—

To draw wind while escaping
 Breath
   (How can I read, listening
To scratchy rock & roll while the moon drifts, listlessly
  Into our sketchy
 Imaginations of the night?)—

If I wrote an "explanation," it wouldn't explain
Anything. Could you, devouring
 The night without tunes?

While little, logical bulbs
Blow up in the dark?

She also writes

In the same poem, called "On Sleep,"
Of the possible, inevitable likeliness
We may all be/become Catulluses
(Read: bereft of means), in contrast to
The well-to-do, like Stein, & so
    Have our poems "lost
    For a thousand years,"
At which time it may well be too late

For "culture," literature, poetry, art &/
Or all the itinerant masters
    & Ourselves, who seem now so perishable
Like ancient libraries, tempting fire

•

When did Balzac find the time to sleep?
Did Balzac dream or brood?

Every poet writes
                One vast novel
Being the whole of the work

Then to still go down to the listening
  Orifices
Whose blood is paper
    Which becomes an epiphany
                    Of glass—

•

I don't like the "cool" poets
I don't like the "interesting" poets
I don't like the "imaginary friend" poets
I don't like the poets who want to be "friends"
    Without knowing the other's work

I don't like the sad poets
I don't like the hip poets

I don't the chiaroscuro tattooed poets
I don't like the benzene emissions poets
I don't like anything
                    I cannot dream or hum

I don't like anything which doesn't invite
Poetry into every inch of one's life,

                & One's body, although I might not fully
        Live up to that
    Bargain

I don't like anything which intrudes on the willing

There are a lot of things that I don't like about
        The way our collective
Culture/Country/Consciousness
        Is going (see
                        Voluminous footnotes).

                                        & If you don't see anything—
                If this poem is lost to history
                                For a thousand years

                        Or is forever lost,
                But still you find it somewhere

Wake up in reverie
Save a leaf (if there are still any)
Become awake to what needs to be broken
Save a person or a city

                Drown in textures

BRIAN EVENSON

REPORT ON LANGUAGE

My ex-girlfriend J., being subject to what linguists call the *pin-pen merger*, could not distinguish between the word "pin" and the word "pen." When they were written, she could, but when they were spoken she couldn't hear a difference. Even when everyone around her could hear a difference, she couldn't hear it, because she came from a part of the country where, apparently, there is no reason to distinguish between pins and pens. Or if there was a reason, they found it simpler to just to utter the same sound and simultaneously make either a pricking motion or a writing motion.

J. went on to be a writer, though later she also bought a dressmaker's dummy—as if she had been confused about wanting to be a writer, and instead had meant to become a seamstress. There was a period, too, where she seemed to want to reupholster chairs, though she never got past the first chair. When she moved out, she left the dressmaker's dummy behind, and the partially reupholstered chair as well. She had found the chair on the curb and brought it in. After the third day, it was partially stripped to the frame. For the next five years it was impossible to sit in. Or, rather, you could sit in it but only at great risk of either injuring yourself or falling through the burlap undermesh and further destroying its chairness.

A dressmaker's dummy has neither digits nor limbs nor even a head. If it were a person, it would be dead. It is a template on which to build clothing for a person, an object imbued with a particular personish shape but possessed of a non-personish motionlessness. A chair stripped of upholstery is still a chair, but one that fulfills its chairness only precariously if at all.

Language, on the other hand, is much more flexible. We make distinctions between phonemes or we don't, we say *pin* or we say *pen*, we slur, we stutter, and still, eventually, we are understood. Or think we are. We muddle our way forward and through relationships with other humans, and then, later, once we realize the extent of our misunderstanding, are left with the objects they have burdened us with after leaving us, or after we leave them.

But in the end it is an easy matter to carry these out to the curb, dust off our hands, and return to a house that feels a little more our own. Or at least, in that moment, it briefly seems so.

REPORT ON THE BIG TOE

There is not a singular word in French for the big toe, which is simply called *le gros orteil*, with *gros* meaning "big" and *orteil* meaning toe. Same as in English. More or less. The theorist B. calls the big toe "the most human part of the body," though he goes on to talk about "the hideously cadaverous and at the same time loud and proud appearance of the big toe." The big toe is that ugly lump that allows us to walk erect, the ugliness that makes us human.

From there, B. segues to foot fetishism.

There is no word in any language for a fetish focused on toenail fungi—which is only surprising when you consider the other fetishes that there *are* words for. My father's big toe has a toenail fungus, which it has had ever since I was a child and which makes the nail unnaturally thick and fibrous. I remember watching my father sit on the edge of the bed and apply drops of a liquid to the toenail, as if feeding it. In my memory the liquid is orange, though I wonder if I am not confusing it with the merthiolate I remember him applying to our cuts before that substance was banned. I believe he continued to apply this to our cuts years after it was banned, but this might also be a constructed memory, holding the place for something else I resent about my father. I remember those details, true or false, in vivid detail, but I do not remember if the fungus was on his left foot or his right.

When I was growing up, my own big toe's nail was prone to ingrowth, if that's the proper word. This was eventually enough of an issue that I had to have surgery on each of my big toes to cut out part of the nail plate. The doctor who did the surgery drew a crude picture of what I realized was supposed to be a toe only after he had stricken out the offending edges of the "toenail" with dark scribbles. *Simple*, he claimed. The picture was so badly drawn that it made me doubt his ability with a scalpel. I remember how painful this turned out to be—not the surgery, which, sedated, I didn't feel at all, but the sensation that I'd feel whenever I bumped my swaddled big toes in the days after. There was a rawness to the pain, a slight queasiness, too, and a strange panic, and sometimes today when I experience something particularly painful, that feeling comes back to me. Not the feeling exactly, but the memory of it, hand in hand with the actual pain.

Sitting here, writing about it, I find, is enough to make other parts of my body throb, the once-injured bits of me that are fine now but apparently still remember what it felt like, as if a particular pain circuit in my brain, once tripped, always remains slightly open.

Perhaps it is in fact remembered pain that is the so-called most *human* part of the body, rather than the big toe—our ability to feel again something that we aren't now feeling, to make present the humiliations and ghosts of our past, and by so doing provide the ground for other forms of memory. Memory is based in pain and offense, just as the human body holds itself upright and proud on a lumped and cadaverous big toe.

THALIA FIELD

from *INCARNATE: STORY MATERIAL*

SWEAT

From the house, hills descended on three sides by road

> hills roads and steep. She lived in the meadow, character-cleared and mud. Mud made the mountain shaky and still when she gazed out the character-door at the clearing, the mud, and the mountain back behind, how old and how glass she is.

That is, behind her the mountain as usual, but before her the glass door and mud and no memory

> taken in and a deep breath and a large glass of water downed to the eye-sockets, to the pocked eye sight through the bottom of the glass. Old is memory when it does not character up. Image is all memory or grass. How she scenes and not one. And as the mud sets up, meadow shakes, grassless mountain high behind, and the three steep roads from the house downhill.

When the sun unchecks and the shadow beneath your arm melts.
When the water is too big for you and you're plastic impeachable.
When the fever in the moon swells the last frogs.

And somewhere on the horizon a Man-of-action cut-out puppeted from where actions are sewn nearly together. Man-of-action's hunger is prodigious after action. The strings which hang him hang him perilously moving. He's more a cut-out after the action of feeling. Only the horizon where he plans his outs beats his heart like a young broken horse but a horizon is so nearly never out as a cut; everyone knows a horizon is only hungry, and every string dangles someplace temporarily while the puppet is barely really. Man-of-action makes a tiny caption of a boat tipping rarely and perfectly. His perfection strings danger or hunger after a sidekick's equal action. Hungry, he is led to any plate and disburses himself gladly, captive to the action of sweetness' cut: a voracious web, scened with insatiable character. All lines, all motivation, all movie. Toward the horizon he puts his look where he barely nearly road off but keeps remembering that he did.

When skin gets wet to the touch and the ancient stones stand up.
When cold is alternated quickly with warmth at the bottom of the alphabet.
When you've slowed to an attic of quotations.

And so forth the hero attaches according to the law of Similars

with boat-horse or army he captions the mountain non-acting in heavy sunlight; hard dew moistening his lips as old as the Catskills, but clean. He puts himself in courses of like-curing-like curing everything he might be found making

"between curl and contraction" his likeness when action meets completing all the necessary and muscular actions planning. Quietly is not action as the hero armors up a planless devastation of torsos in glass motion without complicated glass motions. Character fills his moves as a scene evaporates to dew strings twisting in the managed accelerating of his heart rate.

With this in mind, stands meadow and mud just the scene's effort, minding where she sits, a sight of the horizon cut down by the hills road steep. Now young old might be found arguing the house or a mind made up of mud, drying where grass pokes through final scattered hay. What would a mind do if it captured an act wondering what to make of it or nothing?

The glass door and glass through which she takes pictures stands open where she stands motion open. Old is the down by three roads mud and shaky, character steep, and mud-images she could keep string warm. Today there may be wetness to the standing and an atmospheric pressure without a trace of cloud. Dew is the magic sweat of the world, or the bad word she looks virgin upon. Sun as the mind packs hay, meadows firm up the fallen mountain doorway.

Perhaps after leave-taking the open road, taking leave of her sense of her ageless old home, perhaps-or-perhaps, or never to return up the three roads steeply down. All three are ancient songs forgotten on the Hudson: one for things she can't do; one for things she can't undo; one undone completely.

When mist enters the frenzy of firewood and ignites the changing.
When one ash path forestalls the progress of the flame path.
When downhill is the short amnesia of double-handed string words.

LAND AT CHURCH CITY

from a hovering point over the red clay path (a lane dusted with blistering) her eyes follow him on stages teetering, her wings that is, wet and not quite conscious, his wings really hands playing forward into the past fretted grabable; a there tense ensemble past tense, forward of it, pushing into a path he's grasping: all neck, all keys, into hymn.

at last but faithfully abominable. Her eyes make tiny dervishes on the parched silence, fully parted to let loose a vowel slack in overexposed noon, scratching at opened seeds (he lands without prints for her) so that neither dares count prints, or lay them to lip in seasoned glare. His dance a pilgrim of patterns glaring too holy to mistake for mistakes.

a billboard becomes Seraph the highest angel six, whole wings of calendars open, one for each day fluttering the rocky lane like anything red, like anything she can say mistakes are like, though he's the red one.

one mounting. One receiving. A bird forgives the beating up the entrance, as he could pardon the mention of the seventh missing day. This time holy places gather in permanent redemptions up the canyon turned off from familiar. No amenities. No public utilities. The population is bliss freak, and church.

the town above hangs for him now above, and slightly high that way. High an ordinance of loss. High an anticipated beforehand. High the genetic unfinishable. High the deepest kissed past tense. Roof of unapproachable fire escapes. That nest of churches, for lack of a better word, huddles high in his sight, on its undamnable burning seat, and hers way behind and tipping.

it is left for her to hover atheist and downward glancing. Not a single communion broached with binoculars loaded. Were eagles approaching a mile, a mouse might collapse to a print. But her wings bulk in balancing itchy devotion to whatever, in doctrinal whereby. Feathers aren't muscles, yet oiled for repelling a rain not coming for nine hundred ninety-nine miles or years; same thing, she thinks, same thing.

and below her his knees at the gate lips of ground meet kissing. Avenue the churches or blocks and street churches, for lack of a better word, every structure a church, every never his heart repelling tourists of grace for his soon expiation, turning back a cherub, second-order angel on a self-same map, a winged child mispronounced.

out of stairs he could dispense his own suffering. Churches, for lack of a better word, bow upright to foundations set to poverty, to lift of thrice-born melancholy. One coupon of atmosphere, a bountiful vulture. How a town consumes with lacking better words than churches, yet only consumes churches. Welcome the hagiography of reflected celebrity.

his head lifts to the altar, for lack of a better word, another rumored virgin, what he's lost the chorus sacrificed, losing denomination in their say-so. Churches, for lack of a better word, fake the orange cones at detours consummating. Welcome to your very raptured transience of patterning. Each church re-animates eternity for a slim visitation.

once he gains, for lack of a better word, a body's drunken messenger, wax-wings instantly fathered, his better word falls toward offering. Tar-stained hands fly stones at one heat unimpeachable. Dust red prints wait in the tense of his tentative printing. Still high and hungry, one afflatus a scalding sunlight numb despite excessive longing. Each sweet translation of relics, cloaked in stained glass, balances skeletons before his each translation tarnishes the last translation. These sentences reflect attachments and wide glances from a sky profane of blue, as blank of believing in churches as his city is full. She believes in them on his behalf from a clueless, senseless perch.

sacred aims at blood detachment contain mortal layers of systems. Sins patched of pine tar, mosses which don't mind this rain. Plant the animal kingdom, or any small landing. Cycling bundled roots congest with slippery stasis; an alibi lane in the depth contraption.

but high up in Church Town, for lack of a better name, a stage looses shadows inside the mission, a town unwieldy with churches, for lack of a better word, burdened with them and yet undeniably justified. Shadows and temperatures take umbrage in the testament, kneel beside dusty jubes, rolling beneath carved pews, his attention clots for shadows faithful to permanent dwellings.

his feet are likely and pious approaching scriptured ongoings. His ongoings unblamable statuary, the furnishing of flesh made undiseased. Flight as she thinks her sanctuary in motion, digging from wings into a small repeated phrase, trembling at his faith.

or put one last way: without these churches, for lack of a better word, many denominations force face to city landings; wingspans irrelevant or wholly threaded, he would fret away the last full upholding, undo his full-blooded erection, wait: there could be another annunciation, interrupting flight.

invisible blanks hold the doors open double and barely parted, but do part upon curious muscles. One body makes a street a multitude of church buildings: assemblies and abbeys, apses and mihrabs, cathedrals mandiras monasteries chapels stupas temples; he is aching in worship, and with hands that strive to forgive the height of churches, for lack of any word for faith in height, or what passes unending, she hovers.

ENVELOPE BAG

in general, take the bags off
skin them first, empty of muscle tone
tenacity or fat, the ability to take orders, independently detach them
they're always heavy when they start
with water and membranes and chapters barely visible to outside eyes.

the bags, for a start, were legs once
but now the cells are loose and open, giving themselves room
for growing, giving themselves flushing out, water moving
like a river through a baggie, salmon pounding against rocks
a burlesque of questions, rapidly, their skin soaked and ripping off the bone.

the envelope contains what she wanted to say, starting as a phrase probably
only the tiny word, "hi" or "I" or "I'm" or "you're," something along that line
something as small as a drop of water on burning rock. The word small
and the envelope enormous and the word has room to roll in the bottom
snagging in the creases, evaporate or get lost.

he gets home and sees a stranger futzing, lingering with the envelope
arranging the word so it looks smaller than it is; a word like "or" or "yes"
or else "no" or "sure." Some small word he might pull from the bottom of
the medium-sized envelope labeled "so far" or "maybe," three weeks old
a very medium-sized envelope not yet made of skin.

so the cells are still, as you can imagine, shapely. They cling perhaps:
their original integrity, function, I think, not knowing much about cells
but that healthy they travel in shape and size constantly up rivers, piling up
here and there, but laughing, bottlenecking like envelopes, in a surge
of playfulness through post offices.

but panic spews bags detached and emptied, muscles stiffening
drawstrings on the envelopes, the bags long stockings of legs, taking more
water, or in this case, the little word starts stuttering, attaching itself, not
for meaning, but perhaps to fill its cells, to others, bringing them over
like one brings up mouthfuls.

the envelope becomes what can realistically be called a bag, within hours of
opening, the binge of words, now in longer clusters, but clusters
and invisibility move at odds, to say the least, with clustering trying meaning
the words losing self-effacing habits—words which start as giving, she pours
what she could possibly think, little by little into the legs

whatever, the skin envelope, which takes on bulky shapes of following
thoughts, "oh yea" she adds, for a binge of openness she gorges on, delaying
rest, the bag binged and filling emptily of all that's ever empty, every gift
a sea-signal, narrowly repeating some recollected rush of ocean, "helped"
a longed-for getting, a slow, painful, elaborated

starvation of salmon on the return, there will be no counter-effect, knowing
the monstrousness of binging bags like weirs catch envelopes; eagle-eyes
assume a fatal ending, when cells deform—letters beat each other

past recognition, battle upstream where no dictionary could admit them
grown grotesquely long, jaws distorted, hooked teeth gash on rock

renounced—a stutter of unchecked synonyms, expressing symptoms
full to bursting, the body, legless, still leaking, exhausts itself, brings
one bag to completion, finally to some waiting house, at some odd hour
to the doorstep like a corpse in his absence;
a crime committed in the unspelled name of nothing, the name of a river

the name of fish she only knows by stammering
one dreary hope she's outpouring, swallowing steps
the sound of a baggie in the river being cleaned, water shreds plastic
salmon falling up to meet salmon coming apart, home to a gift
enveloped in sympathy, exhausted by their sacrifice

—a glimpse she can't dump enough trash over, or catch
too few pebbles along the shore, the words should he take them, far ahead
in a bag reversed, the head of a stream—a sample of "okay" or "oh"
spawning a vague purpose, a vengeful puke of rebirth—extinction surplus.

SOFTNESS

What did he mean

when he said "zoo," when he said, "zoo reality is much softer," or was it simply "softer"? What did he mean when he said the zoo was a much softer place "than a palace," that the zoo was softer than a palace and we were the "palace pets"? What was he spelling when he broke brute silence and said we were nothing but pets "sunk in softness"?

What did that man mean, that man, mean as he was, mean to say

with that baby swaddled, with that intimate frown, mean when he said, "that zoo is nothing," as though he could continue to connote that the zoo was nothing "more than a pillow," or really he meant a cruel assessment: that the zoo is nothing more than a pillow's "softness," that softness being "something these animals seem to sink into." What aim his drifting arrow took, his suggestive fingers curled around the rough wool of his senseless baby.

He was bored in captivity, this mean man who came to mean much more to us than he could have when he expressed himself outside our cages "with child"

and us, expecting a mean onlooker as they all are in the particular fate we've come to call onlookers, and what they've come to mean: to come and stand. But this one was meaner and we looked at his involvement, "great" with child and coming from someplace "rocky," evidently not "cushioned," not a palace where he could pet something. He onlooked for a while longer and proposed himself to us, which we weren't sure meant "flocculent" or perhaps "plaint," but in neither case was it a just import. He was just plain lost in what he really meant, and wanted us to mean it too.

Then we noticed another onlooker looking on, this time to this "child-bearing" man rather than to us, doubling our own looking in an unexpected layer so that we were all there extracting meaning from this native man & baby

bred into a version of a mean man, prickly as they come when they've been bored in captivity, when they've lost their wild dream which they do perpetually when they dream "as a sign of loneliness." When they dream their loneliness and call it "softness" and conjure up all he can feel "about his own self-hating hating."

If he weren't so self-hardened could we help him say what he means, rather, he remains before our various cages, saying nothing more than what he means when he thinks, "this zoo is so soft," or "what I wouldn't give for a taste of that effortless." That effortless lie hissing out his lips "time without end"

as much to his tiny infant as to time without obligation he thinks we mean.

Should we suggest the baby go first, to the dry concrete moat, to the piss-reeking "pillow" like a "pillow does"? We mean it when we say "captivity makes us mean" and when we repeat to him that captivity makes one mean "more than anyone watching," or mean "as a stung bull," both. The baby is what we mean when we walk back and forth like that his eyes golden with decisions about the pacing mean; his smallest step resounds in the chiseled fibrous rock of our habitat. Drop the baby man we mean when we think "softness is a value of death, prison, or poisoned time," and we don't mean to bring up softness as a value of escape.

Drop the captive baby.
Drop the not yet mean or meaningful baby and drop the meaning of baby.
Drop the mean and debased watching and
Drop meaning nothing in that jumping tongue.
Drop the baby so the other man can really mean it when he says,
"I would go to the zoo but I just can't stand the animals."

PATRICIA FOSTER

DAY SUBMURGED INTO NIGHT

"Stop," David says. "Pull over."

We're trapped at a stoplight on the strip of a busy interstate exit outside St. Louis, Missouri on a Friday night. Exhausted, we've come to this featureless place for gas and food, hoping for the rescue of a motel room, only to discover there are no vacancies to be found. It's almost 9:00 p.m. We've been driving for thirteen hours, having left southern Alabama at 7:00 this morning, having survived the loneliness of the entire state of Mississippi, the pocked, heartless roads of Arkansas, even the boring flatness of southern Missouri. Now David leans forward, gazing intently into the darkness. "I've got to photograph that."

Above, I notice a bright harvest moon animated by a slip of cirrus clouds in a smooth, inky sky. I glance at him, my artist husband, then again at the moon. "For god's sake, it's 9:00!" I'm crazy tired, my eyes dry and itchy, my mind so dull I can't think of a better retort.

"Come on." His voice is urgent, pleading.

I relent, but also grumble. "I don't know why you have to do this. I'm tired. I want to find a motel. I've been driving—"

"Please, just give me five minutes."

Begrudgingly, I pull into the parking lot of a small, almost empty shopping mall so that David can leap from the car and sprint towards a grassy field twenty feet away. I lean my head against the steering wheel, irritation exacerbating my exhaustion, my arms heavy and weighted, my shoulders aching. I must have dropped off because I don't remember him getting back into the car until he says, "I've got to get it from another angle." He's gazing across the highway, his voice rising with a dangerous hum of excitement as if he's just had a double espresso. "Up there." Such energy grates on me. I want to smash it.

"Jesus, I'm exhausted," I repeat. "We don't have a motel room yet."

I watch his lips twitch, his face a shadow. "I haven't asked for anything on this trip, not a thing."

It's true. Though I've driven the entire way—my choice—David's been a good sport, demanding nothing, taking occasional naps, but mostly keeping me company and walking endless circles around the car when we stop for gas. After cancer surgery two years ago, his legs often ache on long rides—the muscles tight and swollen, his ankles spreading—as if he has residual lymphedema, precarious and insistent. Reluctantly, I steer across the street to another empty lot, irritated that he's so enthusiastic, so implausibly energetic. This time I don't fall asleep, but watch resentfully as he shifts from place to place, setting up the shot, then moving again, setting up another and another and another, never once glancing back. "Come on," I yell out the window as the rush of traffic ruptures the warm night air, the whirring of insects. Still he doesn't turn. I wait five minutes, then yell again.

An hour later at a motel entrance, we're raw with fury, each thundering our wounds, the other a prima donna, an indulgent son-of-a-bitch. My neck, a knotted boulder, stiffens. David squints hard at the windshield.

In the motel parking lot he sulks. "I'll just sleep in the car."

"Don't be ridiculous," I say, irritated that he can be so melodramatic.

*

What is there to say about a motel room except for its blinking brightness, its lights harsh, surreal after the highway's irregular darkness. Just a generic motel room: two queen-sized beds, a bedside table, a desk with plastic ads, a wide-screen TV, a fake-walnut chest of drawers. Silence. We don't speak. In the bathroom, I brush my teeth and wash my face, splashing eye drops into tired eyes, my mind swirling while David undresses in the main room. "Sorry about that," he says when I emerge, my body a barrier of resistance. He says it casually as if "sorry" will do, and I gaze at him stupidly because five minutes earlier I wanted to strangle him. He steps closer. "Sometimes there just isn't enough of me, especially when we're down south with your family," he says quietly, "but when I take photographs, it's like I'm getting myself back."

I nod. I understand. And yet there remains something charged between us, a messy, pent-up struggle that transcends apologies and explanations and makes me edgy.

Twenty minutes later, I'm lying on cool, clean sheets, my shoulders and hips soothed by darkness, a hint of relief though my mind's reeling. I close my eyes. Just let me sleep, let me sleep. And then David slips in naked beside me, wordlessly, insistently pulling me close, his lips on my cheeks, in my hair, on my breasts and we're suddenly making hard, pleasurable love, the kind of ravenous sex we haven't had in years. Maybe it's our anger re-directed, pleasure consuming trouble. Maybe it's the fever of release after a week with my family. Maybe it's just the trip, the two of us crammed in our untidy car and now this, day submerged into night. Beyond us, the air conditioner purrs, the clock drones its precise tick-tick-tick while SUVs and U-Hauls stream past on the interstate, drivers sullen or high or numb, the world dissolving, but we don't care, we don't care.

*

Eight months pass and everything's changed. I shy away from contact, uncertain, afraid of sex, afraid to lie naked in bed, afraid of the pain, a dry burn deep inside, flesh rubbed raw, a searing hurt if we do it and then a flood of guilt. My fault. My fault. Last year, the year of our Alabama trip, I took hormones, a nice little pellet on a plunger, knees up in the bathroom, one hand pushing that sucker right up the hole. Easy as pie. Girl on the go. Efficient. Necessary. I loved it! But months after our trip, my old illness announced itself—a familiar terrain of exhaustion, pain and fatigue—and for a week, then two, then three, I slouched around the house in my black sweater and loose pants, taking naps and over-the-counter medicine, sitting groggily at my desk, waiting to feel better, drinking rooibos tea, waiting for something to change, to be able to work, to read, to think. Waiting. The third week, diagnosed with a severe sinus infection, and later a multi-drug resistant bacteria, and put on antibiotics for six weeks, I immediately stopped taking the hormones, the side effects pitched and rampant: nasty vaginal itching, bloated belly, and worsening brain fog. Candida again. An estrogen nightmare. Ramped up by antibiotics. It turns out that sometimes you can't treat two conditions at once! While David's illness—a rare cancer—was dramatic and difficult, a gaping wound delicately repaired and carefully attended by an arduous, two month recovery—my own illness, chronic fatigue syndrome with its accompanying sinusitis, severe allergies and candidiasis, seems almost fatuous, an intemperate floosy taking up valuable time. My disease is fickle but insistent, leeching energy, dragging me down, my brain thick and slow and stumbling, an old person's brain, until, like some sorcerer's magic, my body wakes up and gives it all back to me.

Secretly, I fear that nothing inside of me works anymore. My vagina has thinned to its current shyness, a result of years of prednisone hitched now to menopause and god knows what else. My stomach is a clench of distress, my brain often revving, shimmering, and then, as suddenly, clutching at nothing. Dumb ass, I call myself. Dry bitch, I think on a bad day, believing I've lost a vital part of what makes me female—the ability to lose myself in sex, to have physical, orgasmic pleasure, to be not just me but us. Perhaps that sounds romantic, a soft-focus lens applied to the intimacy of sex and marriage, a pornographic nostalgia, but it's that precise closeness I miss, the collapse of some tiny part of my separateness.

But why is this my fault? Why do I feel culpable, ashamed? Why do women so frequently blame themselves for the broken body, the wounded self, a little dash of self-loathing with your coffee, ma'am? Why is sexual dysfunction considered taboo, the worst possible thing? Why does no one talk about this in literature as if it's unknown and unknowable, a mysterious curse rather than a condition?

I know that what's valued is defined by each historical period, that what I feel is, in some ways, culturally constructed. In the 19th century, female sexual appetite was considered taboo, a threat to a woman's emotional health, a devouring menace. That damning perspective made women fight tooth and nail to change, but in the 21st century, we've made a pendulum swing that can also pinch and slap: sexual lack is the beast, the unspeakable burden.

No one wants you. You're nothing, unnatural, a freak.

But am I?

I usually convince myself quite easily of inadequacy—I must have done something to deserve this—but today I balk. I want to give this a hard stare. I'm a 66-year-old woman with a chronic illness and a full-time job as an English professor, rising each morning to critique graduate theses, to prep for my literature class, to grade papers and email quick reminders to students about conferences and late assignments. Of course, I'd like to be back in that motel room, rushing over the edge in rapturous sex, perhaps even some "give-it-to-her" bad girl stuff, a relief from my intimate but not-always-sexual life. My fantasies, like those of many women, have always bordered on polar realms of dominance: either enticing submission or demanding dominatrix. If fantasy is all that's required, I'd also like to be beautiful with the invigorating beauty of youth, to feel watched and lusted after, to entice and seduce by a glance, a gaze. The pivot of desire. And yet, oddly, I've discovered that hot sex—like beauty—isn't the only bliss around, isn't the only way to enjoy a marriage that's happy and well. To my surprise, my husband and I also like to lie around naked and talk, stroking each other, gossiping, tangling together, sometimes kissing, sometimes napping, then waking and lying close and reading our books. And then some days, I feel a jolt of desire, a rising wetness, a heat. I straddle my husband on the couch and we make-out like teenagers, eager and dirty, hands touching what hands want to touch.

That's the surface narrative, the easy thing to tell.

Let me write this again: A woman lies alone beneath the covers, her body aching, deflated, the bed a prison, her mind both anxious and dull, her medicines lined up like party favors on the bedside table, pills to treat the symptoms, pills to snuff out the infection, pills to reduce the side effects, pills to help her wake up in the morning, a full glass of water squarely in the center. No cure. Don't touch me, her body says. Let me get well. Just let me get well. And this is the wanting of illness: to leave the dark captivity of pain and depletion, to imagine a quicksilver return to that other self. Why, she wonders, is it always one or the other: desire or absence, health or sickness, guilt or relief, a stark binary equation.

The truth of my life is its inconsistency. I get sick. I get well. I feel sexy. I feel like a dud. I make love to my husband when I can. Otherwise, we turn naked butts to each other and sleep.

*

And yet I suspect something hidden, even embarrassing, a knowledge I don't want to know. I see that the need to define myself —to "be" something in the world—has been more vital to me than pleasure, that work has consumed almost everything that I am. The sudden, impulsive knowledge of this startles me. But why should it? Wasn't I brought up with the wager that the promise of life might be beyond me, that, quite possibly, I wouldn't be rewarded? And once such terms are acknowledged, is there anything left but capitulation or war? Of course I chose war, the good fight, all battles quickly becoming internal, the steeling of the self, the sacrifice of time and pleasure to the shaping of a new, better self, a successful self—autonomous and revered, soft-voiced but indestructible—though that incarnation never quite arrived. Instead, I got ill and the fight shifted to two fronts, though I still believed that if only I could do a little bit more I could make it right, I could still win. Instead, I got sicker, my mind and body a tightly knotted fist.

"You're so tense," people often said to me, their foreheads furrowed with polite concern. "Why don't you try to be a little kinder to yourself?"

Hearing such comments, I went quiet, still, surprised that I appeared so self-defended, so walled off from other people. And yet I knew it was true. What frightened woman doesn't need armor? What sick person doesn't need to be shrouded? Who among us, in work or in bed or in the company of our solitary selves, does not want most, does not desire desperately, to feel well?

*

It's been two days since my husband had his latest blood tests and CT scan, two days since we sat fidgeting in the waiting room at 3:45 in the afternoon, both anticipating and dreading the consultation with the oncologist. This is the worst time: the flurry of tests over, the paper gowns and needles removed and my husband back in his street clothes, the two of us in the quiet, tastefully furnished room. My husband has no symptoms, no visible changes in his body. It's been two and a half years. No matter. Cancer is sneaky, a deceitful invader. The rare cancer my husband had couldn't be detected without a pathology report. And now?

Once in the treatment room, the doctor breezed in, said cheerfully that everything looked good, that there was no sign of malignancy and we could go home and celebrate, though we'd have to come back in six months so that my husband could do this all over again. And then again and again. "Until you've been cancer-free for five years," he said clearly for the first time. I sat up straighter, thinking I should have known. Should have known the reprieve would always be temporary, a six-month renewal like a short-term lease, nothing more.

And now—two days later—my husband seems back to normalcy, back to working on the digital prints he's making, back to cooking dinner, assembling peppers and onions and zucchini and celery and brown rice and chicken, back to working until 3:30 am, getting up at 9 or 10 or 11. Though his eyes look tired, his energy is focused in the present while mentally I'm still stuck in that treatment room, stunned by the realization that I didn't know. I thought that after two and a half years, the doctor would begin to increase the length of time between scans, would begin to talk optimistically about my husband's progress, about the decreasing possibility of recurrence, about cure.

For these two days I'm beset with problems: I strained my right groin muscle running through the hospital parking lot, knowing I might be late for my husband's appointment. Though usually we go together for every test, this time I dropped him off for the CT scan and rushed back to the English Department to teach my class, with plans to meet him in the waiting room before the consultation. I'd almost made it on time, but then couldn't find a parking spot in the ramp, and when I did, I leapt out of the car and ran. Ran in the wrong kind of shoes. Now, getting up from a sitting position, I actually yelp. But my husband wants to celebrate. Tonight, he caresses my buttocks through my pajamas, his hands moving tentatively towards my crotch even though I stand very still, legs together, telling him it hurts even when I try to walk. Certainly can't spread my legs. He strokes my hair and says he knows. He does. And yet I'm disappointed, even exasperated at this new problem. I'd like to say that I feel desire even with pain, but it's not true. Pain trumps everything. Illness swallows up desire. Nothing. No one.

*

Funny how I imagined ending this essay: for the first time in a year, I want to take the estrogen again, to lie on a bath towel and insert that little white pellet. I've thought about it constantly, imagining myself feeling sexually alive, though I know it's not just the estrogen, but the desire for desire, the impulse to want, the imagination revved up and ready: I'm okay, no longer ill. But first I have to repair the damage done by the long-term antibiotics, make the body well, and perhaps more than that—harder than that—I have to turn rebuke into mercy, a soothing cadence, it's okay, it's okay, it's okay, so that when I wake each morning I think of myself not as someone merely useful, but fuller than that—someone necessary.

TONYA M. FOSTER

from *A SWARM OF BEES IN HIGH COURT*

On the stoop, Kim oils
his scalp, parts his hair into
tender paragraphs.

"On the stoop, Kim oils
and parts," a writer writes,
"her legs slash vulva."

What doesn't kill her
maims her, makes her superwo'
man (!) to be studied.

What doesn't kill her
right away becomes chronic
acquaintance until…

Black is black taint
that marks the linoleum tile
she Mop and Glo's clean

"Black is black"—t'aint
that the color line—
"just cause" as refracted light?

They say "bitch" and mean
the syllable to break her
solipsistic strides.

They say *bitch* and *mean*
when she walks by seeming to
think thoughts blind to *them*—

block boys trying on
the tongues of the men they know
to be (.) Come cornered

block boys, trying on
these reins for y/our desires
—bitch, chickenhead

Don’t think the body
don’t think   the body don’t think
by feeling its way

Don’t think the body
in its singular-plural
selves don’t feel your gones

Bodies of young men—
spent smoke, spent casings graph one
among many points

Bodies of young men—
sight-specific installations—
streets, stoops, corners, cells.

Bullets can
pepper a body, like salt falling—
a startled cook's hand.

Rain, clear this
Saint Nicholas hill, like a strong hand,
of lean and wait.

Bullets can
cover a street, a door, the distance
between yours and mine

Rain clears this
up—which is stronger—the grind of
cars or cornered voices?

Bullets can
blot a page, train an eye to
follow thought and sound.

Rain, clear this
moment's deadlock of was/will.
Wash us in do/be.

Blind puddle that was
little boy's blood, cold water
and Mr. Clean clean

"Blind puddle that was
chance for movie chivalry"—
sunlight dries this thought

Blind-puddle-that-was
posit the boy, strutting man-
to-be-been, the gones.

Blind-puddle-that-was
imagine sinews, tendons.
Tongue your wasness.

JOANNA FUHRMAN

from *THE YEAR OF YELLOW BUTTERFLIES*

Terrible to dress in the clothes / of a period that must end.
Frank Bidart

You must remember that certain things die out for awhile / so they can be remembered with affection / later on.
John Ashbery

#

It was the year young women wore blue jeans with carefully ripped holes, holes revealing leggings, and in the knees of the leggings, little rips, glimpses of neon paisley tights.

In the paisley tights there were holes, and through these holes we could see little patches of perfect skin-colored knee-makeup.

In the knee-makeup, there would be always be a gap where the real skin would peek out, and in that gap would be another hole and in it a surgically implanted transparent window revealing veins, and under the veins there would be muscles, predictable bones.

Inside those bones, we could see little tubes, and inside those tubes, there was the beginning or the end of language. I didn't know which, but I knew it was a kind of happiness like a crooked line is happy or like a million crooked lines are even happier.

I thought of it as a great yellow swooping, maybe the music of glaciers melting, or mislaid planets slowly re-adjusting their orbits.

#

It was the year everyone kept forgetting their babies on the conveyer belt. You'd pay the stork for it, then leave it right there, not noticing that it was wailing for breast milk or the past.

So many people forgot their babies that year that they needed to open baby libraries across the country. You could check out other people's if you'd lost track of your own.

I never bought a baby or even wanted to borrow one, but I liked to go to the baby library at my lunch break.

Under the mounds of congealing drool, I could finally remember my own lost babyhood— how blurry it was, how loud.

#

It was the year Goth, rockabilly manicurists applied mini-wigs to women's nails. My wife's nails were blond like a young Brigitte Bardot. They were half hair, half self-lighting, phosphorescent wicks.

In the dark, I couldn't tell the difference between my wife's fingers and an ocean of glowing jellyfish.

I didn't like or dislike my wife's new nails.

They became just another part of her, like the wads of ear wax left on the pillow or the glossy lipstick she applied after eating grilled cheese.

#

It was the year those photographs appeared everywhere: big-toothed Americans smiling next to naked, hooded, bound dark men. We'd see the images printed on T-shirts, embossed on popcorn cartons and caught in the silver, cinematic underskin of our eyelids.

We thought that the image would cause a rearrangement of our dormant atoms, that the lion sleeping in our waterbed would wake and burn a rapturous path out of its oceanic nap. Instead, the powder on our nacho chips stayed the same blunt orange, the ballet dancers remained perched, spinning forever on their lovely, bloody toes.

#

It was the year everyone decorated the outside of their houses to look like the inside, and the inside to look like the outside.

You liked to wear a jumpsuit with an x-ray of a skeleton silk-screened on it. I liked to wear an earring shaped like a decaying liver.

Once I crashed into a friend's wall because I thought it was the sky.

We placed our teacups on a tree trunk ottoman and rested our heads on waterfall pillows.

You were wearing an ocean on your mouth, and I was dressed like the sun.

#

It was the year everyone had dreams about nuclear holocausts.

In Laura's dream the sun turned the color of pomegranates.

In Max's, he hid under a couch with his pet hamster, Sam. Clara stood alone on the roof. Ken ate a cupcake shaped like a mushroom cloud while his friends joked about the end of the world.

From what I remember of my dream, the streets were covered in sneaker tongues, angular wounds, burnt moss.

I cried on the sidewalk with blue sirens.

What I remember might not have been my actual dream. It might be a memory of a promo for a TV movie, the one they advertised during breaks of the primetime soaps my mother said I wasn't old enough to watch.

FRED GARDAPHE

ITALIAN ICES

Way back when, Nero Claudius Caesar, Emperor of Rome, would employ swift runners to carry snow from the mountain tops back to his palace where it would be mixed with fruit juices. If the snow melted before it reached the palace, the slave runners would be executed.

Mr. Domenico Rossi was called the Ice King of Chicago, and his eyes glistened whenever he told the story of his family's history in the ice business. "When the snow would come to the mountains of Abruzzi, the men of the village would climb up to the mountain top. Shovelers would make mounds of snow here and there and then beat it with the backs of shovels until each mound was shaped into a ball. Then they'd drive a pole through it and two men would carry it to the mouth of a grotto and dump it inside. After a number of balls had been thrown down, other men would jump into the grotto to spread the snow and cover it with straw. They'd keep doing it, layer by layer until the grotto was filled." In the summer, from an opening at the bottom covered with plants the frozen snow would be taken out in blocks onto the road, loaded onto carts and sent into towns and cities for refrigeration.

In 1533 Catherine de Medici brought ice making to France when she married Henry III. The chef was forbidden to discuss the recipe, under the penalty of death. Flavored ice was to be a luxury the poor wouldn't taste for centuries. In 1798 an Italian by the name of Tortoni opened the first ice store in Paris. From there Italian ices found their way to England and ultimately to America.

Rossi says an unusually mild winter forced Barrone Celli's ice farm fallow during the winter of 1898. Without work, the men in the village began to wander north. The Rossis, like many others, took off for America. They made it as far as Chicago, joining paesani in the neighborhood surrounding the Polk Street train station. Massimo Rossi settled for work with Giuglio, the right hand man of Zengel the ice farmer. The Rossis, unlike the paesani who were doomed to work as construction gang laborers, had jobs that lasted throughout the year. When the winter freeze stopped the construction trades, the Rossis were at their busiest. In those days ice was a crop harvested in the dead of winter from frozen ponds and lakes. Horses pulled plows equipped with thick, razor-sharp knives that sliced lines into the surface. When the four hundred pound, three feet square blocks of ice floated ashore they would be taken to a shelter, packed in sawdust and stored in ice houses insulated with hay. With a normal winter's harvest the Zengle trucks could carry ice through the streets all summer long. In those days, ice was not consumed; it was merely a means of keeping perishables fresh. Among Zengel's biggest clients were the funeral homes and the City Morgue. Rossi says the old German really made a killing during the influenza epidemic of 1918 and took the opportunity to buy land west of the city. He leased his business to Massimo Rossi and his friend Giuglio under whose direction it thrived until Massimo's death in the late 1930s.

Rossi says there's good ice and there's bad ice. And nowadays nobody cares what they get. Back when he was a kid, nobody took ice for granted and everybody could tell the good from the bad. Then he stood up, walked away from the table and returned with an ice cube in each hand.

"Take a look at these and tell me which one you want in your glass."

"They look the same to me."

"Ha," he laughed. "Now take them in you hands, feel them, tell me which one you like best." Both were cold; one seemed to be melting faster than the other so he chose the other.

"Now smell them."

I couldn't smell a difference.

"Ok, now taste them."

I honestly couldn't taste a difference and told him so.

"You see what I mean," he sighed. "There used to be a big difference and nobody knows that anymore. The one in your right hand used to sell for three times the price."

"So what's the difference?"

"One you can eat; the other you use only to cool things with. One is made from water in the lake; the other comes from a fresh water pond outside the city, and I'm the only one who knows where it is. My father bought that land over fifty years ago and planted a forest so thick around it you could never tell that it hides a spring fed pond. And that's the difference between a Rossi ice and all the others. That's why they call me the king. Used to be if ice had bubbles or cracks or clouds in it the price could be cut in half. I tell you ice is like a jewel; the clearer the better; there are flaws that come from freezing too quickly or poor handling or too much chemicals or gas in the water. Ah," he said, waving his hands in the air, "what do people care any more?"

When Domenico had taken over the business he put his three sons to work as soon as they could wield ice picks. After World War II, there was hardly a house that needed Rossi's ice anymore so the family settled into the side business that had grown out of Mrs. Rossi's kitchen, producing lemon ice.

Domenico Rossi had made for his family a comfortable living through his mixture of ice and lemon and by the 1950s many of Chicago's biggest hotels were his exclusive customers. That was during the days when the city was stealing the land left and right from the paesani to make expressways, medical centers and a new college. They carved it up, Rossi says, like it was the carcass of a hunting kill: drawn, quartered and gutted.

The Rossi property comprised a three story building on Taylor Street. The first floor was the storefront ice shop; the second and third floor housed the Rossi family. Adjacent to the property was a half lot that Domenico used for a garden. The Rossi land survived the first cut, an east west line called the Congress Expressway that ran down the middle of the neighborhood over which soon drove hundreds of thousands of automobiles in a never-ending hum. That's when the neighborhood began to lose its charm, and the residents their trust. Credit was no longer extended on a person's promise to pay; after all, there was no way of telling how much longer any one of them would be around.

A few years later came the second cut, yet another slice right through the middle of the neighborhood, and another endless river of cars running north and south on what they called the Dan Ryan Expressway, after one of those Irish politicians. Soon the neighborhood, surrounded by fenced off highways, became a peninsula connected to the city by bridges over the streams of traffic. Old man DelBella referred to it as the Camps, for he had been a prisoner of war in the Austrian camp during World War I and knew the life of paranoia and despair behind wire fences. Rossi's street customers dwindled down to the handful of regulars that came every day in the summer and the few tourists and former residents that would stop by on the weekends.

The coming of the University nearly wiped out what remained of the neighborhood after the expressways. Rossi has trouble with what's happening in the old neighborhood. They knocked down the low income housing, chased the Italians out, built brand new row houses, and now they want the Italians back. Only they don't want the regular people; they want the phoney balonies who speaka likea thisa, who wear red, white and green and who sell their fancy pasta for ten bucks a plate. "*Come si fa*," says Rossi. "What you gonna do. All the writing in the world ain't gonna make it change."

GEOFFREY GATZA

EARTH REVOLVES ITSELF ONCE AGAIN

—after Pierre Reverdy

Resounding blooms
Blue birds fly north.

In the backyard where everything seems to happen
The squirrel darts through our leafless lilac tree.

Outside a woman is cleaning the table; a man makes fire.
Water streams from a hose clearing the driveway apron.

A rainburst negotiates with a cloud.
The sun abrupts with striking chimes.

RESPLENDENCE

For all the good I do, I could have been a plumber.
Steering dreamlike laborers into a corner to remonstrate.

Unclogging the copperworks with these poet hands.
Seeking gold among the spiders of scum and pubic hair.

The refuse of human detritus piles higher and higher.
For all the good I do, I should have been a plumber.

Digging deeper to find, return to the owner, the lost ring
Dropped down the sink's drain, hiding in the j-tube

Waiting to reflect light again, making glad the hearts
Of the joyless fingers, missing the weight, the responsibility

Intertwined amongst the significant and its signifier.
The shine is the most artificial aspect of a diamond.

OK, I'M BETTER NOW.

Nothing is dead in the house today. Everything as alive as it was before
Falling to sleep. The dust is a micron thicker and the hair on my head
Reaches upwards another notch closer to the stars hidden behind the
Glowing sunshine. We pretend to be alive when there is no work, live
In shared bonding moments over food and television shows waiting
For the other to engage in a flash of sex before we watch a bedtime
Detective show and curl back in the warmth of our day's reward sleep.

The organs churn while the belly turns to sour bells.
The cello lows itself to sleep on the velvet couch lazed.
Hoping to lull out dreams of days gone by, whistlestops
And buggy cars roam the deserts of backyard forts.
I hope these days remain constant in perpetuity.
A hundred million billion trillion flashes recreating
Lackluster, unrelenting peaceable moments in Kenmore.

WATCHING LAST YEAR'S PUMPKIN TRANSCEND DETERMINISM

Even now this cemetery is accumulating.
The hills darken. The dead
sleep in their blue graves,
the grounds having been
picked clean, the ribbons
faded, the pinwheels piled at the dumpster
among wind ripped tiny American flags
as garbagemen come forward for collection:

Now feel tension fail to achieve.
Concatenation transpires.

Tears melt into sweat.
This is the barrenness
of grief; to watch life rot
as we move ever forward.

MINE IS THE SUNLIGHT

I saw him clearly, an old man hovering.
His oil slick of a self
Looking beautiful,
reflecting his wolf
Moon courage,
frostbit in a rainbow.

Colors smear across the horizons.
Motor oil expels on rain puddles,
Slowly absorbing into the concrete pad.

Evaporating into a marriage of fire down
in Florida somewhere. Looking out at palm
trees swaying in the early rains warning of
oncoming warm water storms. He sat down
for dinner, said grace and unfolded his napkinhands

And said to me, that life was a can of cranberries,
Molded into a mechanized horror of a real berry.

GABRIEL GUDDING

WRITING LITERATURE TO BENEFIT NONHUMANS: ON THE FAILURES OF ECOLOGICAL WRITING

There is unhappily in literature, and in the majority of contemporary political, philosophical, and ecological thought, a failure to see the nonhuman animal even at its most extreme limit of suffering.

The very thinkers who love animals and grow disturbed by their mass slaughter still eat them. The very people who pride themselves on their championing of the other, who protest the mistreatment of the subaltern and the disavowal of the suffering of the abject, still tell themselves it's possible to humanely slaughter.[1] The majority of critical theorists, poets, and ecologists who speak of intersectionality, biopower, supremacism, ecopoetics, feminism, animal welfare, and animal farming still willfully take pleasure from the brutalization of our most other others. The majority of feminists still consume the products of animal agriculture, the largest systematic exploitation of motherhood and childhood ever devised. It bears repeating: the majority of the very thinkers who love justice and who would object to the unnecessary[2] killing of animals still eat them and steal their young. They persist, even in their most disciplined thought, as ethical misers and energetic dupes of industry.[3]

---

1. The ethical dualism in the oxymoron "humane slaughter" has its institutional counterpart in animal welfare laws that criminalize the abuse of slaughterhouse animals by workers while protecting their legal right to kill them. Killing in this schema is not a class of mistreatment.

2. Among countless other dietary organizations, the American Dietetic Association (not a liberal organization) clearly declares meats dietetically unnecessary. "It is the position of the American Dietetic Association that appropriately planned vegetarian diets, including total vegetarian or vegan diets, are healthful, nutritionally adequate, and may provide health benefits in the prevention and treatment of certain diseases. Well-planned vegetarian diets are appropriate for individuals during all stages of the life cycle, including pregnancy, lactation, infancy, childhood, and adolescence, and for athletes." From a meta-analysis of decades of studies by the American Dietetic Association (now the Academy of Nutrition and Dietetics), the US's oldest and foremost scientific authority on diet and nutrition." http://www.ncbi.nlm.nih.gov/pubmed/19562864

3. As David Lurie says, in Coetzee's *Disgrace*, "I eat them, so I suppose I must like them, some parts of them."

How does it happen that politically aware people can fail to see the ethical injustice in their own consumptive and cognitive habits? The animal-industrial system functions as the epitome of what Robert Proctor might call an agnotologic economy—one that works by actively inducing an ignorance in both consumers and producers. We can intimately as consumers desecrate the bodies of nonhuman beings by eating them while at the same time remaining unaware that we are eating a body. We can intimately gain mouth-pleasure from their bodies while at once remaining ignorant of the pain and sorrow that the nonhuman animal endured so that we could steal this pleasure. We can feel comfort and love while eating a turkey and while collectively denying the turkey's wish for comfort and love, her desire to play and live, her having been a mother. We can do this despite knowing that they have the same neurotransmitters and hormones we do and that the vertebrate brain is remarkably consistent in its anatomy, such that it is a sure bet the Umwelt of the turkey is similar to that of the pig and that of the human.

We need to feel this. And the arts have an essential role here. Strictly political action is not enough. As political struggle can only be concerned with those beings who are already part of the polis, we can't through politics adequately attend to the subaltern. It is precisely these beings—the excluded, the eaten, the enslaved—who have a need for a pre-juridical, pre-political defense. In a climate of political concern that studiously ignores widespread and systematized suffering, it is precisely the epistemic role of the arts and other modes of critical thought to levy pre-juridical and pre-political means of argument in order to draw distant realities of suffering into the arena of warm concern. In short, humans can no longer be thought the only creatures who must benefit from our literature.

The idea that literature should be written to benefit nonhumans is new. We see no hint of this in western letters prior to now. Book X of *The Republic* maintains that the only permissible literature is that which praises gods and famous men. Aristotle remarks in Book IV of *The Poetics* that literature's purview is the imitation of the actions of men and gods. Sidney's *Defence* holds that literature's purpose is to improve the character of a gentleman. Shelley, Lessing and Schiller all declared that the intent of literature should be to improve humanity. In fact it's been a broadscale and sustained note since the advent of humanism: the project of literature is humanity's improvement. Full stop.

Zoopoetics is a new movement in literary theory and practice that treats nonhumans as individuals with agency, as conscious world-having individu-alsworthy of moral consideration.[4] Think Alice Walker, Kafka, Coetzee, D. H. Lawrence. Think Oni Buchanan and Aracelis Girmay, Les Murray and John Kinsella, among countless other innovative writers and editors actively helping to reconceive our relationships with nonhuman animals.

Zoopoetics is markedly different from ecocriticism, ecopoetics, ecopoetry, and ecological literature in general. Such movements are not concerned with nonhumans as individuals; for them, animals are populations to be managed. When they do concern themselves with nonhumans, the animal becomes a metaphor for some human reality, and the poems, essays, and anthologies in these genres typically express disquiet about threatened favored populations of animals in the wild—wolves, eagles, bison, monarch butterflies—and rarely if ever mention the plight of farmed animals or question the practice of breaking apart families, enslaving, killing, eating and drinking the bodies and secretions of nonhumans. The animal in these works is aestheticized and collective. Terry Tempest Williams, for instance, protests the killing of prairie dogs and owls in the Utah desert, as a part of the general "subjugation of women and nature" in her book *Refuge*, but thinks nothing of lauding the hunting of rabbits by her family only a few pages later as a practice integral to her family's sacred (her word) relationship with nature.

As with the rest of mainstream culture, there is in this eco-centric literature a general disavowal of the suffering of those enslaved and butchered each year for meat, jackets, fur collars, handbags, watchbands, hats, shoes—all commodities unnecessary for, and in fact detrimental to, our health and mental wellbeing. The rare animal who rises to the status of an individual by such authors is generally a domestic pet or a rescued farm animal.

Dozens of poets in a collection of essays on ecopoetics will rail against damage to the environment and the loss of connection to the animal world and nature caused by human hubris but never once mention a slaughterhouse, the practice of meat eating, or the fact that animal farming is not only predicated on human supremacism but is also the single greatest driver of climate change and the chief ecological threat to rivers and aquifers

4. The term zoopoetics was introduced by Jacques Derrida in his 1997 *The Animal that Therefore I Am*, but it has recently been more carefully inflected by Aaron Moe in his book *Zoopoetics: Animals and the Making of Poetry* (Lexington 2013) as a counter to, and a clarification of, ecocriticism and ecopoetics.

worldwide. Forewords, prefaces, and introductions to recent anthologies of ecopoetry and the postmodern pastoral won't mention the slaughterhouse at all, though the bodies of dead nonhumans are universally eaten and worn, and CAFOs are scattered across countrysides everywhere. It is instructive the degree to which thought about poetry's material relation to ecology and animals can have so little to do with the single most potent factor in the history of anthropogenic ecological destruction (the animal-industrial complex), and so much to do with the history and aesthetic politics of the Black Mountain School.

Writing literature for the improvement and benefit of nonhumans isn't some boutique issue, especially when we consider how animal farming is altering our climate and damaging our health and environment. Even for those who cannot intrinsically value nonhumans as ends in themselves, they should recognize that our fate is bound up firmly with their wellbeing and act accordingly.

Not that poetry has any special abilities in this regard. Poetry has in fact been at times, even recently, a force for stupidity of nearly magical proportions.[5]

A stupid art is any art that insists on its own a-ethical or non-political content. Or more accurately, it resists its own already ethically dimensioned content. There is no ethically flat enactment possible in any art. "Literature begins with a porcupine's death.... As Moritz said, one writes for dying calves. Language must devote itself to reaching these feminine, animal, molecular detours, and every detour is a becoming-mortal."[6] Art must contain or elicit the energy of a mortal ethic.[7] A truly minoritarian art will bear a mortal ethic that will illustrate for those blinded to the prejudicial ablation of the animal that one cannot be considered a politically invested or an ethically energetic being, an innovative writer, a feminist, an ecologically responsive or environmentally concerned being, a skeptical thinker committed to the factual, or an activist bent on the cultivation of political emotions, if one eats animals,

---

5. "Conceptual Writing is a-ethical and wouldn't dare make the presumption that it has the power to affect the world for better or worse. Conceptual Poetry makes nothing happen. Conceptual Writing is the Switzerland of poetry. We're stuck in neutral. We believe in the moral weightlessness of art."—Goldsmith, K. The Harriet Blog, April 27, 2010.

6. Deleuze, G., "Literature and Life." *Essays Critical and Clinical*, Smith and Greco, trans. (Minnesota 1997).

7. By mortal ethic I mean not to counter the historical impulse to construe poetry as a will to immortality (there is no need to counter that old canard anymore), but that art's ethic should bring the meaninglessness of the mortality of sentience to the pity of sentience: in ourselves, in other creatures, and the planet's eventual solar extinction.

or any part of an animal. A truly moral art must touch the diet. It is itself a class of food. And it proves the template for food.

Where compassion is not enough, and where critical theory is clearly not enough, a change of diet is sufficient. And where a change of diet is sufficient, an outspoken and lived solidarity with the indignity of the enslaved and eaten is imperative.

A human future that does not acknowledge the injustices done to nonhumans cannot be rosy. Thankfully, a growing body of thinkers, literary and non-literary alike, is increasingly in agreement with political theorist John Sanbonmatsu, who writes,

> A Left or socialist politics which does not place our enslavement of other beings at its center, conceptually and politically, cannot possibly succeed: 'speciesism' is not merely one more 'ism,' but in fact lies at the root of every form of social domination.[8]

Rather than coldly expressing concern over animals as populations, we should, in the words of philosopher David Sztybel, be "'hot' for the individual animal."[9] This new literature does this. And none too soon. Now that we are living through the sixth mass extinction since multicellular life rose on the earth a billion years ago, an extinction caused in great part by animal farming, an extinction, what's more, that is nearly invisible to us, it's time we begin to think of literature as a force that can benefit nonhuman animals too. A zoopoetic literature, which is sometimes straightforwardly veganic, is being written for the benefit of all sentient beings, not just as populations but as individuals, as individuals with bodily and mental sovereignty.

Such a literature will correct our received notions about what it means to share a lived sense of mutual vulnerability with nonhuman animals, to be one among many, not first among few, of sovereign and suffering beings, each of whom, like us, is surrounded by the causes of death. Such a literature will also help us understand that humans need no longer be one of those causes.

---

8. John Sanbonmatsu and Carol Adams. *Critical Theory and Animal Liberation* (Rowman and Littlefield 2011).
9. Personal correspondence.

DAVID HAMILTON

LAVENDER TALES

Last summer I added new perennials to my garden, testing for what survives our winters to thrive in the summer and even spread a little under conditions too shady for more spectacular flowers. I think it was Toadflax—I always intend to keep better records and should check next summer to be sure—that sent up six or eight spikes over knee high, with a small, purple flower wavering at its tip, and proved appealing to someone, I decided, when on the third consecutive morning I discovered one stem sliced off about half way up with the top half left lying beside it on the soil. Maybe "appealing" is the wrong word. Maybe it was in the way of someone else's purpose; maybe he was weeding. If nutrition had anything to do with it, he took very little, the rabbit I found nibbling on the next stem the following morning and every day after until he had topped them all.

It was a normal rabbit, a bunny if you like, who ambled through my garden's boxwood hedge and then just stood up on his haunches, cutting off another flower. I stood on my deck, which gave me elevation enough to look down on him, and for him to see me as well. Which did not disturb him much. He paused for a moment then went back to nibbling until I came down and walked toward him. I got within ten feet or so before he loped off into the brush.

I'd seen him before. Either him or a cousin, never much disturbed by us. We have two dogs, one of whom, the big black one, harries any chipmunk, squirrel, or raccoon in sight, while the other, the small white one, yaps at whatever she sees or smells. Oddly, I've never seen either chase a rabbit though other dogs I've had were avid to do so and never seemed to learn what it means to be on a tight leash. But these two, often free in a fenced-in yard, seem to recognize a rabbit chase as futile. More so than the squirrel? I find that odd.

But my summer-with-rabbit passed and last weekend, with my daughter in Philadelphia, I listened as she remembered visits as a child to my parents, in Missouri, and so a rabbit in my father's garden. It was a small garden of lettuce and peas and the like, off to the west of his house, where someone was raiding his lettuce. Rarely passive, my father kept watch with his shotgun until he spotted the varmint and slew him. "Now let's learn something," he said to Jenny as he lugged a dead bunny into the kitchen and turned him belly up on the counter. Dad sliced through the rabbit's abdomen, pulled out its stomach, sliced that small, slimy sac open, and pointed, "See, he was eating my lettuce." "I've always remembered that," said Jenny, at midlife, with a smile.

My dictionary says that a "rabbit punch" is "a chopping blow to the back of the neck," and I felt a whiff of one as I listened to her, with a grandchild on either side, tell an old story I had not heard before. And I remembered rabbit hunts my dad and brother and I, my uncle and cousin, and a few neighbors—the Narrons and Chevaliers come to mind—had on our farm when I was maybe twice the age of Jenny's six-year old boy. We were a farm family and in those days raised several crops. Wheat was one, a field or two each year, and midsummer was harvest time. Dad ran the combine while Uncle Henry ferried grain wagons to a bin. Dad started by cutting a swath around the perimeter of the field and working toward the center. Lots of rabbits made their homes in the field and with each cut, their haven narrowed. Eventually another pass or two would mow all cover down. At that point Dad paused to alert the neighbors. Whatever dogs might be around were also invited. And whatever boys. There were at least the three of us, my cousin, my brother, and I, and the youngest Chevalier was about my age too. Everyone gathered in the field, spreading out on both sides of the combine, like Cossacks though on foot. A couple of the men carried sticks.

As Dad cut those last swaths, rabbits scattered. They had to break and run. They were fast and the timber not far off, but rabbits tend not to keep running. They run ten or twenty yards, hunker down, look around, and run again if necessary. Meanwhile the dogs were running. I remember them as beautiful, three or four swift hounds running and with every few strides leaping over the stubble, soaring high to catch sight again of a rabbit, then turning in midair to follow it's flight. I thought of dolphins leaping over crests of waves then slicing down through them as I had seen in travelogues shown through the winter at our landlocked library.

The men ran too, following the dogs. Whenever a dog caught a rabbit and crouched on it, a man got there quickly. Jerking the rabbit from a dog's mouth, he gave it a rabbit punch with his stick or cupped its head in his hand and twisted. I was avid enough at twelve or thirteen, and fast enough too, to make a couple of kills myself. I remember one of each kind, and assuring myself, yes, I could do it, before twisting a head and feeling the snap, and the other time, being less sure of how to handle that stick, clubbing a poor bunny until an eye popped out. My stomach lurched as if I'd been pushed off a cliff. The rabbit's eye, still attached to a membrane, lay over his cheekbone rather than in its socket. I never became a hunter, and something visceral of that memory struck me listening to Jenny before I could think to recall any of this.

Nor had I ever thought before to ask why Dad started at the periphery and worked toward the center. He could have done otherwise. He could have cut right across the middle of the field then back and forth working toward both edges. With every round his turn would be wider, and easier to make with that big piece of machinery, and all the rabbits would have been shooed gently into the timber or next field, one on either side. But that's not what happened. Instead we demonstrated how an axiom of my uncle's had wider application than I knew. "One boy's a boy," he liked to say about our help on the farm; "two boys are half a boy, and three boys are no boy at all." So it goes for men and boys and dogs, amounting immediately to a mob.

What followed was a feast, rabbits skinned and grilled outdoors and shared around a table made of two old doors on sawhorses as the sun fell beyond the timber along the Missouri, which was our horizon. "We got seven and a half," I remember Dad gloating, "nine and a half" another time, a half having gone to a dog. We weren't subsistence famers, but Dad and Unc still struggled to get a farm started after watching their parents lose theirs in the Depression. The rabbit feast was not just indulgence.

About a dozen years later, I was fresh out of college and teaching primary school in Barranquilla, Colombia. It was an English speaking school, its small clan of teachers a mix of locals and North Americans with the latter group constantly changing, each of us coming for a year or two. One term my closest colleague was a young man named Cort. He had the fourth grade homeroom; I had the fifth. He wore black turtlenecks, even in tropical heat, thought of himself as Brando, or as "beat"—Do the two go together or make an oxymoron? I've never been sure of that—and he spoke warmly of his motorcycle, which he had left behind and may have longed for, for he left after that semester. Before he went, however, he presided over an Easter celebration of his own devising.

After our assembly and parade, with all the students in their Sunday best—not as brilliantly white as First Communion, but close—Cort led all the kids out on the playground, a broad, sandy lot, and showed them an Easter bunny. We'd have a race, he said; the winner would get the bunny. So he lined everyone up across the playground, stood in front of them showing the bunny, a very white bunny, then put it down and blew a whistle. Several dozen third, fourth, fifth, and sixth graders ran storming. I remember it like the final scene of "Suddenly Last Summer" when "Sebastian Venable," uncredited in the cast and whose face is never seen, is overwhelmed and torn apart by a horde of Mediterranean teenagers. The bunny ran a few feet, then stopped and hunkered down, and I never saw it again. Only dust rising from children converging on it.

I see that compared to my father I'm much too passive. I had no foreknowledge of Cort's plan, but I could see it shaping up and knew better. I knew it was a dumb idea, and cruel. I knew pretty much what the bunny would do. But I didn't step into the scene and stop it. An overall posture of hesitance, too often my story, was part of the reason. I've never written of it before either and have told very few. I may also have thought, what in the hell am I going to do with that bunny if I take it off Cort's hands? Actually, I only wonder that now. I don't remember it crossing my mind then any more than it may have crossed my father's to shoo rabbits from the field rather than harvest them. Mostly it was just disbelief. Is this actually going to happen? Then it did.

A couple of years later, my young wife and I were in Virginia where we lived in a very small house on a farm a couple of miles from Charlottesville. The house was an old grain storage shed, renovated for renters like ourselves. It had one room upstairs and one down with a kitchen and bathroom annexed to the downstairs room. Mice loved it. Plenty of grain remained in the cracks. Occasionally we'd find one in the bathtub, an old clawfoot, in the bathroom off the kitchen; and once, when I lunged for it, the little fellow started circling the tub as if it were a cycledrome, his self-generated centrifugal force lifting him up its porcelain sides until, after several circuits, he leapt from the rim and disappeared down a radiator grate.

It was there that I heard a rabbit scream. I'd seen rabbits in distress before, but I had never heard one scream. We had a cat, somewhat better at catching mice than I, and hell on rabbits, especially baby rabbits, and it was the season. One morning I awakened to a scream in the yard. A banshee? Not that I'd ever heard a banshee. High pitched, wavering, pleading perhaps, so I climbed out of bed and ran downstairs to find out. Stepping into the yard in my shorts, into dewy grass cool at dawn, I circled our little house to find our cat, a white cat named "Pues" from our time in Colombia, face to face with a rabbit. Pues held a baby bunny in her mouth, and the mother rabbit, just about Pues' size, stood up to her, nose to nose and, I think, pleading. Pues had paused, not knowing what to do. Nor was the mother rabbit able to attack. That time I did intervene. Taking the baby from Pues' mouth, I released it into taller grass, its mother following. And I took Pues indoors in a small attempt to restore order. But there is an order larger than any I could impose. Pues was an outdoor cat, and by then she knew the location of the nest. I don't remember another scream, but I expect she did her part to control the local cuniculan population.

Which we did affect, inadvertently, though likely not for long, somewhat later. One weekend, my wife's sister and her husband came for a visit. They were city dwellers, Philadelphians. And they brought along a rabbit in a cage. A big rabbit, a lush, calico rabbit, he must have been twice the size of an ordinary garden rabbit or a white Easter bunny. He seemed twice the size of Pues and had a powerful kick. When annoyed, he would turn his back on you and lash out like a mule, with both feet at once. Pues kept her distance. My in-laws were tired of him in their Franklin-era row house on Addison Street, little larger than our farm shed. It's possible that their whole motivation for a visit, for they never came again, nor to any other place we lived—Ann Arbor, Iowa City—was to release Thumper into our woods. I watched him amble off into tall grass and brush but didn't follow. What in the hell would I have wanted with him? I imagined a race of superbunnies soon terrorizing the neighborhood, the rabbits having become the Cossacks, though I suppose a fox or bobcat cut that threat off soon enough. But for these lavender tales that my daughter's memory summoned, I'll trade whatever Toadflax, linaria purpurea, comes up in next summer's garden.

ROBERTO HARRISON

nature as music

there are others in this walk through the ferns
a sun moves to integrate smaller infinities
one more background is resolved and then sees
what the number welcomes to the others

and what we have to subsume. when the stars count
and the integers portray themselves as people
that they knew the traditions of light dressed those patterns
and that others removed themselves from the heights

and from the depths. and one of us would announce
to the earth that the lessons of the underground
would remove our faces in order to love, and that the earth
protected itself from the songs of the machine, and that they knew

the circle would fold to the other side. we sang the neutral cave
of the lesions of the ghosts as they returned and as we all
removed our bodies from the fabrics of intention, we remembered
our own dissolving flesh in the retrial of the promised satellite

that the trees held and that we networked into the fires
of our cut sentences, where the machine would recuperate
its losses for a diagram and for a network, as the link
to our deserts improves that they only survive to be less themselves

than he was on that first day. the attack of the electronic
engagement that startles the tiny world into revolving
the animals, that they were more to the equation of the porous
neuter eggs and that they belonged to sorrow, one animal

like the bear, one animal then like the removal
of the seas of our horns, or like the sands that force function
to the song, and like western corn in its natural harvest of control
that they do not see and do not relieve their motions

as the end of life. their promises would not reveal the other world
and they would not announce to the car that they hurt like the street
as one moves there to the snow. one of it would see and one of it
would scar the traveling ice from the room of its intention, as two would

to their own desertions what the spiraling cub attended to it saw
the occluded pattern. then the call to the motion would bleed
and the call to the winter would remain what determined the support
of the machine. one of us would talk of it and decide for the colors

their own intended consequences. what more do I dissolve to grain
the saddle and become one spoken in many, like the forgiven minerals
and that they saw themselves as one being. their only desert and their only
forest would remind the eastern light of its own structure, that they own

a receding color. they were horrified to discover the song of function
and ability, as they knew no way to welcome their crossings, their trees
like an offering and like one who stands and sleeps. there are those, and there
are many who became and did not see, and they welcomed their own

disappearances as a return of destructions. they have one more weapon
it calls themselves to the mineral, they have no known language and they
became and they went. one of us was one of them. we saw others and we were
beside the dividing lines of the numbers. and those of us did not attend their

only wave. they had themselves protected and they moved to sunrise to remain
like the last word and they moved to the night to intend their own crimes
as a softening corruption of the stellar fields. there was no one there who spoke
and they saw themselves as the end of all answers to intend the services of the forms

of their equal lodes. they were woven then to the pattern of the intentions of a ball
as they were more than a word. the interior mask of the computer is a message to the lives
of their servants, their only increase one of these that died in the lake. one of us
saw them backing for the light, and one of us did not attend to the crimes. we were

the only action that would solve their time. we are the functions in the seas of attrition
as we spawn the sorrows of another form. one of us would move and one of us would
intend that we saw and responded to the move, the longword, and the sequence
of determinations as we collected those aggravated and assumed like a name. their

opposable desires would not intend the circumstance or home of the greenery
and decide which of us were one. those infinite ascensions and their internment,
like the war of bodies and their only action, like the growth of pins would attend
and dissolve for nothing. one of us would see and become and one of us would not

that the season would remind itself of the trouble and pain of the wheel. their fossil
would destroy the line and their promise would not engage the cockroach. they saw it there
as one was to dissolve. and they saw it there as one was to arrive
with nothing of the weather. those of us there would not dissolve again

and would not send again our engagement with the screen. there is no one
to be in front of and no one there to answer. and those of us would not see
as the stomach of their ascension would not remove its own death. then the command
would attend and would become like that to the sea. and one of us would move there

to the ocean. confusing faces would not speak. those of us of humans would not speak.
their approach to the writing became less of itself to remain the more of the end. and one of their
lines would make the technical light of its known quantity its own disaster and would not attend
to their woven wounds. most of us would amend to itself its own mountain. those of us

who were there saw to the becoming of the night. we knew the others would not attend to them.
we were more than the single door. we arrived to count and to stand. we were among
the others at necropolis, with smiles. we knew the engagement of the war would not retrieve
their memories. which of us was there with the light? we knew that the others were gone

ELIZABETH HATMAKER

MALIBU HIGH (1979)

D: Irvin Berwick.
Crown International Pictures.

Spec: 1 video field, one head pass, vocal assault, a complete assembly revolution of sound and R-rated nudity in 1 field, 1 screen, 1 car.

In diegesis, 1979, far outside frame,
kids are post grainy post worry, seizure, post angry
new grit burnout gobbing out of reach sub-studio
Hollywood or less on less for lesser gyration yet
gotta think of dwindling labour class
on screen then air-bourne. Eye flicks and shudders.
This loss of opportunity for badness. No class cred
for fucking bad at the Rubidoux,
Mission Tiki, Motor View
Hi-Way Drive-In in Santa Maria.

Poignant truth yet penetrated mean acquisitive
exploitive relics w/o virtue; economic mechanisms,
will create surplus of labor, callous synthetic approaches,
"Reaganesque extremism in policy
and style." Film heroine—dumped by her boyfriend
for rich girl. Her w/o accompanying thrashed
angry soundtrack and she don't care about
new world order, de-regulation, transition noise to smooth to easy to
active resistance through careful commoditization. She
punk w/o larger stratagem, no job but fucking in
our coming sync crisis, low frequency of ideological failure, it
taints outside drive-in, it chokes at
panopticon easy post punk voice of death of
post punk him him him what

she gonna do in weary drone not this
drive-in, this sound-addled
offline mechanical body
mangled backdrop, torque of consent w/o dignity.
Rust can be fatal, crummy
oxidizing suggests nationalism, give and take of ownership
sudden attack on dignity—on your knees now—slow
assent to the global market—on your tits now—show me show me and
shut up
—and violated like copyright all stupid nostalgia.

In the mise en scène, in
her roomy compartment, in the blueprint of fragile consent. "Her metal
heart erodes
under half-hearted plot," reads the tag-line. Our hearts sink
then glide on an 118 wheel base. Solid, solid, baby. Don't
doubt our fine engineers' reputations.

And what she think about what with some punk's
hard shine on her low tits? She curls in,
ready for mechanical sodomy, ready for its sound-on-film
to inflect her voice, feels it not quite fit her cavity.
Her eyes follow third rate action bad family, always Reagan at the helm,
finally always then-obligatory compliance with world order and then here's
the scene when she kills her hs principal, blows up his heart with her tits.

In the field, easy to observe glassy-eyed repose
Humiliation, promise of future tense—listing under slacks-wearing jackass,
his attempts at funkiness seizing at ignition
jam her on weary ecosystem, he leaves her and then
a series of lesser vo-pros low wage bullshit job lump kids with
syndromes w/o cure Reagan's revamp of 1601 Elizabethan Poor Law pram
crappy car, hep c., the punk ass next to her, one hand on
her tit, fist to her nose, dark beautiful voice scaled
down, growling, quaking, seizing the gravel
of his bad future in her ear
and she want to blow the heart outta all our fucking
pointless visual rage as she ignores him for screen, her downfall so
expected no break in audience conversation. We could time her life-cycle to
bad plot deadly click bad transmission pulse count.

No archive got words, impression shit,
her rusty after-impression barely registers as a solid, barely economic
change. She
ideological object bad-faith economy or something or slut's failed
technological innovation. Her impression push-button cough of meaning,
sudden jerk on her suspension.

In the movie, she's Kim, not that not knowing
should make us all guilty and all though nice name
when she the loser through drive-in speaker,
low radius AM/FM, a Revox tape machine records, slow grinding
pitched to EMS Synthi-100, Wollensak tape loops unacceptable
for modern recording practice like sounds from her future boyfriend's
past decayed factory slither like party reel-to-reel, easy for better houses
being funky. Effect is
half-listened unremarkable I itch.

A new visual field: Eye punk for sluts,
low-grade bullshit for sure, over dubbed by lyicon half-tit
embedded lead and synthis, not even growling four-eye headlamp,
vox pop male beaver rust lookey.

Industrial Revolution constant from production through
transmission; "there is no need to build in a safety factor." She extinct from
post family
economy no daddy without shiny private sphere rusty
mechanical grasp of wardrobe, sound, verb structure,
Breasts shake wearily in sockets like dirty change, it's the reverb
of the image that grates, it's the incorporation of
her entire assembly.

She puffs out like bare life, you say, she dumb
as bloody shit on the elegant soundtrack. Her bumper erodes grassy
spoiled California eco-system. She is lead in the needle record
no one hears except that sounds way too romantic, way too much,
friendly—yes salubrious—pre-exchange, pre-lumpen particle. Instead she's
"single revolution in which the assembly records or reproduces
complete and [breathe hard here] un-segmented field"—yes, she is
signification about the commerce of all y'alls women and beats go on.

like saturation outperv technology is anachronistic
heavy groove wear across her tits, we hear the echoes,
the girl in drive in outside screen she is fine handling
torqueflite and sweet 230.2 cid and sweet and still not sure why she's
there in a car with a vo-pro punk who sees her outside his dead deep voice
rage against trade policies not favoring him feeling small
and shit mainstream and she, she hardtop, engine voice,
distracted viewership, shut the fuck and and watch watch
analyze color reference burst at 358 mHz
at moderate temperature in 20 doomsday years American Studies
is dead and gritty means the body of waste and all.

And her politics got nothing, her flat vowels got no traction, no no
she ambient noise like a rusty belt around her image. Her cultural fall is
monaural residue on your windshield. The sound from the engine rolls on:
"eyeball-drilling sound!" And her lack of interest is laid out on conversion
fabrics, class perpetuated shag, special individualized mass-produced
private space
rotted drive-in fields. "Modern girls should buy their todays" reads bill-
board lexicon. No shit it's
only subversive consumption. Aught to be at a multiplex anyway.

And I'll tell you another thing about all the things about making her as
hard as possible, more dirty word on the proletariat. "At least
I don't gotta pay for it," Kim barks rust belt accent. Bad light rotted
metal terrain. All flesh is force, MS to CU, a breast of blue light to dinner
music,
the symbolic over the bloody Wollensak, her use of breast, the triangle is
an open
economic system, a half-beautiful woman, cruel-toned words: Pram face.
Dumb-shit. Rusty van
socket. Oily voice of transmission, Bendix Electrojector, pirate technology
of girly.

In film, Kim, she sexy MG Midget, an improbable Jaguar, giving you the
triumphant finger, her
sound far gone to waste. In her mangled wreck resides gender class
ideology eye-socket—
even in your car, buried underground w/case of Schlitz in your rusty
compartment.

Sure, her something off argument, so soft core blasé, so downward
mobility
dole shit after hour bad spec, wrong economic vision. She laydown,
gross-out on the floor, a misalignment w/appropriate workforce ambient
so the wire says. Yet surely
there is revolution merging subculture pollutant-born congenital disease as
her breast puffs out to the vertical synchronizing pulse finally once more
before expiration quietly in
the editing bay.

QUINTUS HAVIS

MIDDLE-EARTH TO MISSISSIPPI, SELMA TO SAGITARRON

I write because I hail from a land of breath-drinkers who feast 'pon my vernacular and fart farces, while speculative hipsters wear masks of coagulated blood called neutrality howling me into an inaction they call fair play, an inertness they alternatively name "moving" and "powerful" as if my pain were the mortar of a schoolhouse, from a village where our menfolk were made sacrifice to a hateful God and loathsome porcine priests whose glock nines spit sermons that implore immaculacy or scream a fatal inertia, cherry-hot and heart-seeking like virginal passion, my hands up in fearful praise, because I am ruled over by men who would bust a gat in the sky just to watch the galaxy fall, where Mother Sea was raped and named perpetrator-victim because of the rolling tide of her hips and the wetness of her vital pussy, so I write celestial charts and ship blueprints with sharp wings to cut through the bullshit, with hot and crude language to fuel that motherfucker, all to astrogate the cold gaze of stellar eyes watching hard and suspicious behind nebula curtains, my words the seed sewn to grow a new Genesis begat by a Mother, Daughter, and a bad bitch from NOLA out there twerking to Sissy Nobby and Big Freedia, 'til we are snared by thin folk whose profile is pearlescent and vanishing and whose whispers ride slave galleys pregnant with a fearsome ugliness down the canals of my ears while pathetic ghouls that would steal our very lives for fun and profit sew the seed for trees bearing the strangest of fruits, and so I write to bend the temporal line before me, hitting chronological corners in a candy-painted Caddy with lowered suspensions and chromed out rims, bumping both Lil'-and-Ra-Kim passing by Thomas Jefferson hollering for me to let him ride, while Lupe Fiasco shakes his head over so-called jezebel antics and sourly lotions his ashy dick in a galaxy far, far away where, long, long ago, the lone last black woman in a blanched universe watched a damn dark people rise like a black fist from the heart of darkness to be cursed as darkness incarnate and die gobbled up in a great mouth with alabaster teeth sharp as vorpal blades that snicker as they snack.

PETERSBURG FREESTYLE

On the corner of Washington and Sycamore, rabid and drunk from a bite of Mad Dog 20/20, Lamar and I daydream Seagram wishes and cannabis dreams, where we hollered at august sexual thaumaturges who alchemized ambrosial pussy to slake the throaty aridity of thirsty niggas and exercise obese pockets down to a crack fiend's sylphlike physique, where stick up kids post up like picket fences, where drug dealer swamis charm addicts hissing for the next fix, where BGs stomp Scantron bruises on rival colors to earn gangbang certificates, young niggas with hoop dreams deflated, and with no reflections of themselves on television, head to the land where razor blades and glock nines are situated.

O Petersburg! Where squaw civilization fell to civilizing swords, where filibuster bullets overwhelmed the arguments of stone arrowhead words, where Col. Wood's erection-expeditions probed the depths of damsel wilderness to create the Confederate umbilical cord, where Union armies tamed abdicating blacks into trench diggers, where History won't shame those white men by mentioning them lowly niggas.

Praise Virginia, where slave graves will turn parking lot for the glory of Tiffany windows, where my friend will be ignored at a funeral because her white husband could never leave a nigga widow up on Crater Road, where homeless niggas will hunch, spines bending parabolic arches to calculate a degree of warmth, where even supreme mathematics will lack proofs that'd help a nigga's books balance, where, on the corner of Washington and Sycamore, in the cockade of the union, my nigga will nudge me and cry:

I LOVE NIGGAS
I LOVE NIGGAS
I LOOOOOVE NIGGAS
CUZ NIGGAS
ARE ME

EZILI AND THE INFINITE DEATH

The supreme mathematics postulate that adding one god to one earth summed a reality. What follows are mythopoetic equations, the blueprints of a divine machine.

Ezili Freda, her of full lips and round hips, swayed into fiction in a gown of night, bearing a necklace of shimmering starlight and three rings crowned with swirling nebulas, one for each husband: Damballa, who forged her a mirror of sky, Agwe, who snared them from the maw of space as it yawned the cosmos in its slumber, and Ogoun, who forged the rings and necklace all. And here she stood, at the twilight of consciousness, her flesh the richness of tender earth, her twist-out on point, her shoe game vicious in them Red Bottom heels, adjusting her attire and twisting this way and that to make sure that she knew what the boys were watching when she walked away.

And for that, the eye of great God opened to gaze and lust and plot, as thirsty motherfuckers tend to do. He approached her with that Atari to discover she only played PS4. And he gave his all, with his Colecovision rap, his Neo Geo smoothnesses and 16 bit NES spit, yet still fell short. Wrathful, he howled he didn't like her anyway, the bitch, and she's obviously a slut and even though she was pretty (for a dark skin girl), she wasn't even all that, all out to impress like that, ass, titties, dressed like that, and just like that, His sword swung, and divided her into pieces and He subtracted his favored chunks.

Lo, and almighty God trapped the world in illusion, dooming us to witness lustrous brown as exotic toys or exotic filth, and to see women accoutered in holy ebon flesh as an organization of parts as opposed to the sum of a more divine equation.

This pussy was the route used by colonizer cum to lay the foundation of the world.

Ezili Mapiangue awakens into fiction half-dead on a bed of Tuskegee needles. The goddess of birth, damned in substandard hospital rooms and cursed for a shivering crack zombie by doctoral-wielding arbiters of life and death. The scars swarming her body conjure time from the deadly genetic memory of cotton fields and poll taxes. Her contractions writhe to the rhythms conjured by demigod progenitors of jazz, blues, and rap; howling wolves and muddy waters tumble forward in an amniotic symphony fronted by five fabulous brothers, plus one. My, my.

God has already been here, and lo, we witness his wroth. Lands that follow His footsteps use black birth records to chart the trajectories of small backs falling into prison bunks like lightless meteorites. The fiction of Mama Ezili is elided for one more pleasing to God's eyes; a horror of family trees split, of tyrannical mothers mocked by men garbed in drag, and of gentrification-as-colonializing-warfare, running niggers out of neighborhoods and their own culture. This horror-fiction will come to one day allow a white man to report that the plantation was a place of love, as he considered the joy Ezili must have felt, having her babies ripped from her womb and replaced with a limbed and opaque whiteness.

This pussy was the mortar that cemented the world into being.

Ezili Quvenzhané sailed into fiction astride beasts of a southern wilderness. She skipped on lily pads across avuncular, watchful waters to play games with cunning cousin snakes, learn wisdom from grandfather snails, and nap on matronly alligator tail pillows. Twin afro puffs bopped a gleeful dance with lightning bugs in the evening listening to cricket bands jam du-wop to Madam Twilight.

Ye, and the Lord smote her with a crimson word: "Cunt." And so she fell in twain 'pon a bloodstained carpet.

This pussy was the open house, to show interested alabaster pinpricks gentrifying night just how much could be theirs.

EVERYDAY JARGON

Race (n, adj)

(1) The indelible mark of history.
Ex: "Why is he writing about this again? He must be one of those blacks mad about slavery; just let it go, God."

(2) A signpost used to navigate social situations.
Ex: "Roll up the windows."

(3) An excuse.
Ex: "This is why niggers can't have shit!"

Color-blind (n)

(1) A state only inhabitable by the privileged.

(2) A lie.
Ex: "I don't even see color; I see humanity."

Diversity (n)

(1) A thing claimed, not owned.
Ex: "We pride ourselves on the diversity of our campus here at ISU…"

(2) The name of a situation which involves tokens.
Ex: "My hometown was very diverse; Olive Garden and Taco Bell were right across the street from each other!"

Minority (n, adj)

Racism (n)

(1) A thing that doesn't happen here.

Threatening (adj, adv)

(1) To be spirited without effusive joy.
Ex: "I don't see why he's so threatening; we're just talking about how Obama's election proves racism is over. We learned the lessons of race relations from the past!"

Race relations (n)

(1) Dead niggers.

Minority leader (n)

(1) A reduction of ethnicities to a mass body with a single face.
Ex: "We blacks need a leader these days to help us."

Exotic (adj)

(1) The function of dark skin.

Ex: "These postcards make Dubai seem like such a fun and exotic place!"

(2) The function of accent.
Ex: "Oh, you speak so well! Where are you from?"

(3) The function of dress.
Ex: "That veil those Arab bitches wear? Shit is hot. So fucking mysterious!"

(4) The function of posture.
Ex: "LOL, your gangsta Facebook pic is totes funny, Becky!"

Sexy (adj, adv)

(1) Fetishized.
Ex: "There's just something sexy about a woman who can cook. There's just something sexy about Obama's swagger. There's just something sexy about African accents."

Commercialize (v)

(1) The moment of colonization.
Ex: http://www.youtube.com/watch?v=ql-N3F1FhW4

(2) The disarming of counter-culture.

Militant (adj)

(1) To be agitated about issues regarding your subordinations
Ex: "I don't see why he has to be so militant about Trayvon! It's up to the courts. Who knows what that kid was doing."

Dick (n, adj)

(1) A compliment
Ex: "Haha, dude, you're such a dick!"

(2) A comment on how power is wielded
Ex: "I feel like everyone tries to make me out to be a dick just because I'm saying the plantation could have been a place of love. Why couldn't the mammy love her master's son?"

Pussy (n, adj)

(1) Fighting words
Ex: "We'll see how much of a pussy I am when I beat your fucking face in!"

(2) A comment on how power is wielded
Ex: "Don't be such a pussy! Call them out on that racist shit!"

Faggot (n, adj)

(1) When one fucks the wrong thing

(2) A comment on how power is wielded
Ex: "We totally raped that fag today!"

Eloquent (v, adj)

(1) When one is competent in speech

(2) When another is shocked at said competence
Ex: "Wow! Obama speaks so well."

Midol (n)

(1) Xanax for women

Bitch (n, adj, v)

(1) When a man isn't manly

(2) When a woman is considered so

Sexually Empowered (adj)

(1) Slut

Male Gaze (n)

(1) The voyeuristic eyes of God and America

Female (n, adj)

Retard (n, adj)

(1) When a person acts silly.

(2) Terrifying

(3) Invisible

Rising Intonation (n)

(1) The tucked tail of communication

America (v, n)

(1) Enter Arby's

(2) Purchase potato bites (a brown pod, fried, bearing yellow cheeses and decimated bacons)

(3) Dip in ranch

(4) CONSUMECONSUMECONSUMECONSUMECONSUME CONSUMECONSUME

GREG HEWETT

BLINDSIGHT

Never considering how his light is spent,
the blind climber tastes the height and sheer of cliff.
He summits, triumphant. The vista resounds.
Once a blind poet saw war clear in stanzas
weaving and unweaving heroes and horrors.
No camouflage can hide us from his vision.
Light denied, the physicist could see clearly
the structure of atoms, the complete absence
of empty space. How full the world looks beyond
the flickering tyranny of the visual.
When light lapses from my room I find myself
virtually lost. In blindness deep and far
vision grows visible and the dark world wide.

SKYGLOW

When it's clear, I miss the stars.
Since their exile from the sky
I have navigated okay. Thank heavens

for GPS, and when I get nostalgic
I still have deep space
as my screensaver. The dark has left us too.

In another time
we might have met by the river under a river

of stars.
For now

we spin filaments of light into profiles,

drawing each other
through something resembling time and space and dark.
Let's call this something something vague and mythic
as the ether. Let's say we're ethereal.

Whoever you are now texting me, when you open
the actual door I might not mistake you
for all that you've uploaded.

The TV flickering violet behind you is aura enough.
Glow-in-the-dark stars pasted to the bedroom ceiling are a big plus.
No matter. The whole universe is made up
of just 2% visible matter and I am
looking for something beyond the naked eye.

SEVEN FISH, THREE TREES, TWO MEN

Maybe numbers are invisible, but look
over there, seven
fish swim in the uncountable water watched
by a man seated alone in the shade of three trees,
though none the same—oak, ash, beech.
We sense numbers hiding in our very breath,
in a line of poetry, a measure of music
running through our heads.
The truth of, say, zero, negative two or
algebra is outside of us and all of nature,
yet somehow the absence of another man
is more present to him than the school of fish
he is watching, and the vision of the two of them
dwells there in the negative space of the trees.
If he could compose the right words in a line,
he thinks, or just come up with a simple equation,
he would have him back. But numbers and death are
different undercurrents of this world filled with trees,
fish, people, and so many water and so much words.

MEMOIR

It is and it is
not is not the way
we tell stories here.
We want it just once
upon a time yet

the man at the door
of this stanza is a ghost

of his former self
and a monster from

time to time. Something's
about to happen

though it's difficult to tell
anything at all.

On days the fog lifts
it isn't any clearer.

Eucalyptus pollen and
malaise drift down over all.

It's apples or oranges
in the wooden bowl.

Under this fine patina
we're general as statues.

The air blurs
motive and gesture.
A hand raised means anything.

No journalists are camped out
to get the story

of our metaphoric crimes.
It's easy to imagine

there's no prequel or sequel
or spin-off to living so

uneventfully,
no story

arcing toward rescue,
no happy ever after,

but at least
I never promised
you Armageddon.

AT THE SAME TABLE

Memory tells me
I see us

still sitting
at that same sidewalk table
but do I really

have that image or
don't I

also see
the table and wine
and you there

from the same
point of view
as then and not see

myself? If I were
to call you

all these years later
I am still sitting
at that same table

for you, although not

as I would see it.

If you want
an image of what
you once called

my soul, then listen
to all that I see,
it's right there

in my body voiced,
translated
into you.

THEY MAKE ME PLAY THE MINSTREL

Only they've placed me on a deserted island, beside a lagoon,
my blackface slowly melting under the moon

made too bright and strong
for the Technicolor takes of my last song.

It's for my own good, they say,
this isolation, you never know what people may
be concealing, even in the middle of the day.

FOREIGN FILM IN FOG

No desire in sight,
you take a streetcar to the end, to the beach.
The ocean is a TV with the picture turned off.
There's nothing to see but a neon marquee pulsing through the thick air.
You enter and find yourself in a long foreign biopic about a brilliant mathematician who
lived a century ago and had bad luck in love and a hill on the dark side of the
moon named after her,
and when you go out into the world again
clarity greets you like a well-rehearsed shark.

LILY HOANG

ON THE EATING OF TAILS

Once I wrote a miniature book that I called a novellete that I called "Webcam Sex" and it was about webcam sex and it was written in a style that was a mockery of Tao Lin and Marie Calloway because I was bitter and this was years ago and does anyone even care about Marie Calloway anymore? and a publisher offered to publish it and I was very happy about this. The publisher who offered to publish it wanted to publish it electronically and "Webcam Sex" would launch the press's eBook series and this made me rather pleased. I was pleased because he is a model literary citizen. I wouldn't call him a hero but I admired him greatly and he did all sorts of good things for indie lit and I liked him immensely although I've met him only once. Maybe once, maybe never, but I'm pretty sure once I have shaken his hands and maybe spoken a few sentences but I can't remember, not for sure at least and I have a terrible memory and I take Xanax and that certainly doesn't help improve my memory but it does feel awfully good and often I wonder if this is what people without anxiety feel like but no—it's just another chemical euphoria and I don't think of any consequences, I can feel only the standardized immediate relief, its predictability: how calm will slip through my body and in. I take Xanax but I don't take it often because everyone else loves it and I only like it but I take it when I need it and I take it for fun and when I need it sometimes I don't take it at all so I can save it for fun and anxiety is an explosion and it is a crushing and I don't take the Xanax and I reject amelioration, I reject feeling better, I fester. I deserve it. And once a blog accused me of cronyism because on another blog many years before I had written a comment about how I don't like to submit to journals because I hate rejection and the person took this to mean that I never submit to journals and every single one of my publications must've been printed on the back of cronyism and this was obviously ridiculous or I was in my hotel room crying because people can be so hateful and they can be so mean and I don't take a Xanax and the person who wrote the blog sent it to my chair and I had only had the job for a month and already—this. Maybe I met this publisher once but I can't even remember and so let it be known that it was not through cronyism that my book on webcam sex called "Webcam Sex" was accepted for publication. Except that it was solicited.

Pause.

"Webcam Sex" is not going to be published because I pulled the manuscript because recently a series of fingers were pointed and a number of names were called and this all happened under the bright lights of social media and gossip is unavoidable even though I avoid the news. One very prominent finger was pointed at Tao Lin and years ago when I read his book *Richard Yates* I thought I would be sick but my fingers kept on turning the pages even though I thought it was reprehensible I kept on reading and this embarrasses me, which is why I write about it here. Everything about me embarrasses me and everything else embarrasses me too and I feel empathetic embarrassment as real as my own embarrassment and I wish I could just walk around totally invisible except that we all write for a disgusting hope of immortality even if we are not gods. And we are not gods and I am no god too. Something that really embarrasses me is that I smoke cigarettes and I never smoke cigarettes at work because I think it will make people think less of me and it will make people judge me and all I want to do is fit in and all I want to do is pass for one of them and when I first got here they used to invite me out and now they don't anymore and to Dorothy I'm like *I'm too weird for them* and she's like in total agreement with me and so she doesn't say anything even though we both know I want her to say that I'm not too weird and that I'm ok and all I want is to be ok. And it's totally stupid that I care if my colleagues know I smoke cigarettes and it's neurotic and it's insecure and I am so insecure and even my boyfriend tells strangers that my biggest problem is my insecurity to total strangers he says this and he's right and I have imposter syndrome and I want to capitalize that like Imposter Syndrome because it is real and it is harsh and I wonder what will happen to me when I'm revealed as an imposter, how bad it will hurt and where. Dorothy texts me one morning and her name isn't really Dorothy she's asked for a pseudonym and I've written about Dorothy is dozens of essays and now she wants to be a pseudonym and I don't want this to hurt my feelings but it does and I understand and I'm calling her Dorothy because they both want to be where they are not now, which is here, and here is hardly a facsimile of Oz but with me, and Dorothy texts me one morning and it is early and she tells me a guy we both know has been implicated in the sex scandal that featured Tao Lin but fires being fires only spread wide and now—this. I don't respond to her text. It is, after all, still early. But even more than early I wanted just to ignore the text and ignore the name because the name that Dorothy texted me was a name we both knew but even more than that he was a good literary citizen and he was going to publish "Webcam Sex" and it was slated for release and soon. And there was all this sex scandal and I don't do research. I don't find out what's been said or by whom. I just know that his name is in the circus ring and the feminist in me wants nothing to do with any sex scandal where the issue at hand is consent because consent sometimes is meaningless and I know this and I wish I didn't know this but I do and I want nothing to do with any sex scandal, especially one with Tao Lin and any of his people. The good literary citizen editor is not one of Tao Lin's people but his name was billboarded anyways. The sex scandal started on Twitter or maybe it was Tumblr and it definitely made its way to Facebook and I just want to turn off my iPhone sometimes but Dorothy is deep with gossip and I rely on her for news if gossip is news and it is. I talk to Dorothy about the publisher and I talk to her about "Webcam Sex" but I don't talk to her about webcam sex even though we are best friends and I would tell her anything. I ask Dorothy for advice and she says pull the book and she says I don't need a book so bad as to support this publisher who we both used to think of as a model literary citizen and I don't even know what he did, just that it was a sex scandal in a day of too many sex scandals and maybe feminism is associated somehow but all my spotty information it can't be related to feminism or maybe it is but really I am just ignorant. Dorothy says to pull the book and I get an email from the editor who solicited "Webcam Sex" and the editor says the publisher is innocent and I believe him and I remain ambivalent. I talk to Molly about the situation and she says the young feminists are schooling us on the definition of consent and she wonders out loud if an unvocalized no means rape. If silence equals consent. I talk to Molly and she says I should publish the book now because if I don't publish the book now people in the future will think that I only wrote the book because of the sex scandal, that I was using the sex scandal as fodder, that I was capitalizing on it, and I don't really care what people think but just for the record I wrote "Webcam Se" two years ago two years before any stupid sex scandal. I talk to JMWs about "Webcam Sex" and it is especially good to talk to him not just because he's a stud but mostly because he has heard me read "Webcam Sex" when I read in Tucson with Mike Young and we read on a porch and it was full of grad students and the desert is lovely there and JMWs sports a pool and a hot tub in his backyard and after the reading we are all intoxicated and in the hot tub and I am not disappointed that I go to bed alone. JMWs says I should write about this whole thing and I should post it on *HTMLGIANT* and I say that I'm sad *HTMLGIANT* is closing down and it's not because of the sex scandal at all but the timing connects the dots even when they are just two dots, floating the fuck around. JMWs tells me I should write about this and it should be big and this could be my last contribution to *HTMLGIANT* and I could go out like an explosion like boom like jazz fingers simmering down and I get all riled up and then I never write the post.

Pause.

I tell JMWs about how *HTMLGIANT* used to be this escape for me back when I was in a shitty marriage living in shitty towns being miserable and then *HTMLGIANT* happened and I jumped into the Internet and there, I made friends when I couldn't make real life friends I made Internet friends, writing friends, friends who are still real life friends today, if only on the Internet, or: I have always been afraid of snakes and in Vietnam snakes are considered lucky and they are a sign on prosperity and peace and snakes eat mice and I guess there must be a lot of mice in Vietnam and I am a lot more American than I'd like to admit but here I am admitting it: get that snake away from me! And I tell JMWs that I think it's notable that two women of color writers are telling me two very different things about "Webcam Sex" and in Vietnam and in other places including here snake is used for medicine too and the publisher is a white man and there are all these sex scandals and do I think any of this really matters? Is this an issue of race and gender and all those other oppressions too? Is it ever about anything but? JMWs tells me I should start my own *HTMLGIANT* but it should only feature hot women of color and he doesn't mean hot as in sexually attractive but maybe he does and he probably does like ninety percent but also ten percent hot as in intelligent and full of feist. Right now I am sitting in my sunroom and there is a fire going and all across the country there is snow and just last weekend I was in Houston with my boyfriend and we biked all around town and now I am back in the desert and there is a fire because the night is cold and I am lonely. JMWs suggests I put "Webcam Sex" up on *HTMLGIANT* in its entirety as a free download and I think about it and I ask Dorothy what she thinks and she doesn't use the word *dumb*, per se, and Dorothy and I work at the same school and now I am Associate Department Head and now Dorothy is Director of the Creative Writing Program and don't all these titles make us sound so legit? and we both wish we were just professors again sans fancy titles and loafing around my house writing emails and gossiping. Used to be I'd sit in my hammock for hours and read Joyce and I was never trained for this position and I spent the first two weeks of the semester weeping every day after work. Whereas I didn't know it at the time I bought a bicycle and the bicycle saved me—no exaggeration, I stopped weeping when I started biking—and fuck you it's a fixed gear and once I was in Boulder and Mathias came up from Denver and I remember walking with him and his bicycle and I liked how the pedals moved as the bicycle moved and that was when I wanted a fixie because Mathias had one and we have tattoos together and he gives the best hugs. I was weeping for August and in September I had my fixie and I don't really care if you're judging me because I ride every day and I am hungry all the goddamn time and I am sitting in my sunroom writing this essay and there is a fire going and above the fireplace there is a painting my friend Stevie made me back when we both lived in South Bend when he was a grad student in print making and I had already graduated and was adjuncting and then I was Visiting at Saint Mary's and he painted the painting on particle board and he painted a pile of crushed PBR cans and there's a devil man with a chicken foot meditating and he thinks *Acid rules* and there is a rattlesnake man he thinks *Ride the snake* and back when we lived in South Bend together Stevie used to married and I used to be married too and I guess the past tense is just another thing we now share. For Christmas this year I would like to ask my boyfriend for a Houston bicycle and for him to not break up with me again. I don't deal well with rejection and he doesn't care about money but if I had to choose—I can buy my own fucking bike. In less than two weeks I will go to Iowa to teach at a college and the title is fancy and it tickles my pride a little—*Visiting Distinguished Writer*—and there is nothing distinguished about me except maybe my gray hair and it's really only because I'll be Visiting Distinguished Writer that I can afford another bicycle, my lifestyle being just outside what my salary can afford, and recently I've been thinking more and more that I would give up the tenure track if my boyfriend asked me to move to Houston and all he'd have to do is ask and he won't, I know he won't, and all he'd have to do is ask and I'd give up this tenure track job that is the carrot and its cake too. The first time I read from "Webcam Sex" I was reading at Brown and Cole Swensen and Renee Gladman were teaching my book *Changing* and it's crazy that anyone reads my books and every more wild that people are teaching it and those two heroines and at Brown of all places and at dinner Renee was explaining astrology and she explained fire signs and she used cups as figurines and in one the Fire sign is in the middle and everyone congregates around them and in another the Fire sign is the leader and everyone follows and then she gets to Aries and she lines everyone into a huddle and Aries, she says, and she throws my Fire sign right through everyone and I am the smash, I am the brick the shatters glass windows. Aries is fire and the year of the snake is fire and I was not born in the year of the snake but according to fairy tale the animals of the zodiac were crossing a river to win a race and the snake was not a good swimmer so he was a stowaway on the horse and the horse was not winning but he was not losing either and the horse crossed the river and was about to cross the finish line and then the snake jumped and EEEE and that is how the snake beat the horse and the first time I read from "Webcam Sex" I was reading at Brown and I got off the plane and texted my friend Michael who was teaching and I'd see him later, after dinner with Renee and Brian, and it was seasonable in my b&b so I took a nap and inside my nap I had a nightmare and I never talk about dreams but this one was special and in the dream I was in a house and it was kind of like the house in Mark Danielewski's *House of Leaves* as in the exterior was smaller than the interior which was expanding as I was walking and then I was running and I was being chased and I knew I was in dreamscape and so I wasn't scared and I lofted around even though I was scared but it was just a nightmare and I was safe and it was fine and then I woke up because I needed to pee and I looked up the house and I found it right there on Google Maps and I texted Dorothy and we FaceTimed and I was like *Isn't that weird?* and I was like *Want to see?* and I flipped my phone around so she could see my laptop screen and instead of the house there was a webcam recording me sleeping and I could see myself having the nightmare and I could see my eyes flute and I could see my fear right there on the screen and then the recorded me opened her eyes and looked at the real me and that's when I woke up for real. None of this is in "Webcam Sex," which will not be published, not any time soon at least. For the time being, it will sit in my DropBox and occasionally I will open the file and scroll through the pages and I will regret that *HTMLGIANT* closed down when it was the only space for me on the Internet and it was a space for so many writers of my generation and now it is gone and even when it comes back it will not be the same it will never be the same because there is only the one and replication is not duplication and a snake dumb enough to eat its own tail will die too.

LILY HOANG & BHANU KAPIL

from *ON PUNCTUATION, DESIRE, AND THE POST-COLONIAL BODY*

THE COMMA

The comma faces backwards, toward[s]: the origin of the sentence and thus: of time. An: horizontal inversion. A meat hook, I said, upon which: the content of the sentence is dragged and spent. A soft tissue, shredded, as the carcass passes from hand to hand. What are the subjects of your sentences? How do the commas abrade them? The comma provides, in this sense, a resistance: to the effortless forward movement, societal movement, of the sentence. I made a parallel to post-colonial life, and then corrected myself, positioning the comma as an anti-colonial device. I shall pause there, with some interest about what you are thinking: about meat.

If: the comma faces backwards, it is a meathook upon a meatsentence. But if: the comma faces backwards and is a meathook upon a meatsentence, the comma is a delayal of the inevitable: what is to come will surely come, even a meathook cannot prevent fate. Each sentence is already a destiny, a destination, which will arrive, regardless of our desires—as readers, as writers. To read and to write is mystical, and what is more romantic than destiny?

Today, the subject of my sentences are women, women who half a lifetime ago were subjected to an event, and now, half a lifetime later, what is causality? Do events impact? Sentences are not events, they are situations. The comma is the event, in its silence.

The comma is not the equivalent to a rest in music. It is not respite. It is not breath. It is the sentence, pulling you back, making you desire: .

There was an article today about trans-generational trauma as a kind of imprint, transmitted genetically—a form of memory not held in the nerves—from mother to daughter. I am generalizing. My friend, Andrea Spain, a post-colonial scholar, sent me the articles—a kind of evidence for the kind of work happening—the women in your sentences, and I guess, in mine—in other domains.

That memory: is it a form of affect then?

Now I am very conscious of not using commas as I write these sentences to you. I like the model of silence, and think of the comma, then, as a glottal or swallowing motion. A peristaltic urge or reflexion that is not, as you say, analogous to music. I don't feel the desire or the destiny—but rather, the sentence like a bit of "pavement," as Virginia Woolf wrote in her Diary on the first day of winter, "over the abyss." The commas are the places where the tarp, the pavement, the bed sheet, are fastened, perhaps, to the ground. Have you ever been edited for your over-enthusiastic use of commas? If there is a fate, then I know what it is and I want, at all costs, to delay it. The meatsentence can only end badly, even for the man in the fedora who just ordered a ham sandwich at the delicatessen on the corner of Ruislip High Street and Eastcote Road. Now I am in England, now I am in my childhood, which happened in a near-parallel space to the time in which I am writing this. The comma does something physically to the materials but it also deploys them, don't you think, at a given rate? Is this cadence, is this rhytmicity? I can't tell. I like it better when we call it something else, matching it more closely and intimately to the stories we want to—tell.

I have parataxis tattooed to my chest. The comma—despite my bad-mouthing—is my best friend, as though the mark itself feels. I too hazard my use of commas here, which is opposite to my feelings on our chapter on the colon. There, I used it freely. There—here—I used it openly. Bhanu, I lose discretion here for a moment: I hold my urine. I do not relieve myself. When I do, I am toileted for a minute and there is no resistance. I am comfortable with a perpetual state of discomfort, holding it in. My mother tells me Vietnamese people endure pain better than all others. This, I internalize. I swoon for. I make it my partner in life. How does this relate to the comma? The comma similarly causes me discomfort. This is obvious. Each time I type it—here and in other writings—I try to avoid it, and then, fatefully, I place it: where it belongs.

Bhanu, I write this to you sitting outside in the Land of Enchantment. It is sixty degrees and sunny. I am knitting a scarf, for a pretty boy, contemplating our conversation. The pattern for the scarf: k1, *yo, k2tog*, repeat until last stitch, p1. The pattern makes a fabric of holes: where has my sentence gone?

The man in the delicatessen: suppose he ordered only a cheese sandwich. Three cheeses, five cheeses: gourmet. Grilled. Seared openface. Is his meatsentence without hook?

What type of post-colonial body are you? Did you have parents as I did? In my life as a child, unlike the colonial meat of Swann, there were no commas. I had three options: practice the piano, study, take a nap. A nap is a comma only to a pedestrian, a flaneur, the leisure class.

Bach, yes. I was an awful student. Both my parents were born under colonial British rule; my mother was eight when the civil war happened, as the British withdrew their ships. My father, well. That is another story. Poverty trumps war. You can be so poor that it makes no difference who is in charge. "There were no commas." A butchered swan: in London, in the second world war, they ate the meat of zoo animals, distributed to neighborhoods as a ration. Tiger, zebra, swan. The Queen's swans, recently, I saw on the news, captured and eaten by "immigrants." They were taken, from a park. I like that you assume I am not, necessarily, a progeny. The commas slow these stories down to the point at which they might, could be, are: told.

My friend Richard Greenfield texted me, on our chapter on the colon, having not read it: I hope someone said mis en abyme. That's what I think about. I respond: Bhanu just mentioned abyss. I tell him I will write about this. What is abyss? Is it: the ellipsis? Or the potentiality of the comma, extending.

My people are infamous for eating domesticated animals. It is not rumor, my father tells me. And then he tells me stories about this man or that, never himself. My people are poor still, but even poorer before, that was when they ate their animals: destitution. I say my people fully acknowledging that they are not, never were, I am out here on my own, enchanted with our grammar. Honestly, my meat has nothing left to claim.

The man in the delicatessen is always Russian. To withstand, to keep it in—and let it go. The comma is a gate. It is a fluctuating gift. The boy receives the scarf, the man orders a cheese sandwich, yes.

PAUL HOOVER

THE BOOK OF NOTHING

Nothing isn't empty.
It fills a room so completely
it spills into the street.
Everything comes from nothing.
Something, poor something,
stands vacant at the door.
A rose opens and opens
until its petals fall.
Then it seems vacant,
like a room with one chair.

Beauty is always fading.
We know an object best
when it starts to disappear.
Words are here but nothing,
meaningful sounds passing
then nothing but pleasure.
Light and space are something
passing through the trees.
A cry is heard in the distance.
It is something briefly
and then present absence.

A background seems like nothing
until a figure emerges, from what
seems the beginning.
But there is no beginning.
Something always comes before,
receding here, approaching there.
Only you remain
to bring it back from somewhere—

that shade of blue in the hallway,
black depths of the water.
Yellow fires, gray earth, and green
of wheat are something: actors
without equal, cock-crowing town.

Everything nature says
is ancient, careless, and cruel,
but it has no concept of nothing.
Leaning against a sunlit wall,
it projects casually something.
A mirror out of doors
catches the eye because
our eyes are in it, because
it seems to eye us
as part of its nature.

The overlord language resides
there, too: a stain, nerve knot,
with its incessant naming.
It comes into being, breathes,
then fades away again.
What was that? we ask.
Did you hear something?
It was nothing, says the cook.
A ghost, insists the chaplain.
It was dinner, says the hen,
so philosophical lately,
and always about one thing.

WRITTEN

The written stone rests
in the unwritten river;
unwritten rain is falling
over the written town.

Nothing written today,
but tomorrow you'll be written
as you sit in your room not writing.

Lo, it is written.
Pollen writes on the stamen.
The man writes a child
in the body of the woman.

Your eyes write the view
into the window,
but it doesn't stay forever.
It returns with you into the unwritten.

All that means is written.
Lo, a tiger of a word
has escaped its cage.

Our quiet words
wait beneath the stair
for a reason to speak,
an edge or fold or cause
to remark. *Oh*, we say,
no way and *no how*.

This is how the world begins,
dark branches written
against a white sky.

The written stone rests
in the written river;
written rain falls
over the written town.

WHY IS QUIET "KEPT"?

They are crying out in restaurants,
so delighted to be speaking,
they appear to be insane.

But we are the silent types,
who hold speech within
like the rustle of gold foil.

We eat our words and swallow hard.

There's nothing much to say.
The knot's in its nest, breathing.
A hand thinks it's a bird.

The world "nows"; it doesn't know.
The world "wows." Then it snows.

A word arrives, silent and upright.
It stands in profile against a white wall.
It's here for safekeeping only.

Keep quiet, mice.
A cat's patrolling the area,
with drones and more drones.

The keys we carry unlock us every day
and lock us up again. Hushed is the ward.
Now conjugate, please, *to werd* and *to werld.*

One of us has just conceived
the sum for infinity: plus one, plus one.
In the cosmological phone booth,
there's always one more.

The fishing report's too thick to read,
but its cadence is that of a god.
Waves and ships are passing.
We can barely discern the semaphores
flashing through the fog.

And here are the ones who walk the walk and talk the talk,
blackening the day with news, with news.

DARKNESS OF THE SUBJUNCTIVE

If it hadn't rained, we would've gone to the beach (Phuc Tran)

If we were in infinity, we would be everywhere,
even inside ourselves, as taste resides in the walnut,
and the walnut resides in the shell.
Then we would thrive inside the subjunctive,

where nothing happens but dreams of being,
as paradise dreams of its inferno,
the inferno of cotton candy.
If only the world had ripened, like a pear,
it might have melted the mirror in me,
delivering its softness to the hard road of the mind,
sixty miles from town.
And if our grammar were even to our heat,
comma, conditional phrase, comma,
we'd be addicted to the sentence,
sentenced to an exile that sees, hears, and thinks,
and is often mistaken for love.
Trees are chronologies;
every leaf shines, and in turning over it winks an eye:
if, *if*, and *then*. The world is possible meaning;
the world is possible, meaning:
I might have been an elf, had I been elfin.
But I am not an elf. I am a giant with tiny hands:
would, *could*, *and should*.
Had I been winged, I might have flown
from industrial field to pastoral alley
on great woolen wings, with the blue face of a bee.
Then it would have been said, "He is repairing to his persona"
or "He is retiring to his future."
I'll copy this by way of the stars, reflective.
Get back to me by facsimile or dream of climbing a night ladder
to the place of ideal size, near a town of simple affection.
If we had been born, lived our lives, and died,
we might have existed. On the side of darkness, infinity;
on the other, a sixty watt bulb.

TIM HUNT

POEM WANTED TO TAKE

a Selfie—one that would show
just how unique he was,
enfolded in some special

scene or centered among
faces all his Facebook
friends would have to know—

arms across John
Ashbery's shoulders on the one
side and Carl Sandburg's

the other, his phone
holding itself and Siri's
cheerful "Cheese" drawing

a triptyched instant
into a sentence
of smiles that read right

to left and back again, oh
in any order, please some
order, Poem thought, as

he slipped his hand down
to pat the trope of John's
ass, while basking in Carl's

comradely squeeze. Oh, yes,
not an instant, please. Please
some story, and all his friends

clicking "Like" as John
and Carl went back to their pages
and he floated on in this

pixeled instant. Ah!
Being. So much better,
Poem thought, than

Truth or Beauty or the
Dancer dancing
in the dance, all those

old puzzles in the tricky
analogue
of analogies when something

was real and something
was not. Oh, Siri,
thank you.

TRUCK STOP IN KANSAS

What thoughts I have of you tonight, dear Allen, as I drive the endless plain of Kansas, dulled by the road, wishing the horizon's thin moon would look my way.

Needing coffee, a tank of gas, a place to pee, I pull off the interstate into the truck stop. The aisles are bright: fluorescent candy, cassette tapes of all the Country Hits, not just Reba and Brooks & Dunne but even Ernest Tubb "Waltzing Across Texas" and Hank Williams for the really lonely. They gleam through the shrink wrap.

And, yes, belt buckles, gold and silver, bull's horns and rebel flags and some of tasty turquoise, and all the bumper stickers you need to make your truck a poem, and next to the cash register, but discretely to the side, the aspirins, the creams for all itches.

Where are you, Allen? I saw Walt Whitman leaning a moment on a mop, but now he's gone.

In the café I cannot sit in the section marked "Truckers Only." The men across the railing wear Lees and cowboy boots. They have big bellies that tilt their buckles toward their feet when they stand, but they are sitting, elbows on the tables: eggs sunnyside and overeasy, pancake stacks of dark butter beneath the syrup, ketchupped hashbrowns bacon sausage, the coffee steam and Marlboros.

I am drinking coffee, black; I want to put sugar in it but don't. I try not to stare across the railing as I catch bits of gossip I do not understand and the jokes I do. They know I am not a trucker. I know some of the jokes are offered for me.

And as I look out at the idling semis, that is when I see you, walking quickly truck to truck, pausing, then darting to the next, as you offer blow jobs hoping for love in return.

Ah, dear old sly chameleon provocateur who would be our father. Come, ride with me. I am going to Wichita, and I will let you chant me all the way there.

And if you want, we will park beside the road and walk out into the field, imagining the wheat golden in the sun as we hold hands and watch the stars.

Even then we will both be lonely, but not alone. And perhaps this time the war really will be over. You said so that other time, and I believed you as I stumbled through your words in prayer.

Forget with me a moment the black waters of Lethe. Forget with me a moment the green automobile, the empty cottage. Forget the actual America we have become. Then we will walk back to the car and drive on to Wichita.

GODZILLA'S WIND CHIME

This is what YouTube is for: moments
We know are stupid but aren't quite—
Mismatched contexts clanging like untuned
Scraps of iron as if Godzilla somehow
Found a tree big enough to hang that wind
Chime he'd been making when the camera
Wasn't rolling and let himself feel sad
And alone before putting on again his three piece

Suit of anger, talons fumbling the Windsor knot,
sighing at another day punching the clock.

So what *did* we do with such moments before
We were digital, or those that *still* happen
As if we are back again in a land of land
Lines only, having forgotten to holster the cell phone
As we step to the center of the empty street—
The high noon sun, the stare down, hand poised
To reach, draw and squeeze off a shot, and there
We are with nothing to click, as the moment
Sneers, turns on the heel of its cowboy boot
And sashays into the saloon for a shot of rye.

OUTTAKE FROM *THE SECRET LIVES OF DOBIE GILLIS* IN HOMAGE TO MAYNARD G. KREBS AS IF HE WERE NOT A SIT-COM CHARACTER ERASED IN HIS ERASURE

Bongos between
sandaled feet, dirty
socks wrapped
against the cold, Maynard
holds the paper cup
of lentil soup, seeing
for once the blackbirds
pinned to the park's
gray tree limbs and
wearing the cold that is
not their cold, but is,
as they do not pretend
to be cats and kitties
pretending they are
somewhere, some
thing. Like
Wow, Man.

KENT JOHNSON

INTO THE HEAT-FORGED AIR

Far from the Rappahannock, the silent Danube moves along toward the sea.
John Ashbery

Far from the Pirin, the pointy Appenines plummet toward the sea.
The grey and mauve Virungas undulate pleasantly, much like
The Darlings in their slumber. Chuckling nomads make lean-tos
Within the Schwatka. Troop carriers rust their wheels
On the Taurus, and jackals roam
The Toba Kakar. The Sentinel Range is white with
Dust, as are the peaks of the Ahaggar, covered in
Dust. The Tibetsi are grey and dry as bone.
The Sierra Madre is neither sentient nor unsentient.
Whilst the Titiwangsa appear to walk in the sky, the Verkhoyansk
Splash about in the sea. The Mackenzies are phlegmatic,
Almost diffident beneath their weathers.
Eons have crosshatched the Silvretta Alps,
Pure porphyry. Ophitic basalt predominates
In the Aberdare; its radiating crystals of feldspar recall
Dandelions in seed. Not so the Hafner Group, whose pure
Slate is uniform and dark. Slowly, the Koryak
Crash into the Kurai. The grave and dry Drakensbergs
Couldn't give a darn what anyone thinks, but
The Glarus crackle companionably in the sun. Bombers draw
Vapor circles over the Lesser Khingan. People die of thirst,
Fleeing over the unforgiving Rockies.
The Pegunungan have never been climbed,
Sheer and crumbly their needle peaks.
The Bergamo Alps are sheathed in mist. The Massif Central
Is imposing from afar, but palm-fringed are its valleys.
The Kunlun are huge. The Glockner Group tilts
Forward and laughs, like a girl at an angle, held up
By a gale, while the Rieserferner Group is one of

The shortest ranges of the world,
Likewise the tiny Angokel.
Still, the Sistema Penibetico goes on forever.
The Rhaetian Alps eat climbers like candy,
Yet the Cherangany are mild. In the Brooks Range, ferns
And cairns become abundant; giant sloths are joyous on the
Plessur. The Ratikon is all hollow, a carapace of slate.
The Wetterstein has a ruined tavern half-way up. If there is a
Geological example of neurosis it is the Brenta Group. Not so
Its neighbor, the Karawanken, serene and languorous in its smooth
Rock skin. Strangely, the Dolomites are made of limestone,
As are the Ortlers. Migrants trek down the Cottians, carrying
Torches. The Mont Blanc Group is famous; the Cairngorms are
Covered in primeval pine. The Caucasus are stern and dark.
The Carpathians span five countries, all once members of the
Warsaw Pact, but the Juna are smothered in crows and the roaring of
Caws. The Pyrenees are sullen, aloof, though this
Is all part of their insouciant charm. Even as the Altay turn to mud,
Night envelops the Nulatos. Chinamen jump with a thump
On the Jotunheimen, while the Sierra Morena blushes
In the evening, powdering its breasts with cloud. The Svecoffenides
Are lugubrious, a lure for poets. The Table Mountains are flat,
Awash in runic trash. No one can believe the Golden Mountains.
But the Stone Mountains are airy, made of chalk, tunneled and
Hollowed out like Swiss cheese. The Bystrzyckie Mountains are
Unknown, devoid of life, while the Urals are vast and crisscrossed
By capillaries of gold. The Vosges, avant-garde of ranges, has not
Much changed since the invention of photography. The Appalachians
Are growing smaller by the day. The Wicklow Mountains were once
A redoubt of the IRA; now they are mottled with ocotillo and
Mesquite. The Endless Mountains end abruptly on the outskirts
Of Harrisburg. Meth labs crumble like sandcastles in the Green
Mountains. Adult stores are buried under strata in the Smoky
Mountains. The White Mountains are full of wind. The East
Catches the light; the Rubies have knife-like ridges.
The Shoshone Range loves to whisper its name on the wind, and
True to its name, the Snake Range is full of them. The Toiyabe Range
Bakes its rocks under the superheated sun. The Endicott Mountains
Release their small snows, teasing the streams. More children are lost
In the Black Hills than any other range; at least half are found years
Later, in the shadows of the Punamints, mendicants with no

Memory of their pasts. The Anti-Lebanon is covered with checkpoints,
But not so the Otztals. The Tian Shan are so trodden, whole areas
Are like sponge; still, the Tatras are slick and hard. Deer bed down
In the Elburz with the lion. From above, the Hindu Kush look like
Sutures, raised and purple, along a thigh. Snowcranes turn to ice
On the Hida, blown upward by massive drafts; they fall like toys,
On the hot stones. Sunnis squat in caves in the Safed Koh; in every cave
A little cage, and in every cage a sparrow from the Alleghenies. Prayer
Wheels make clacking sounds in the Western Ghats. Strange concussions
Are heard deep inside the Zangezurs, though no one knows why.
The Vindhya Range is mute, intractable, along the spine of India:
How does consciousness arise? The Cordillera Darwin swarms
With thistles and ferns. Black helicopters fly over the Cordillera Negra,
Never to be seen again. The Cordillera de Lipez is hollow, its rock
Thin as eggshell. The Cordillera de Sarmiento is a block of stone.
The Sierra Ventana is covered in dust; it blinds those who would seek
Meaning in form. The Cordillera Pelada is covered in blue dust.
The Parcell Mountains are taut as a bass string, even when covered in dust.
UFO's hover over the Sandias. The Sierra Nevada is sprinkled with corpses,
Turned to quartz, while the Torngats have Sasquatch, otherwise known
As Bigfoot. The Superstitions are dotted with radio dishes, but tiny elk
Rut in the Kigluaiks. The Eje Transversal has nothing to say. The Anvil
Range smells like wild cabbage or fennel, and the Glenyon Range does
Too, though more subtly. The Bitterroot puckers its lips
In the rain, and the Cabinets hold many wonders. The Gallatin Range
Is lousy with moles; the Garnet, its sister, is 90% iron. The mountains
Are indifferent to our yearnings, our joys, and our sorrows.
The John Long Mountains look like a boy praying toward Mecca;
Bats prowl their starry skies. The Castle Mountains have
Been reduced to conglomerate clods of granite and chert,
A hilarious hulk of hubris. The Klamaths are retiring
And diffident, but no less noble for that. Great howling
Armies clash in the Ouachitas, but the Nadaleen Range
Is encased in dust. The Ozarks are conflicted between
Tradition and modernity, though the Chilkat Range
Is a lizard's dream. People climb the ten thousand paths
Of the Himalaya, seeking who knows what. On the Schober Group,
Lava flows upward and downward. The Niedere Tauern
Just sits there; no one knows its true nature. Amazingly,
The Lepontine Alps run upward and downward and in all directions.
After entering the Sumava, it is said not a single person meets another,

For there is only the activity of the Sumava.
Hands are pressed to cave walls deep inside the Anti-Atlas.
The Granatspitz are puny next to the Thurnwalds.
The Montes Rook, towering and hermetic,
Form the smiling mouth of the frozen Moon.

PIERRE JORIS

RIGWRECK

A THROW
what do we know, what can we know?
OF THE DICE
of science, of love?
only the facts, that is to say
only effects
NEVER
can this happen
NEVER even if, can this happen
in science, in love
EVEN WHEN CAST
Indra's net of love,
EVEN WHEN CAST
money's net of stone
what do we know, what can we know?
What has caused this gulf
between water & oil, you & me
IN ETERNAL CIRCUMSTANCES
(no circumstances are eternal,)
AT THE HEART OF
of this rigwreck
What will we know?
We know only effects / have to choose
the causes
A SHIPWRECK at the heart that the
gulf widens
between water & oil, you & me
fish & water, me & you
that the
Abyss
between water & water, you & you

me & me, oil & fish
widened then whitened
there is slack growing
raging underwater in the heart
underheart in the water
on the brain
what we know is oil & water don't mix
what we know is fish & oil don't mix

what we know is you & I have to mix
what we know is you & I have to live

under an incline
clinamen of a warming clime
an angle not an angel tells us
me & you want to live
even if despair desperately soars
& gets an angry rise
form the phantom pain of its own planet's sore
broken wing
a second-hand angel singing Ecce Homo,
Ecce Homo, though not so Sapiens,
conscious liar,
beforehand relapsed, liar, liar, not released from wrongly steering
the flight of this planetary love affair
no use repressing the outbursts
of this lethal love affair
cleaving the bounds
of this oily love affair
at the root of greed
set the rig afloat
a ship finally a ship
the impossible change
for deep inside weighs the admission of impending disaster
the shadow hidden in the depth
by this by this arrogance this arrogance
at the root of greed this arrogance
at the root of arrogance
this love this love for more
a more always spelled out in money
blows the rig up this morning

will blow the world up tomorrow
there is no alternate sail
ship earth in space / space ship earth
the only raft for dumb sapiens
who has to learn to love
this imperfect raft
there is no alternate sail

dumb sapiens has to learn love
has to learn to adjust
has to learn to look   to the spread
the spreading of disaster
has to learn to jump
its yawning depth
as great as any abyss
between you & me
the hull of a rig
the hull of a ship
careening from side to side
turns over & is for a moment cathedral
burning church of the worship of money
brightly floating death flaunting love
rigwreck rigwreck
a catastrophe here now,
the circumstances local & global
not eternal only this now
cannot grasp the hawser
opens a gulf
between life & death
a millimeter uncrossable
a BP centipede monster
at the heart of this rigwreck
abolish   abolish
abolished responsibility
Moloch, Moloch
Moloch —
rules, Moloch
rules
all rules broken when Moloch rules.

MICHAEL JOYCE

from "ARRONDISSEMENTIÈRES OR A ROUND HERE"

UNDER THE SIGN OF A (1er/20ème)

On marche, march on. Little soldier, petit soldat. Monsieur le miroitier, c'est mon parrain. The boy in the mirror and the man in the moon are one, le cylope dans le miroir de Clair de lune, clearly here our hero: Hamid, known as Sami, son of the imaginary Haroun the Baker, maker of Kaab El Ghzal, Dwiyrat, and Makroud, Detroit Michigan, avez vous vu ma mère, have you seen my mother, Madame Maman, if so tell her, please, that I am lost in this city, or rather that it is lost in me, ou bien que c'est perdu dans moi.

All night on the airplane he watched the lights from others' screens because she wouldn't let him watch his own, listening to the engines rise and fall and watching the tall ladies make their way along the aisle in the dark stepping slightly sideways and looking down at the sleepers and the movie watchers their faces washed in the light. He asked her why not but she said he had to sleep because they had a big day once they landed.

Once somewhere in the night when she seemed to drift off, he felt for the screen in the dark, watching carefully lest she stirred while meanwhile trying to figure out where to press to turn it on but the moment his hand went out she swatted at it, Arrêt, she whispered, Dor, ma puce!

He didn't speak French and she knew it, and wouldn't teach him any more than he'd learned in the two-week "tasting menu" of language lessons at the Waldorf school. You can pick it up on the internet, she said, and instead made him take Chinese and now he was lost in Paris. Maybe he could find some Chinese person to help him if he remembered how to say anything other than Nǐ yào bú yào gēn wǒ tiàowǔ? or Jiào jǐngchá! Although the first would be good if he could find some Mii to help him over Street Pass on their 3DS's. The second he did not want to think of.

If anything happens, find a policeman, she had told him. Just say *oh so coors* or *shwee purdue*, making him repeat it after her over and over again like she knew what would happen.

What did happen he did not know. First there was the long line in the dim light at the airport before the glass booth where she had to lift him up on her hip like some giant doll so the guy behind the window could be sure that his face matched his pass. It was embarrassing and she said it was because their names were Algerian although that didn't make sense since the guy himself was some kind of African.

Vous êtes Française, Madam? the guy asked when he looked at hers.

Americaine évidemment, she said and pointed to the passports.

Something was going on but Sami was too tired to ask. The African guy stamped the two passports and yawned, tossing them through the glass slot like someone dealing cards.

Au'voir Madame Saharicain, the guy said and, wiggling his fingers, beckoned the next person forward while she fumed.

All this for some reason made her even madder, because when they got through the glass gate into the customs hall, she muttered, Reub quéquette! and spat on the marble floor in a way he'd never seen her act.

It was then that she put the passports in her purse even though he complained that he wanted to keep his in the thing with a pocket that she'd made for him to keep it safe on a string around his neck or what was the point of having it.

I'll keep them with me for now, she said, 'cuz we'll have to leave them at the hotel desk once we get there.

But when they got to the hotel it turned out that they didn't have to leave them after all, which she thought at first was because the room wasn't ready but then the guy convinced her they didn't do that anymore, at least as much as Sami could figure out what was going on, her nodding away like a bird and saying okay, *dakor*, okay, *dakor*, a dumb smile on her face.

First, though, there was were the trains and the trains, the one from the airport jammed in standing among German and American tourists wheeling huge suitcases into one another and a whole school group of Italian high school students laughing loudly and taking up all the places where you could hold on to stand, their backpacks whacking each other and anybody in their way. There were also more Africans, not travelers but night workers on their way home. Somehow she found a way for the two of them to stand next to the doors, their two rolling overnight bags before them like a fort to keep anyone from standing there. Sami was so tired he could have slept on his feet but he felt he had to watch everything especially each time they came into a new station on the way to Paris and the sad-eyed Africans came and went in the early light. You know you are African yourself, you too come from nomads, she had said once when they saw a Taureg guy all wrapped in blue once in Greektown along Monroe Street back home in Michigan, but that didn't make any sense. By Gare du Nord he could hardly keep his eyes open and they had two more trains to take she said and she wanted him to take her hand because of the crowds but he didn't want to seem a kid and so he promised to stay close to her. People kept coming at them like in the battle board of Mambo de Chocobo in Theatrhythm Final Fantasy, which was, so far, the only real game he got, except for the Mii ones, after she gave him the 3DS for Christmas.

Then after not being able to get in the hotel it was back down into the Metro on the train and up some stairs and along a long corridor and back down stairs to the train again, she fussing over the little white subway tickets she had bought at the airport, telling him to make sure that he held on to the one he used to get on in case the cops asked to see it when they got off, all this after they'd already seen two cool guys in skater hoodies fly over the turnstiles on one hand way back when they first got on.

You mean les flics, he had said and she laughed in the way that made him feel dumb, especially there among all the French people, instead of seeming proud of him like she meant.

Those guys would say feuks, she said, blushing a little. Anyway don't fill your head with all that nonsense.

When they pushed their way off the second train and finally came back up on the street again everything was gray and it was raining in thin, cold lines. They went along a wide wet sidewalk among people rushing under umbrellas and not looking where they were going then ducked under a long stone arch and came back out into the rain and a huge stone courtyard where crowds of people wound like a big snake in a great spiral line around a glass pyramid.

Merde, his mother said, and he knew what that meant but he wasn't going to give her anything to laugh at. We'll be here all day, she whined. He stamped his feet.

Just then some guy came up out of nowhere and tied a blue and pink string around her finger like a ring and demanded money and she grabbed tight to her purse and began to yell at him in Arab and in French and then these gypsy ladies swooped in out of nowhere and started chirping, circling the two of them and swatting at her sleeve and one trying to untie his backpack, when out of nowhere like Superman this handsome guy comes up shouting at them followed by two cops who seem to have bubbled up out of the crowd. By then the guys who tied the ring on her and the gypsies are gone like they were never there and the handsome guy is talking with the cops who haven't bothered to chase after them and he takes his mother's hand in his and shows the string ring then peels it off and throws it on the wet stones and all the while she's saying nothing and doesn't seem to get it that the handsome guy is hitting on her as much as he is helping them and the next thing you know he's leading the two of them back out through the arch and down an escalator to some fancy mall with a food court with a McDonalds and an Apple store and a Virgin record store and an upsidedown version of the glass pyramid and then another not quite as long line for the museum which the guy ignores instead walking the two of them directly to the ticket window like they are VIPs and then shows the ticket lady some card in his wallet and she gives them two tickets and they are in, while he's waving behind them.

Eh bien, c'était vachement magique! she said.

Well, that was pretty magical, Sahar said to him, and, not here more than five hours, she was beginning to wonder whether it had been a good strategy, let alone fair, to take such care to raise Sami colorless and transparent in a multicolored world like some jellyfish bobbing along a coral reef. In a way he arrived in Paris with less in his backpack than his grandmother and grandfather had brought forty years ago as pied noir refugees from Oran. Still hatred had increased fortyfold in this world just in the past decade after what happened in New York, so much so that she thanked whatever gods there were that his American blood diluted his North African enough that people already thought, at least when he was out in the world without her around Detroit, that he was Italian or, at worst, a Jew, which of course he was, albeit not in the way such things were accounted now in America, and not certainly for a fair-haired child of olive complexion walking hand-in-hand with a dark Sephardic woman who could as well be his nanny as his mother. Mais dans ces quartiers this was, perhaps, a different world, or at least she hoped as much, though to be safe she'd written her name down as Sarah M along with the name of the hotel for this miraculous malāk who had plucked them from the maelstrom, but who surely had been sent from the goddess.

It was to the goddess that she was taking now this her foremost creation, a creature fashioned of her body, her desires, her dreams and the dreams of exiles of generations, this new-man-to-be, her first and only—fatherless!—son, to present him there, to dedicate him to the mother of us all, even before presenting him, god willing, to her own mother in the final days of her diaspora, her hegira, half-blind and alone there in her small apartment au quatrième étage for years now after the death of Sami's grandfather, years after they cast out their only son, the kadeshim, on account of his impurity, years, also, after her daughter left for her own new world, a new man already stirring within her.

It was crazy, Sahar knew, as soon as she read on the web about the protests that caused the Louvre to promise to exhibit the stela rather than repatriate it as the Algerian activists were demanding, to have run out right at that moment two doors down from her bakery to consult with the Lebanese travel agent, Fatima, to plan such a trip to see the thing the moment it went on display; crazy, too, to make these plans without letting her mother know or trying somehow to contact her brother, perhaps through Facebook or some kind of Parisian gay site. But something had shaken her to the core, a recognition, the moment she saw the image there on the screen. She felt the same as she had the moment she knew, only hours after conceiving him, that she was pregnant with Sami and, just like then, had begun to mold images of the stela out of sweet dough in the same way she had sculpted little pastry figures of her child—blasphemy in any of her or his traditions—slipping them quickly in and out of the edge of the oven while no one was looking and, after they cooled, tucking the brown creatures into the gris-gris she had stitched back then to protect him from the djinn, the same ornate fabric she had converted now to decorate the outer cover of the nylon wallet she had sewn for him to wear around his neck to carry his passport and—with its own small wafer of etched stone within—to bless him before his grandmother.

And now, after navigating impossible stairways and rushing through ornate galleries without really looking, pushing their way through crowds intent on taking cellphone photos of images they could buy in any of the postcard kiosks spread through the museum, and finally finding the small deserted corridor off the main hall of Near Eastern Antiquities to which the goddess had, she felt certain, spitefully been isolated by curators resentful of having their hands forced by protestors, they stood before the great mother herself, first in a line of mothers without nations, husbands, religions, even names, the downturned crescent over the round moon of her head like an umbrella, the comma of the crescent hovering just above one upraised arm, sinewy caduceus thrust upright from the other, this bar of her arms resting in balance upon the trapezium of her skirts, the ensemble of her centered below the unmistakable letter A, the beginning of all.

Look, Sami, see, here is what we came for, Tanit, the mother of all that will be, the mother of your mother and her mother before her.

Je pensais que ma grand-mère, elle s’appelle Eve.

GEORGE KALAMARAS

LETTER TO DON FROM GUNBARREL

for Don Byrd

Just five or six ant turds up the road from Boulder, Don. This town's name can fill a person with buckshot. Jackrabbits damage crops so bad, that in the West they'd been rounded up and driven into pens for slaughter. The long bones in a bat's wing correspond to bones in our arm, hand, and fingers—the thumb is short and ends in a claw. I won't say it was a dream. It was all so green. Green the dark. Green the hills. So green the Gunbarrel graves stayed gray. There's a veterinarian here, whose office is connected to a taxidermy. Remember, Wallace Stevens placed a jar in Tennessee. Duncan taught a summer just five or six ant turds from here. His mother was a falconress. And he was your teacher. And you, mine. Do this simple equation of pain: 1 + 2 + 3 = 0. My mother too is a falconress. Here, remove my hood and tiny jangling bells. In the marsupial possum, only thirteen embryos can possibly survive, one for each magical teat in the warm of the pouch's dark. Try dislodging the tiny things with nail polish remover, and you smother your own dark sound. Crickets have been known to eat paper, cotton, linen, furs, even rubber. Paramecia are slipper-shaped protozoa, covered with hair-like cilia that move at the rate of ten to seventeen beats a second. Still, we can't see enough to measure them except with a special scope. On the other hand, among the other significant unsolved problems is the development of human genitalia. In Boulder, genitals count, especially among the beautiful young. Gorgeous sway of this hip and that. And how fast we age. When it rains, a certain fish up the canyon gets its name. If Stevens loved chaos, order courted Williams. I do not say this lightly, but I have a taste for thirteen ways to eat Don Byrd stew. Some wingèd thing mounted on the knotty pine wall, which had muffled my mother's wrist? A clinic *and* a taxidermy? We aren't already whole, even when stuffed with lice? One civilization is always rubbing up against the next. One species of healing and display. Count the ant turds it takes to get from here to there. Somehow, we didn't get hurt.

THE DRINKING CALF

"'What did they die of?' I asked.
'Whatever,' Keith said. 'Cold, most of them. Probably some pneumonia in the calves. Some of these cows probably died of old age.' We came to one creek crossing and Keith elbowed me. 'Look, he's getting a drink,' he said and pointed. A calf long dead lay with his bloated head bobbing in the burbling little creek, a macabre counterpoint to the mountain iris and daisies blooming on the banks next to him."
David McCumber
The Cowboy Way: Seasons on a Montana Ranch

Amazing new love. Cut every earth, little one. Names to be named. Names to nerves. Yours, unwept. The kept, the retreat. No desire spoke of lingering. At least at the creek. Cross our mouths out with stones. Here. Drink from my. Hear. Take from me. The tearing apart of the hand. The cup of it and gone. Trees told me so. Awl-shaped spur. Larch. Cottonwoods. Goodbye lip. You time their hair. Lesions on a ranch. Your time, Hereford hair and brushed. Eat time good. Sad her die and sad her urge. The scrabble of it and clutch. Whatever cold there is in the world is a cold snowing of bones. Some likely died of age. Most, of cold. One creek. Two. How daisies later then and iris. How the bobbing head blooms. *What do we die of?* I asked the mirror, slantwise through the throat. *We come to one creek and cross it*, was all I heard in the burbling below. A calf. A long dead calf. Dead long in the now long grass. Alcohol be salt. Be sad. My, she, the. Clutched moon-sorrow bathing the killing in Big Timber. In Butte. In the deep-down of White Sulphur Springs. Sinks on a ranch. Across the meadow, all the way to the Evans. On the north-of-the-road. The dead and the rarely far from where we are. New calves in spring. Say our mouths finally right. Say the word as if we could. Say say say it as if it could barely be. Yes, being is a state of be-bloating. Death, less so. Though particles of grief plow down the ground. To be twenty-three days old, barely tongued and licked. Dry. Begging for suck. To reach of it and bawling and clutch. To sleep sound in our beds while the world possums its mouth out with stones. There was a little rat once played dead. There was a little rat taught us disease. There were cancer and nerve endings in the human pit of the arm and eight lymph nodes that absorbed the wreck of the breast. Caught in the track. Cut this way, that. Husband, wife. Stitch the rails under the arm all the way west. The healing cut. The world is dying and much less dead. Scratch scratch as if the final breaths below the skin therein. Most of them cold. Some of them old. Many little ones dying, just feet from the creek. Pneumonia before not many breaths at the bale. Hay. Alfalfa. Root-rot in the irrigation ditch. How light borne dark. How in of a.

The dying and the barely breathed. How *slung* you! How *dare* we dip the hand in the oiled dark! Eagle and hawk, turkey buzzard, badger, at the gutpile, tearing out the delicate juices of the eye. The gist of the jaw. Bloated calves and more. Cut every letter of every earth. How animal of us in the human swoon. Here, little one. Sink into me. Drink from my. Eat from the. Hear the pouring apart of odd organs of light. Galaxies of gall. Of human moons in the cool. Of the urgency of the herd. At creek's edge. Miles from the spur. Something simple in the give and rinse of the cupped hand. Something not less sweet. Sad her die and sad her urge. Sad the edge of sight. Amazing new love. Twenty-three days not yet named. I will you always your brief loving of the earth. Cocked at the creek on the axis cut. Whatever bloat there is, is a slow moment of bone. In sickness and in death. Till tilt us do part.

THE CLARITY OF ANY SADNESS

After sustaining any infraction, find a way to direct it toward dissolve.
The Sutras are full of such advice.

Try this : place two words, equidistant, against the friction of your speak,
against the stricture of stick and stone.
See how your own insides thrive on the plants that lush outside you.

Get on your knees while kissing your knees.
This is an esoteric teaching I am not at liberty to clarify.

Then separate the string bean part of your heart from the tough potato
skin.
Boil the butter and pour it, clear, through gauze into any jar of your
choosing.

This is not a recipe for sadness. The elephant is already in the broom.
I have been using the tail of its massive silk self to clear the way.

SYMPOSIUM ON THE BODY'S LEFT SIDE

A range of discourse toward an ethnopoetics.
A riddle are guessed in the transmitted mistake.

And so we gathered, gnawing our beaver paws.
It was the right brain, the proper strain of thought, that guided my reason.

I appreciated the format of a 366-day conference.
On February 29, we all pretended it was March.

Biting the back part of the body, the upper left leg and thigh, had its reward.
I could carve myself for a month and didn't have to speak.

Someone keeps phoning but will not leave a message.
We can rest assured it is not Ezra Pound trying to turn our pain into a Koyukon riddle.

So, formula my best guest effort. Cut away all parts of slipped-speech grief.
Talk to me backwards in riddle meek and speak, in the cumbersome membrane of the translation of the internal organs of game animals displaced in the domesticated bodies of the butchered herd.

ON THE BRINK

High Park Fire, Livermore, Colorado

Say one day you wake up and your wife has cancer. She's rubbing your arm awake, sadly shaking her head, treed like a possum by a pack of hounds. Say you're getting a second opinion twelve days later, and the waiting room cable news says the largest wildfire in Colorado history is a mile from your summer home, though—fortunately—still on the other side of the river. You see the metaphor but detest the cliché—the fire raging in her right breast. The biopsy must be wrong. The report incorrect. Once you even read that you used to sleep throughout the night. That the owl nesting in your chest clocked its head to follow every moment of the moon. Say the moon was your friend. That it worked overtime to coax the fires back up into the milky mouth of night. Cancer this, back-burn that. Where do the birds from the Roosevelt National Forest go when their trees immolate, when their inside-night can no longer nest? And the foxes? The mountain lions, coyotes, and deer? Yes, they evacuated the neighborhood animals—Gabriele's mustangs, Jessie and Pete's two burros with that sad sad burro stance, small and complacent with the load. Nineteen wolves up the Poudre River now recline in caged runs in Greeley. Someone is feeding them road-killed deer once a week to supplement their meal. Sue calls with news of the *Coloradoan's* headline, *Glacier View: Community on the Brink*. The doctors are most definite. Evacuation is a must. The tumor board at the hospital swirls like three fingers of Yukon Jack asking the amber back-burn to wait. Someone is on the brink, and it's not just your wife. Something is always eating you from inside, trying your high wire of light. The weather is hot, your age report still hopeful at fifty-eight and sunny. Disposition is everything. You follow the drama 1183 miles away. You follow the drama at your side. How can we ever understand the gift of thirty-five years together and counting? MRI, PET scan, HER2-negative. The life-saving burn of radiation. Dye that illuminates the riverous cleansing of the glands. You've always loved learning but some details hurt. Say that hurt was whole. That the possum up the tree just took the branch toward shiver and splint. The mouths of the hounds cry joy, even as your marsupial self longs for the pulsings of the pouch. Say the luck of three, that the third surgeon's opinion is best. That you walk in the door from that relief only to hear that the fire jumped the Poudre, tore up your meadow in a 200-foot high wall of flame, and took the house. All in just twenty minutes. Life is fair. We have no way of measuring our mouths, the how and why we cry. If we could just say it right we could save the world with a spur. A five-pointed star twirling, heel to tongue. Where do the animals? How do they go? How might the night clocking my sleep draft down and stomp out the spot fires of the brain? The burros look sad for a purpose. It must certainly be in their job description: *Here, humble ones*, something must have told them, *carry the world's emotional load with quiet calm, giving it back to us with the sad of your bull's-eye glance.* We are always looking into ourselves even as we look at others? Say that's right. Say it's not fair. Say the fire should never have jumped the Poudre in the first place, that it should have never entered her breast. Glacier View is burned, burning, burnt. The glaciers in the distance are still there, high above the rise. Snowcap moan above the singed and stinging earth. What is hot and what is cold. What is torn and what is whole. What is burnt and, oddly, still most beautiful.

BHANU KAPIL

PARTITION

One day per room. It's raining.

My mother's mother put a hand over my mother's mouth, but my mother saw, peeking between the slats of the cart, row after row of women tied to the border trees. "Their stomachs were cut out," said my mother. This story, which really wasn't a story but an image, was repeated to me at many bed-times of my own childhood.

Sometimes I think it was not an image at all but a way of conveying information.

This is something that happens in the second room, in the city that the room belongs to, and it functions (the information) as a grave.

12:20 on the third day; notes from the glass coffin. *Schizophrene.*

Because it is psychotic not to know where you are in a national space.

Imaginal technology for the map of the day is timed to open. In this way, the psychiatrist can work economically with three kinds of black space at once. An economy is a system of apparently willing but actually involuntary exchanges. A family, for example, is really a shopfront, a glass plate open to the street. Passers-by might mistake it for a *boucherie*, splashed as the customers/ butcher are with blood. Transactions frozen in place beneath a chandelier of the good knives.

A map of three black days and beneath it in pencil a sentence.

The date and time; 12:20 on the third day. It is a London suburb as seen from above and recorded with dyes: an indigo house leaking its color into the grid like a cloud. The house is visibly blue, pinpointed on the grey image which is cross-sectional, warping and pocked with industry.

This tissue overlays a police map tracking calls to domestic disturbances in a three-mile-radius of the Southall Broadway. In turn, a local government map of the London Borough of Ealing, of the ethnic origin of a borough-wide population, overlays a Social Services map, in which different kinds of abuses are recorded as having happened in particular homes.

The blue house has made a cell-like choice to distinguish itself from the other cells, a transformative property that has no value, ever, in the time it happens in, though it gives the map hard value.

12:20 on the third day and I'm eating in the node deep in the pock of the grid. Here is the food I was given and here are my teeth, moonlit, despite the hour.

A speck of violet light behind the ear. Since childhood: attenuation. It is a soft craziness and she's not sure why it happens now. I found her once, in the Queensbury Gardens, down on all fours in a bed of tulips and crocuses, observing the light coming through the scarlet membranes of a petal. I was walking to school after coming home for lunch, and I saw her, an Asian woman of some kind, murmuring. We lived at that time in a white neighborhood but sometimes you encountered them, flecks and drifts of free-able matter.

"He dragged her down the stairs by her hair to the room where we were eating."

I cannot make the map of healing and so this is the map of what happened in a particular country on a particular day.

Deep in the map, I put my fork down and feel my jaw and teeth swell up. This is blood pressure: a flow, reversing itself, but I can't quite manage it, the information. 11 a.m. to 1 p.m. You pig, you kid.

STEVE KATZ

BLUES BORROWED AND BROKEN

Sun go down I
Hate to see it
Evening on Gulf
Northwest wind
My baby no more
Baby for me   blow
Away crooked dreams
Blow away clock
Of Fridays nor

HIGH ON THE HOG

Grab your pencil, hold on tight,
Here comes Melvin down the trail.
He rides his screaming brush hog
That spews stones and branches
Fifty feet in every direction. Melvin
Sits in the tractor cab above
The fracas, red-faced, tall, and tipsy,
Always ready for mischief, he seems
To sing under the clamor of his hog,
And spins his lusty wife, his beautiful
Daughters, his son so tall and willing
To cook. They spin off him and away
In directions unpredictable, at speeds
Only love can measure

IMPROVEMENTS

for Blossom Dearie

The city grimier, the poor
Be needier; though streets less
Crimier, gunners are gunnier,
And that's not funnier.
On the stoops, stoopsitters
Be stupider, as is all things
And everyone else. Creeps much creepier.
The bombs bomb bombier and the farms
Aint farmier. The ocean's slimier,
Where we are right now looking out.
The nature world alarmier.
Our karma seems much karmier.
But moms aint marmier, nor dads be
Homier. We know some wisdom comes,
And the wisdom's whizzier. Here's
The middle way again, and the
The midst is medleyer. Some metals
Are heavier. Fur no furrier. Our
Muddle, way murkier, sink-holes
Sinkier. The riddles, riddlier.
Evelyn noticing the changes on her
Skin still insists the rain is balmier.
This balm is irritating. Some main course
Floats our way. Our waiter, weightier.
Come into my garden my sneezing pet.
Here the tequila's tackier, and love, please
Be pleasier. Here the irish moss crests,
On the waves with plastic jugs and styrofoam,
Washed onto the smooth conglomerates.
Our beach not beachier; but gannets
Are back and gannets do dive, gannets
dive, and their dives are divier.

YEATS UPDATES

You are old
We are grey

leave my book on the shelf

write your own book

Now

back to sleep

WHAT HAS BEEN DONE

All praise to Duncan Mustard who built
My simple bed of pine boards and rough
Slats and four thin square legs.
He included two deep drawers that slide
Without apparatus. He used no nails, no
Screws. The slats are unfinished, rough
To keep the mattress from slipping
In my agitated sleep, or when I'm with you.
When we romp, we hump, we wriggle.
The mattress stays. All praise to him!

All praise to Duncan Mustard, slim, elegant,
Handsome despite himself. He built
The convertible futon platform
That as a couch is comfortable against
The back, and if you pull the pegs so
The platform lowers, it lies flat and level
For the futon. With sheer technology of mind
He drew the curve that makes this possible
Then cut the base to conform. He used no
Screws. He used no nails. All praise to him!

All praise to Duncan Mustard who made
This simple bench that is so refined. Three
Birch boards finished and joined, no nails,
No screws. He created the best angle

For the legs to make the platform stable
And strong. All praise to him!

All praise to Duncan Mustard who extended
This deck with juniper boards that hardly rot,
And set in the ground around the deck three
Hearty posts from which can swing both
Clothesline and hammock. Here he used some
Nails, and here some screws. All praise to him!

All praise to Duncan Mustard, who with Alison
Laid the shingles on this house like a carefully
Woven overcoat with a stylish crenellation
To separate bedrooms above from all rooms
Below. The shingles lie flush and alternate.
They protect the house from rain and
Ruinous wind. All praise to them!

All praise to the Alison Mustard who weaves
Her fabrics of silk and linen, of soy and hemp
Finer than silk, at her loom away at the top
Of Cape Mabou road and as I write and as you
Read is dying the thread to arm the loom. She
Will weave the scarf I throw around my neck.
All praise to her!

All praises to Duncan and Alison Mustard
Who rule the empire of nowhere of where
They are on Cape Mabou road, anti-despots
Of the woods, just emperor and empress
Of wherever they be. All praise to them!

WATER WORKS

To be more precise my pride
Is not for the water itself
But for the idea that back
Towards the dimming
Of the twentieth century
I was capable at least of this.
I could lay the pipe

In the streambed
And climb the steep
Hill through jewelweed
And tangled snags and sink
One end of this PCB into
A pool high up then siphon
The water from this tiny
Brook that hasn't yet gone
Dry ever to guide it to
The house where it gives
Good drink good shower
And will soak the beans
And boil the eggs

FOR ED DORN

Dear Ed

This is to thank you
For the white rose
You invoked before
You split forever

Perhaps you will
Next time be more
Botanical and remind
Us that it grows in

The phosphorescent bog
Of words and blows
Relentless as all
Vocabularies disarray

KEVIN KILLIAN

COLOR IN DARKNESS

She didn't read all of his texts, but who could? They pored out of his fingers like Rachmaninoff. In *Newsweek* it said that the average teenager sends and receives three thousand texts a month, but what they didn't tell you was that some teens kept writing more and more even when they turned twenty, and this boy seemed like he's never slow down, and she didn't have the time to consult her cell every moment, so some she ignored. He had to know that, never said anything. Even when they were together, in the same room, he'd be texting her when he could have just opened his mouth and spoken. It as comforting to think that he was always there, like hot and cold running water in their apartment, this stream of text, so delicious and refreshing. Even in the car on the way here, his little fingers kept flailing away, so organized and precise. She wondered if there was a way to go back to the very first text her had ever sent her, maybe the first or second week of school, the text that leapt so electrifyingly into her cell as she and he sat, thirty meters apart in the crowded lecture hall, as Marina Abramović herself stood humble on the stage, acknowledging the applause of every student and professor and adjunct in the whole arena, so humble, and she herself was clapping so hard that her palms were turning red—were rawing, was that a word? How could you help it, Marina was so inspiring and she'd never thought she would lay eyes on her, the great genius of endurance and patience, and the phone in her hand started to buzz and to give off that ring, just three little notes, a triolet, ding-a-ling and she glanced down at her screen.

—Boring! Daddy always said every dog must have its day… Let's get outa here go to Boom Boom.—

The girl didn't even know what Boom Boom was, but across the vast assembly room filled to bursting with applause, a youth stood and adjusted his scarf round his neck and picked up his, you wouldn't call it a knapsack, it was more elegant than a knapsack, he picked it up and stared right at her in the half-light like Christian Grey commanding Anastasia Steele to come with him right now. The boy looked familiar, maybe, but had she seen him in real life or was she thinking of one of the boys in One Direction, the band that had her obsessed her girlhood? He looked British, she decided, no, Scottish maybe. Already he was texting her again. Juliette u have 32 seconds to make up your mind: Boom Boom or Bore Bore? n u look like a smart chick.

That was years ago, two at least, and now the boy and the girl stood huddled together in the shadowy corner that you might call the "playa" of the bar, outside, under the marquee on Halstead Street. To the west they could just see the last bits of the evening sun dribbling into the skyline, and she shivered a little, mostly from the suspense, but also because he was taller than she was and she liked the propinquity of their bodies, even when she stood in his shadow. They were close in age and close in disposition; their friends said they were like brother and sister, but sometimes Juliette thought that they were actually twins, for she now knew the planes of his face, his cheekbones, the thickness of his eyelashes, as well as she knew her own. They were so familiar and dear to her. His moving fingers, flicking still, in the Apartment 9 "leather texting gloves" she had given him for his 21st birthday. They had corrugated finger pads guaranteed to find the correct buttons quickly.

"And did you see his face when he drove up?" Ben whispered, his voice rumbly and even raspy in the dimmed sunlight. "Bet anything he expected a couple of grown-ups. Credit-card holding, fully employed, adults. Did you see his face, did you, when he saw we were kids?"

Eyes rolling, Juliette nodded, though in reality she hadn't noticed anything special about the driver's face; she felt guilty or even stupid for not being aware, alert, alive as Ben. For one moment she thought of prevaricating, of lying in fact, but then she remembered she needn't with him, her spiritual twin.

"Guy looked normal to me," she shrugged.

"He was appalled that two teenagers use Uber gift cards! I looked at him and I was like, 'They were a present from Santa—a big old sugar daddy Santa who knows when I've been naughty and he likes it that way."

Just then the line seemed to surge forward and Juliette felt that familiar rush in her throat, and she started the pat down of her pockets and camera cases and everything hanging off her shoulders. Knowing that in a few minutes she'd be face to face with her models, with the fairest of them all, Beaver, the divine Beaver, seemed to short circuit her neural system. Lean, mean, six one and cut, and uncut, Beaver was the crème de la crème of all the dance she'd been photographing for the last five months, ever since Ben had introduced her to the delights of the strip club.

"My head is gonna come off," she said to Ben. No, she better text it, the noise was incredible there and he wouldn't hear her. One, two, three, the great gilt painted doors flung upon from within, and upon the threshold the sly, mocking face of the proprietor gleamed on them like the man in the moon. "People let's proceed at a mad pace, the show can't begin without you."

Quick quick quick, read the message on her screen. Right shoulder down, Ben to her left with his left shoulder down, they stormed the line and made for the great warm darkness ahead—vague colors shimmering just behind the invisible entrance. "Slow down, kids," groaned one old queen, as they raced past the losers. "Taint no taint worth such a hurry!"

Uh right, but she needed to be as close to the tiny stage as she could get, to sit on its lip if possible, but sometimes the bouncers pushed her off and down to the floor. Very sweet they most of them were, but they had their orders.

White beams of light began to spill across the lip of the stage, and corresponding pools of pink light plucked at the nylon curtain, like a huge shower curtain, that divided the performers from their fans. "xoxoxoxox," Ben wrote. You could see his mouth saying the x's and o's, a foot to her left. "zoom zoom at boom boom."

A crash of synth broke through the solid wall of drink orders—Kylie Minogue's sort of dub step anthem "Skirt," in which the singer laments that lust had made her skirt fall down—this was such a good omen, Juliette thought. "Be my supernova, take whatever you want; let me bask in you like you're the rays of the sun."Could any other girl singer express the raw feelings she harbored for the inaccessible Beaver? "Do you have a flask?" she texted Ben, a glass of cranberry juice in her free hand.

Electronic signaling threw pink and green pin drops across the nylon curtain and then a specter gleamed out: she could see part of Beaver pushing his big bare chest into this slick wet surface, and she screamed out loud. Felt dumb instantly, or sooner than instantly, but Ben squeezed her hand and joined her in screaming, urging her to scream louder, her throat filled with sensation, tremors, delight. Grinning, Beaver pressed his mouth against the plastic and seemed to suck it in, a hole appeared in the murky glaze, and it was his smile, an open hole to this throat. He was like a god come to earth from some other place beyond the glass—like Poltergeist, but not evil like Poltergeist, a force for good. In a flash she had Ben's old Canon AE I revved up, snapping fifty shots a minute.

"Jesus Christ," she muttered. "Know what, I think I only have, like, four rolls of film!"Love of, or lust for, these Boom Boom boys had brought her into this all-male territory, but she was hoping to make them all famous and without any film, it was going to be a catastrophe! Men in gold suits approached the writhing, wet, naked apparition of Beaver in the oil coated Saran wrap curtain, and pulled it to shreds. Now he was revealed to her, almost all of him, a pair of ugly cargo pants clung to his hips, down to mid-calf. On her right, Ben stood texting someone furiously, his thumbs flashing like castanets, his hip cocked to one side and she knew that meant he was at least a little turned on. Perhaps a new boyfriend? Quite soon after they'd first met. Juliette knew he wasn't interested in girls—sexually that is; he made a wonderful friend. Rather like partners in crime. She'd thought from time to time that Ben didn't even know exactly what he wanted, but they were both young and both "questioning."Tonight, be my supernova, take whatever you want.

Uh-oh she was definitely out of film and fuck! Very soon Beaver would be down to the torn jockstrap into which she had stuffed, over the past two months, dozens of five and one dollar bills and now and again a twenty, dusted with cocaine, when she had one, but as a student neither she nor Ben were loaded with $$$ except for their student loans and—What the hell was she going to do, her camera was gaping in her lap like an unsatisfied vagina! She wanted to turn her portfolio into a show, into her MFA show, and the boys encouraged her to photograph them again and again, as long as she kept tipping they were happy. She used black and white film, even though in some cases the color was so exhilarating, Beaver's gold lame trunks, the black and blue "Z" tattooed down Zorro's chest—but she believed that in some of the prints you could actually still see the color clinging, like a drowning girl, to the darkness of the deep blacks she got in her darkroom. Color adjacency, they called it, the tendency of color to remain, even after the extreme expunging effect of substituting black and white for color film. It was like tar melting in the hot August sun, and the bubbles rise rich and black and in the black the colors of the prism visible, faint pinks and greens and electric blues. "Or are your eyes fooling you into thinking you're seeing color?" Ben argued, at the lab at school, when she'd grabbed a print and held it out before them. He made spooky sounds and pretended he was dead, a ghost, mournfully calling after her, pursuing her through tacky studio hallways, "C-o-l-l-l-l-l-o-o-o-o-r in the dark-k-k-k-k-n-e-s-s!" Beaver was shaking his whole package directly over her face now and she felt so helpless, she couldn't do a thing, completely cockblocked, and then her hand buzzed and a text message rolled itself out on her iPhone, "Look in yr pocket."

Ben of course—she glanced over at him—he'd vanished, but she checked her pockets and they were filled with Kodak's best old school black and white, a dozen rolls at least. And Ben wasn't even a photographer. Just a kind of angel. Quickly she reloaded and slid the palm of her left hand right around Beaver's hard, coked up dick, and with her right hand and her teeth she took the shot of a lifetime. He winked down at her, she shot him again, and everything was in the frame, her hand, his hard-on, his face bobbing above like the sun, in black and white but his eyes, blue as electric robin's eggs in the nest of his visage… She remembered Ben coming to her in his boxers, asking her to take a look, he needed her approval, he rolled down the waistband and he'd shaved all his pubes, but for a little tuft right over his dick, the bristly looking thing, insouciant, looked like a shaving brush, the old school kind her dad used, whipping up a creamy jug of shaving cream with this assertive brush. Ben: What do you think? Juliette: Is it in honor of Beaver? Ben: Kinda. Juliette: It's his trademark. Ben: Zorro has his like this too. Juliette: He's just a copy cat. Then, when she saw this look in Ben's eyes, a look something like hurt, she rushed in and explained she didn't mean to say that Ben was a copycat… And even if he copied Beaver they had learned about Sherrie Levine and appropriative strategies and Kathy Acker and—Ben pulled up his boxers and sat down next to her and they watched a bit of *Orange is the New Black* together, but she could tell he felt restless, resentful maybe? It wasn't like him to drink in the afternoon but he poured himself a jelly glass worth of peppermint schnapps.

That was like his anger drink. Juliette put the TV on pause, shoved herself closer to him on the loveseat, put her arm around his neck. His lovely bare neck. "Do you like Beaver?" she whispered. Ben nodded. She didn't speak for a minute, and then finally, "Like I like him?"

Where was Ben? His scarf and his flask were still on the stage. It was like he had grown into his shadow, like the old cartoons where you could peel your own extended shadow off the floor and bring it with you. It was like he vanished into a hole Backstage? She could still feel the heat of his hands on the metal canisters of film in her pockets. He was just here! She was busy, of course, shooting fast as she could, trying to keep on top of the rushes of power, But at least a little part of her mind was thinking of her twin brother and how precious he was to her, how he had emboldened her to go for what she wanted, to make art from it, to check her dark places and work out of them. Maybe she had done something for him too? She couldn't think about that now. Beaver was strutting downstage, his bare butt crumbling into the dark faster than the Duchamp *Nude Descending a Staircase*, contraposto, on one foot then another, it was like he was twerking, she wanted to tell Ben, she texted him, "It's like he's twerking," on top of a click, atop the barrage of clicks from her Canon, to the music, the nostalgic jam she'd loved in high school, yellow diamonds in the light/ now we're standing side by side/ as your shadow crosses mine—had he left her here? Took off with a trick? Had he made sure she was happy, fulfilled, beautiful?—what it takes to come alive

Maybe he was waiting for her out in the alley, filling his nails, checking his e-mail, combing his hair, registering the street action? There was an old Zen prayer her parents used to say sometimes, they called it the Sandokai—a prayer that now bounced back and forth in her head as Beaver's perfect ass, with the little seahorse adorning one cheek, walked away from her, click, click, click,

In the light there is darkness

but don't take it as darkness

In the dark there is light

but don't see it as light

Light and dark oppose one another

like the front and back feet in walking…

DAVID LAZAR

from *OCCASIONAL DESIRE*

DEATH, DEATH, DEATH, DEATH, DEATH

it is life which is the Great Unknown
E.M. Cioran

My mother has become a kind of painful signifier of her own absence in the years since she died, a symbol of the way a wound effaces the cut while not healing. She died when I was in my early twenties, starting to reconcile with her, after years of self-imposed emotional exile. This, what felt like diabolical intervention, has haunted much of my life, and left me with a permanently acute appreciation for ironic near misses, almost happeneds, and slight fluctuations in the warps and woofs of circumstance. In short, I think I have come to appreciate, shall we say, in not always the healthiest of ways, how circumstance is connected to loss and how it is inscribed commonly, frequently, frequently painfully as an ironic marker of the Big Loss behind me, and ahead of me.

I was talking a while back to a writer friend who said that she didn't think that coincidence was an interesting category of experience to write about. I was struck by this (one is usually struck, in fact, by coincidence), since sometimes I think it is the only thing interesting worth writing about. Oh, not in a mystified woo-woo kind of way, as in some guiding spirit outside ourselves leading the co's towards incidence. But in the sense that we manage to find delightful surprises and combinations, strange pairings and meetings, and then are forced to do the work that is our continuing important work: finding meaning in experience. Everything means something, after all. Even nihilists have an ideological template.

When I fell on the ice this winter I was more or less in the same position my mother was in when she died. Arms at my side. A woman walking by never breaking her stride said, "Are you all right be careful." And I immediately thought, "Horse is out of the fucking barn on that one, honey." I had a huge hematoma on the right side of my head. I had been distracted that morning because I had woken up with a lump on my chest, surrounded by a large area of internal bleeding. And I was rushing to meet my divorce lawyer. My hands were in my pocket. My hands always seem to be in my pocket, some internal huddling mechanism. But everybody in Brooklyn knows it's stupid to walk on the ice with your hands in your pocket. No way to break the fall. I wasn't all right and I wasn't careful. The lump turned out to be a benign cyst. The bleeding was oh so mysterioso. The concussion still gives me atypical migraines on the right side of my head to go with the atypical migraines on the left side of my head from the car accident I was in after my last relationship. "Every day a little death, in the heart and in the head" (Stephen Sondheim).

Today is the fortieth anniversary of the death of Robert Kennedy. He was the first politician I fell in love with. There was a string after him, whom I worked for: McGovern, Bella Abzug, Ramsey Clark. I wish I were in love again. I don't think I'm capable of it anymore. But Bobby was the first. My brother and I pleaded with my mother to vote for him. I remember watching a press conference in the living room, and waiting on my mother's response, she having told us she would if he answered a certain way about Israel. Apparently he did, and she said, ok, she would, and we said, hooray. And then the Ambassador, and there is something differently sad, pathetic really, about a child's presidential hero being assassinated. It's something like the introduction of death into a political family romance. The next month, my family traveled to California. As though paying subconscious homage to the loss of innocence, we went to Disneyland and stayed at the Ambassador. Walking back to the hotel one evening, I ran ahead to a newsstand to get a paper. (We always had newspapers around. If I can lose myself in a newspaper, my anxieties, existential or petty, tend to diminish.) Soviet tanks had gone into Czechoslovakia. Back at the hotel, I stole an ashtray from the lobby, and wrote Bobby on it in magic marker when we got home.

Bo Diddley died yesterday. "Who Do You Love." I love my son. A ragtag group of friends in places that look like an idiot was throwing darts at a map. It would be fun to start naming them. Like an Oscar speech. I wonder which ones would be embarrassed, and which amused. I love the younger me, that boy who needed his mother's love so fiercely. As Charles Lamb reminds us, we need to take care of our younger selves. How they can be tended, it seems to me, is various. They may need befriending, or they may need foster parentage. But they simply cannot take care of themselves.

My grandparents lived downstairs, in the lower apartment of our row house in Brooklyn when I was growing up. My grandfather died when I was eight. I remember being taken to the office at school because my father was there; if you hadn't been a bad child that meant someone was dead. It was a kind of minor celebrity to go home from school in the middle of the day. I remember being pleased and sad, feeling queasy because I felt kind of excited about being pulled out school. I felt guilty. Of course, it didn't take much. I was breathing. My memories of my grandfather define fondness, define the benign. I remember him rowing me around a lake in the Catskills, his strong old tanned body, and Russo-Siberian face. He didn't say much, but spoke with a gently firm authority, a thick and deep, melodically accented English. I remember eating herring with him in his kitchen. But I don't remember too much else. And he essentially lived with us. And I was eight when he died. Neurotic that I am, this has translated to how many years I need to live to have my son accumulate significant memory of me before I die. If he gets pulled out of school, I want him to feel deeply wounded, though not traumatized.

Next year I will be my mother's age when she died of lung cancer. I smoked for many years. Every day, etc.

I was spending an afternoon with M.F.K. Fisher and she heard someone say she was going to kill time. She became furious. "Killing time is an expression I abhor," she told me. "No one should kill time. There isn't enough of it, for one thing. And of course, you can't anyhow." She had advanced Parkinson's disease. And although she was still completely sharp intellectually, she would go into full Parkinsonian freezes, bodily fugue states that would last between twenty minutes and two or three hours.

One of my ways of keeping my constant mortal fears at bay (reminder: check out etymology of "keeping at bay," and checking out etymologies, derivations, the everyday digressions of mortal distraction, is one of the essential ways of keeping my constant mortal fears at bay) is to read *The New York Times*. I started reading the *Times* when I was morbidly young. I like using the phrase "morbidly," which is a deathly phrase, but also a neurotic one. If the Freudian shoe fits. I was on a date recently, and described myself as "morbidly punctual." What did I mean by that? I'm not even quite sure, but aside from the playfulness, and even perverse pride, I think I was implying an obsessiveness bordering on fear, a fear linked to death, that if I were late I would put my life in peril. Late to his own funeral? No, that if

I were late, it would lead to my own funeral? That being on time keeps me alive? In any case (digression is escapism, keeps the angel of death at bay) I started reading the *Times* when I was eight or so, and when I'm in the *Times*, I feel safe, feel like I'm in a world that's familiar and ironically calm, even if reading about the most calamitous events, the most morbid deaths or disasters, writ small or large: tsunamis or self-immolations, crane collapses or just plain men and women collapsing. I'm in there, reading, my eyes are moving, I still have the Op-eds, or the Yankees, movie reviews, the obits (especially the obits—hey, I'm not dead—but I don't like it, get queasy if anyone dies too close to my age, which has gotten more ticklish as I've entered my 50's). When I go out to work, as I've done much of life, grading papers, starting essays or prose poems, messing about with almost but not quite working, I always try to get the *Times* to start off with to soothe my daily anxiety about starting the day. Starting the day in a world not my own in which I'm not dead or dying.

Death is a bland word. It should hiss and call for the speaker to recoil, the listener to back away. Cottage cheese, when it goes bad, should die. When we go, we should curdle.

Priests and fools say
We are but animate clay
Just rude vessels
Housing immortal souls
But the dead only quickly decay
They don't go about
Being born and reborn
And rising and falling like soufflé
The dead only quickly decay
Stephin Merritt, "The Dead Only Quickly Decay"

Alternately, in the nineteenth century, John Brown's body lies "a-mouldering in the grave," attributed to William Steffe, or that greatest of all songwriters, anonymous, tried to establish the parameters of the body's victory's over the soul. When I was a boy, I was a bit puzzled and excited to sing an exciting song about rotting in the grave. I wasn't sure what truth was marching on. Just that I was celebrating a body rotting in the grave. Truth was what really got buried.

JOSEPH LEASE

STAY

when I

squeeze your hand I'm squeezing

her hand—his mother

in the room—his

mother's me—

—

He's dying—

He's dying—

He's asking

Why

I

Love

Him—

—

when I

squeeze your hand I'm squeezing

her hand—the whiskey on

the table, the

rabbits in the

yard

at night—

—

"Even on mornings when I don't see

you I'll see you"—you will go, I will

follow, I will stop, you are with me,

you are with me—and there he was,

throwing his face at his grave—

—

property is death: they had a body crammed in
a mailbox and it was just a blue suit with bones
            sticking out:

—

your
            stain of
faded
            storm
light in
            my mouth:

—

the face in the house—your lips slip the
night—your face slips your eyes—your
eyes slip your yes—love like flying—

—

my father

rain

becoming

rain

rain

becoming

rain

—

He's dying—

He's dying—

He's asking

Why

I

Love

Him—

FRANK LENTRICCHIA

from *THE ITALIAN ACTRESS*

Part III: Still Life

A room, thirty by sixteen, with a ten-foot ceiling. At its mathematical center, bought and mathematically placed by those two: the black steel table, two feet high, six feet four inches long, and wide enough for a body of average width. One body, not two. At one shorter end of the rectangle, a window, floor to ceiling, seven feet wide: a view to the Adriatic and a deserted beach in winter of white sand. Draped. She readily agreed to the purchase of a camcorder to document the extended labor of transformation. From the room as we found it to my desired aesthetic end: the room as proper set of the action.

We remove drapes and rods, fill the holes. At the other shorter end, a door, mid-wall. All walls papered in a gold-flowered pattern, with blue background. After enormous effort, the wallpaper is removed—many layers beneath—how many decades? What did Garbo see? What did JFK? Down to the original paint: a pale rose. With power sanders the job is completed when a fine smoothness of white wall is achieved.

The electrician removes the antique chandelier at the center, overhanging the table; installs track lighting. Two parallel tracks running the length of the room; four fixtures in each track; fixtures spaced three feet apart and hanging a foot below the ceiling. Between the parallel tracks, over the table, on a separate short track, a fixture hanging over the table's mathematical center; hanging low, four feet above the table's surface and bearing a bulb of hospital operating-room intensity.

We paint to execute my plan for the desired end of geometric abstraction. The two shorter ends of the rectangle—the wall of the window and its opposite, the wall of the door, in mirroring black. Except for the door: white with a vertical black bisecting line, three inches in width. The mirroring long walls feature white fields trisected by black bands two feet wide, floor to ceiling. We do the ceiling in high-gloss black, in contrast to the flat finish of all walls.

The hardwood floor of rich burgundy offends my purpose. The original finish is sanded off (by hand, by Isotta), and refinished with three coats of specially concocted white stain—sealed to a high gloss with three coats of polyurethane. Atop the gleaming white floor, below the radiant black ceiling, the black steel table positioned so that its long sides run parallel to the long walls.

Adjacent to the door, black steel shelving holds the digital recording deck and two servers connected by cables to all cameras and to the monitoring laptop in the other room. Four security cameras: one perched on a tripod at the window, focused on the sea and beach; two others mounted (by Isotta) on the long walls at their midpoint, halfway up the walls, opposite each other and taking in the table and the actors, but not each other.

The main camera is set upon a tripod five feet from the table at its long side. Opposite the window wall, at the other shorter end, mounted (by me) at the very top of the wall, at its midpoint, the fourth security camera. Thanks to its high privileged position, it takes in the other three security cameras, the main camera, the black steel table and what it—the lovely black steel table—bears. It sees all but is itself unseen. It sees the entanglement of exposed power cords and cables that carry the digitalized images. My privileged fourth security camera declares that the image-maker, Jack Del Piero, is also here.

Should the actor on the table wish to lift his head—he did, once, briefly—he sees the window—and through it, the sea and the deserted beach in winter, of white sand.

After day one, she no longer bothered with the two five-pound weights that she'd curled daily, many repetitions, throughout the two-month period of preparation.

***

Security cameras: footage in black-and-white: A lean man with shoulder-length hair, blue jeans, loafers, black t-shirt, removing main camera from tripod—holding it at his face and focusing on a couple standing the other side of the black steel table, against the long wall. He motions them to step slightly to their right so that the black band is behind them and then motions to make a space between them so that the black band, two feet in width, separates them. They do so. He smiles. Gives them the thumbs-up sign. This is what the main camera sees: Two adults, late twenties, early thirties. He in a tuxedo, a red flower in his lapel; black shoes shined to a glassy finish. She in a custom-designed white gown, spaghetti straps off the shoulders; poured into it; breasts; waist; hips. Movie stars arriving for the Oscar ceremony. Glowing in living color.

***

With all preparations completed the week before we were to begin, we had nothing to do but dine at the hotel, at a reserved table beneath the signed photos of diners who mattered most to me: Antonioni, Fellini, Visconti. During the first of nine courses—it was always nine, seven days running—call it the Roman run-up to day one—he, Sigismondo, says, "For the truly fortunate, Piero, life's best end is an important death. Think of Diana, think of Jesus Christ Almighty, think of JFK. The suicide bombers." She adds, "Tristan and Isolde, Paolo and Francesca, but not our predecessors, Sigismondo and Isotta, who died unimportantly." I say, "Isotta, I'm guessing, is the Italian rendition of Isolde?" He, with a sly grin, "Yes, and Isolde expired over the warm corpse of Tristan. Tragic lovers." She: "Isolde was a fool." "Were Paolo and Francesca,' I inquire, "also fools?" He: "They were cheating on Paolo's brother, Gianciotto the Deformed, who had sent Paolo il Bello in his deformed place to win her hand. Il Bello was a Malatesta, an uncle, shall we say, of Sigismondo, five or six generations removed. The handsome one, of course, did not tell her that he was a proxy for the ugly one, who was also, do not forget, a Malatesta. The wedding day comes, the deformed one presents himself as the husband-to-be with a hard thing and she assents? Are intelligent people to believe this? After the marriage is consummated, Paolo and Francesca consummate their affair. Gianciotto discovers them at it and with his rapier qualifies them as tragic lovers. This is the story told by Dante and Boccacio. We are sure only of the slaughter—he killed them." She: "Where is the evidence that Paolo was handsome? Where are the photos? The films? In the twelve hundreds, Piero, consider the medical care, the dental situation, the diet. The red meat night and day." He: "Consider that Il Bello was forty years old when they met. In the twelve hundreds, at forty, you are a disaster, my friend." She: "In the absence of visual evidence, why believe the writers? The legends? The camera supplants the word. We don't need the writers." He: "They will believe what you will show, Piero. That we are in truth beautiful people." She, pointing to him, "He is a Malatesta, and the handsomest man in all Italy. And what am I? Chopped liver?" He winks at me. Blows her a kiss. Says: "I am, like all legendary lovers, eager to be deceived by the right woman."

***

The man strips naked. Tumescence revealed. She strips to bra and panty hose. Removes bra, but not panty hose. Small, full, buoyant, upturned, nipples erect. Main camera goes dark. Security cameras: the lean long-haired man placing the main camera on the tripod; adjusting focus; fixing the angle; the naked man moving to the table; lying on it; lean man gathering the clothes, but then thinking better of it and leaving them heaped where he found them; exits. Main camera: man lying on table; touching himself; stroking; she pulling his hand away; straddling him now at the knees; bending over; taking his penis in hand; stroking: one, two three, four; bending closer; lips sufficiently apart, but does not proceed to the promised end. Stands. Removes panty hose.

***

I'm stunned by her appetite. He and I eat half of each course—she all that is put before her. I say to her, in an idiom that clearly neither has heard, "Do you have a hollow leg, Isotta?" They laugh and he says, "Your sexual mind is very interesting." She: "Can you fill up my hollow place, Piero? Can any man? Will Sigismondo? Soon?" He laughs so hard that he cries. She: "In this rare kind of art, which we will together make, sexual intercourse, they say, is necessary." He's convulsed.

***

She moves up his body—straddling now his thighs. Rises on her knees. Over his thighs but not over his penis. Takes his hands and pulls him up, without visible effort, to her mouth. Tongue in his mouth. Releases him, slowly, without letting go, without visible effort, to the prone position. He's ejaculating—she's sliding quickly down his body trying to avoid the gush, the gushes. She picks up panty hose, wipes her thigh, wipes her pubic hair. Inserts her finger in her vagina. Inserts same finger in her mouth. Finger again in vagina. He opens his mouth as she brings finger close to it, then pulls it away. Tumescent again. Gloriously so. Slides her finger through the small pond on his abdomen. Brings finger to her mouth. Parts lips, then wipes it across his forehead—making the sign of the cross.

***

He: "No special occasion for her, the way we eat this week. For as long as I have known her—every day of the week such quantities—like this she eats, like a ..." She: "Say it. Yes. Like a pig who becomes enormous for the purpose of being slaughtered. Beware, my dear fellows, of riding this comparison too far." I ask, "But how do you stay so svelte?" He: "Such a sexual mind you have—are you always so sexual?" She: "I feed my heart, Piero, as do you, on spartan fantasies of a distant future."

***

She's handcuffing his wrists and ankles to the table's legs. Hard again. He turns his face to the camera—chest rising and falling in deep, slow rhythm. With panty hose she pats dry the sweat on his forehead. He nods. Her mouth is smiling. He nods. Table between her and main camera—she's sitting on floor. Takes his hand and kisses it, open mouth. He turns his head to her. She shakes her head No, pointing to camera. He turns his head to camera. Erection unabated, in the twelve o'clock position. She leans over, kisses him on the forehead, open mouth. Hand on his shoulder: massages, three seconds. With her forefinger touches—one second—tip of penis. His hips rise suddenly—a violent thrust—thrusting—straining—lifting his body from the table's surface. Security camera: Holds the position while she walks around the table, circling many times, as the security camera at the highest perch watches her stumble, almost fall, over cables and cords—panty hose in hand.

***

He: "On March 1, we belong to the ages." I say, "I'm just another camera-bearing atheist." "Not just another, a genius," she says, "soon to be bulwarked against the only death: eternal anonymity." He says, "I lied about my birthday." I answer, "You're repeating yourself." He: "My actual birthday is Christmas Day." She: "This also is a lie." He: "On March 1, from the shit hole of the world's unknown, in the Easter of our art, we are all resurrected. In your case, Piero, as you well know, from the shit hole of minor celebrity. We ascend. The three of us. The newest saints of atheism." She: "This is not a lie." He raises his glass and says, "Cent' anni hardly covers it." (She belches.) She says, "They shall kiss our images."

***

She holds pantyhose before him. He nods. Lays panty over his face, arranging with care, crotch over nose and mouth. Pulls up left breast hard—bends her head down hard to it—tip of her tongue reaching—finding it—licking nipple. Takes legs of hose—wraps each hand twice. He lifts his head—looking at window—sea, beach, white sand. Security camera at window: A couple there, hand in hand, a child romping in the cold March surf. Does he see this? He's hard. He nods. Moves behind his head, sitting on floor, wrapping hose once, twice, thrice tight about his throat. Pressure. Hands, wrists, forearms, biceps. Ten seconds. Her eyes closed. Her lips apart. Her pelvis moving. She rocks back. Her feet in the air. Looking down and in—to her vagina. Thighs—high up—awash. Twenty seconds. Pressure released. A passage of twelve seconds—he's conscious again. He's hard again. Repeat the process. Repeat it. Again. On the fifth repetition, just prior to loss of consciousness, she screams as magnificent jets of semen flash under the lights. Security camera: She comes about—standing now in front of him—begins to masturbate. He watches. Main camera: Sits. Continues to masturbate. She's screaming in orgasm. He's erect again. She's catching her breath, face flushed. She nods. He nods vigorously. Takes hose behind him. Wraps it around his throat. Heavy pressure. Ejaculation. Hold. Hold. Hold. One minute. Hold. Involuntary thrashing: head against hose—legs, arms against manacles—body against his desire. Ejaculation. Hold. Two minutes. Hold. Hold. Involuntary urination. Hold. Involuntary defecation. Hold. Four minutes.

Convulsions at the end.

Eyes wide.

Mouth agape.

Drool drip.

***

ANDREW LEVY

from *MEMORIES OF MY FATHER*

BRIGHTER THAN ANY MAP EVER SEEN

Meeting you is very hard

The uncompassionate

Compassionate

Everything takes on a kind of halo

What would you otherwise pretend you never had?

Comfort their

children too

The main idea brought to the table was death

That is your last gift

The voices of the world becoming quieter and fewer

It is broken into pieces

It's not the love I have had
But different

Pages interspersed with inserted slips of paper
The buffer gone

Stricken

I'm speaking about flesh
This sleep of instants

It's seldom I have been as happy

SPEAK UP FOR YOURSELF

themselves from happiness

knew that inside your father

a very tender person

that nothing lasts

themselves from happiness

a person who went into hell

who survived

Now helps me build

MY FATHER SAID IT COULD HAPPEN HERE

The world is an ephemeral impossibility

It ships unemployment

Like rancid potatoes

Creates out of absolutely nothing

Hangs our debts in orbit

A plethora of government security measures

In the human intestinal tract

Their demographics give us diarrhea

Fecal-factory-concentration-camp-facilities

A military junta rules

—

When war is debilitated to the point of insolvency

Like everything else, what then?

The turnkeys mow the grass

"We have just hired a bunch of immigrants to help us fly"

Is something wrong with my business?

Season after season internationalists

Have new corporate addresses

Perpetual war

—

They've still the energy to kick a small man's ass

He quickly changes subjects

You butt in without a word

Then find the crowd absurd

To me, no real man ever paid any attention to such things

He seemed to possess a frightening ease

with the substance behind it

It doesn't do any harm

to think it over

It's not freedom but ain't

The integrity of the irreversible

Of the inevitable decision

To match what is already known

The expression that will occur for everything possible

Write that down?

The purposefulness

The duration

—

To whitewash the face

After having desecrated

Where I was

is effortless

requires distance

can be turned off

leads to in

Accuracies

Carrying dead children and each one

a different story

(Choose one where it applies

or pick a different one for you)

The difference

blocked

from the running

of time

TOM LUTZ

PLOV DAY IN TASHKENT

On my second day in Tashkent I found my way, with some difficulty, to the old city, the *eski shakkar*, laid out on a human scale, a pre-Soviet, pre-automotive scale, just east of the big Chorsu market. Much of the construction is straw and mud, with saplings helping to brace it, very medieval or even earlier in technique, although here and there the repairs were fairly recent. Some of the alleys are just wide enough for a donkey, and in many ways life hasn't changed for 1000 years. The butcher shop has carcasses hanging unrefrigerated, craftsmen bang away with hand tools on leather, wood, and metal. I stopped to chat with boys and men along the way, usually without more than my tiny Russian as language. But one guy, around 65 or so, with one wandering eye, and both of them thyroid-large, his sparse hair slicked back, had lived in Detroit and Chicago. I said I had had a hard time finding the old city, and he said, Oh, yes, it is a very exclusive neighborhood! Like Hyde Park! he said, and winked at me. A half dozen boys had gathered around us. Like Dearborn! he said. I asked him where the center of the old city was. Oh! You want the center of *eski shakkar*, he said, with a big smile. No problem! Here, follow me! And he strode three steps, I followed. He stopped short, held out his arms. Here we are! he said. The boys all laughed. You are a comedian, I said. A comedian and a cosmopolitan. He laughed and slapped me on the back. Exactly! he said. That is what I tell everybody! That I am a cosmopolitan comedian. Still, they don't believe me!

Along one deserted street a woman and her daughter were standing at their front gate. I asked if I could take a picture. They giggled and waved me off, but the daughter asked in English where I was from. I said America, and the mother excitedly shouted into the family compound, something that included the word America, while she waved her hand up and down at me, meaning, wait here. A man of 55 or 60 came out, in shorts, wool socks and sandals, his naked, paunchy torso sweating—he had obviously been working at something—and said, Ah, America! and they all seemed extremely pleased. They ushered me into the family compound. Please! he said, and that seemed to be about all of his English. The daughter told me that she had an older sister living in Washington. Washington! the man said. He put his arm through mine, speaking to me in Russian—every once in a while he asked if I spoke Russian, and I said no, nyet. He pulled me into their courtyard, and told the daughter to tell me I must stay for dinner. America! the father kept saying, beaming.

The father—Mr. Amidov—had been starting a batch of *plov*. Like running the barbecue in the US, tending the backyard *plov* cooker is a man's job in Uzbekistan. Shaped like a wok the size of a small Weber grill, and attached to an LP gas burner, the *plov* cooker is a permanent fixture in the courtyard, and the man was cleaning it out in preparation for a new batch. It was Saturday, *plov* day, and they apologized for the need to keep working. I had made it clear—they has no English, the daughter left for work, and I used up my little Russian immediately—that I hoped they would continue, and it being such an obvious thing to say, we all understood each other. I also made it clear I was interested, that I wanted to know how to make *plov*, and he encouraged me to take pictures.

Plov is the Uzbek national dish, and as the name suggests, it's a version of the pilaf found all over this part of the world, from Balkans to Kenya and from the Middle East to South Asia and beyond. Alexander the Great first encountered it in Bactria, in current day Afghanistan, the first major valley south of where I was. It is more than a food, it is an institution, it is heath, it is hospitality.

The first step is to cook the fat. The best, I was assured, with some mimework on the part of Mr. Amidov, was the tail fat of the sheep. He did not limit himself to mime, but talked a mile a minute. He was one of those guys, a talker, and sometimes he would say something in Uzbek and then translate it for me into Russian, a constant patter. His wife knew to talk over it rather than wait for an opening. He was a constant enthusiast, and his indomitable energy carried us across all the linguistic chasms. Sometimes, after he asked me a question in Russian and I answered in English, he would translate my answer to his wife, who nodded that she already got it.

He turned the heat up under great curds of the tail fat in the pot until the grease was partially rendered, then simmered piles of peppers and carrots and onions he threw in, all peeled and chopped by his wife and daughters beforehand, along with some partially cooked—he made me try one to see that it was still partially hard—dried yellow split peas. To this was added a liberal palmful of cumin seeds. Then he added strips of mutton, a dozen or more whole heads of garlic, pepper, coriander, and barberries, with another palmful of cumin seeds. At each step a standard marital comedy was acted out—everything the husband did, he did wrong. The wife corrected him. He waved her off, muttering, and did it the way she said to. Too much of this? Not enough of that? A spat, an argument, and then he did what she wanted, trying at the same time to insist that it wasn't because it was what she wanted. Meanwhile the pot simmered, and he gave it an occasional, proprietary stir.

Mrs. Amidov brought out a large, light-blue plastic bowl of rice, wet from rinsing. By now there was a half-gallon of grease, simmering a *confit* of meat and vegetables, redolent and rich. With the rice, the marital battle commenced again, he dropping spoonfuls of rice into the fat one at a time, she motioning that he should just dump the whole bowl in; he stirring and considering the proportions, she motioning to take the rest; he objecting to her tone and taking a couple more ladlesful, she saying oh, come on, just dump it in; he stirring the pot and contemplating, then taking a few more gobs, explaining to me that it was important to get the proportions just right; her sighing heavily and pushing the bowl back at him, him rocking his head side to side, taking half of what was left in her bowl and mixing it in, and again turning to me and saying something about the right ways to do things.

In the end all the rice had been put in the cooker, with a final eye roll by Mrs. Amidov. He made a dozen steam spouts in the rice mixture with the handle of his wooden spoon, then covered it with a porcelain bowl that didn't quite come to the edges. He then went inside to get a second, bigger metal bowl to put on top of that. While he was gone, his wife poured an extra bowl of water in, and put a finger to her lips. He dropped the second bowl on top of the first to act as a lid—I'm not entirely clear on the purpose of the smaller bowl—and then we waited for the rice to cook.

He called into the house, and a young son came running out and scrambled up a large tree in the courtyard and came back down with a big plastic bag of cherries, which we sat and ate. The son disappeared back into the house. Another daughter came out and started peeling hardboiled eggs and slicing them.

We went into a kind of breezeway, not quite inside, not quite in the courtyard, where the daughters, it seemed, had laid out a table, with big loaves of round

Uzbek bread—another point of ethnic pride—and a salad of shredded carrots and pickled long-stemmed mushrooms. Picnic! Mr. Amidov said, happy to have found another common word. The kids never joined us. I asked why, saying their names, but their parents waved it off. We had a very spirited discussion about our respective presidents. Theirs, Islam Karimov, was a Soviet functionary who has ruled, extending his terms and holding bogus elections, since independence in 1991. Thumbs down. Then we went through the US presidents, and Obama got thumbs up from all of us—they were being a little cautious, gauging my reaction, and Obama was still pretty new on the job. Then Bush II, who Amidov called Leetle Boosh, when they saw my thumbs go down, they heartily joined in. Then Clinton got big thumbs up, and the elder Bush a mixed, but mostly up reaction. Clinton, clearly though, was the guy they really loved, and I didn't understand exactly why.

The *plov* was done. We went back into the courtyard, and the lids were pulled off, a last batch of cumin seeds was tossed in, it was lightly disassembled—the heads of garlic came out, the hunks of meat were pulled out and sliced. We kept talking about the US presidents. They thought that my description of Leetle Boosh as the devil (I made horns on my head with my fingers) was going a little too far, but not that much. But Beel Cleenton! He was the best. They made a big bed of the basic *plov*, then arranged heads of garlic, strips of meat, the slices of egg on top, and we sat back down to the table.

We moved from politicians' names to place names, proper nouns being the safe haven for languageless sociality. The *plov* was spectacular—deep, deep flavors, and, with all that fat soaked up by the rice and peas, incredibly rich. I managed to mime a description of Los Angeles, and they praised Samarkand and Bukhara, places I was headed. I brought up Andijan—in 2005, the government's security services had opened fire on a demonstration in Andijan, and while the government claims 187 were killed, other estimates suggest more like 1,500. There are disputed versions of what happened—the government floated both the idea that Islamist radicals attacked the police and that they were merely quelling a prison break. Some regime critics suggest it was an attempt to put down a color revolution, and others that there was an internal struggle within the government that was played out in the street. The US condemnation of the attacks led to the closing of a major US base in the country and closer ties to China, which approved of the police action as necessary in the face of Islamist terror, afraid that Hizb ut-Tahrir and similar groups would spill over from the Stans into Uighur-dominated western China.

Andijan, they agreed was a shame, *but*, Mrs. Amidov said—and she made like she was putting a scarf on and started bowing and praying, mimicking an observant Muslim woman with sarcastic salaams—and then did a *phooey* gesture. I asked if they were Muslim, and they said yes, of course, but—and again she put on the imaginary headscarf, then wagged her finger—they didn't like fundamentalism. They were—we somehow managed to get this concept onto the table—secular Muslims.

After dinner we moved into a kind of parlor, its walls covered by rugs, or tapestries that looked like rugs, with a chandelier and what looked like upholstered trim along the ceiling—all more sumptuous than I expected, probably the formal dining room. The table held what seemed like an endless supply of three- and four-tier candy dishes. I had eaten so much *plov* I was afraid to move, and certainly afraid to eat any candy. It was a mix of homemade things, local brands, boxes of samplers, and international, mainly American, individually wrapped candy bars—Mars, Snickers, KitKat. We talked about currency problems, the way the economy seemed halfway dollarized. The problem, Mr. Amidov said, was that the government won't admit there is inflation, and so now, at 3,000 som to the dollar, and the biggest available denomination being a 1,000 som bill, the $200 worth I bought when I landed made a stack a foot high. Using dollars is technically illegal; so is trading dollars for som on the street, where you get twice as much for your dollar. Both are the norm.

Mr. Amidov was either a mechanical engineer, I learned, *or* he was a retired mechanical engineer, and he was also, in his spare time, *or* full time now that he was retired, a maker of hats. He had a dozen frames, made of hammered and steamed felt, out to dry on a rack in the corner of the courtyard, and they looked a bit grotesque at first—I thought they were some kind of animal parts, something visceral about the pale stretched material. He explained how he made them, some of which I followed, and then showed me the finished versions, the kind of hats a Russian prime minster or dandified Afghan president might wear, with several textures of wool including that very tight curly stuff, shiny and black, and some with fur as well, all extremely well made. He sold them, he told me, to a fancy shop for $20 a piece, which I could tell was quite a lot of money for a wholesale hat in those parts by the way he basked in glow of the number. I said, because I wanted to make it clear that he couldn't give me one as a gift, that I wanted to buy one from him.

For the first part of the day, I was fascinated by the way he just kept talking, as he did his interpretive dance to make himself understood, and thought his constant garrulity charming, naïve, but over time I realized it actually worked—that somehow, maybe because of deep phonemes? deep grammar? deep homonyms?—I started to feel I understood what he was saying. So I started, too, speaking everything I was thinking, as did Mrs. Amidov, who, although she observed normal rules of decorum in relation to me—she only talked when I wasn't, and vice versa—her husband's flow she treated like an ambient television soundtrack, something you could attend to or ignore at will. He seemed to never notice that she was talking, unless he objected to what she was saying, at which he would turn and correct her. We all chattered away, and by the end of the day it all felt like family, and in the struggle for comprehension, it was as if we were all fighting heavy accents, nothing more.

He, as I had suspected and had tried to cut off at the pass, insisted I take a hat as a gift. None of them fit, which was a bit embarrassing, all just a little too small—I have, for some reason, an enormous head, I think from my mother's side; my Uncle Gerald's head I happened to notice once as a kid, watching them talk, face to face, was twice the size of my father's—and I think on his end it seemed like a lapse in the hatmaker's art not to have the right size available—but none of that mattered. He insisted that I not pay. I said, no no no no, the *plov*, that was from the heart, and I appreciate it from the heart, and there were great protestations of mutual love and respect, lots of gesturing to the actual heart, but this, I kept saying, this hat, this was separate, this was just business, and *bizness* is, of course, one of the most international words we have. All the way out the door, he kept insisting—the children had magically reappeared to see me off—that it was his gift, pushing away the proffered payment, but at the last moment, he let me slip the bills—two twenties—into his hand at an angle his family couldn't see. We had a gentleman's agreement, all of a sudden, as he took the money, but I wasn't entirely sure what it was. His daughter wouldn't have seen the handoff anyway, being as engaged with her phone as any teenager in America, and the son had already disappeared. I suspected I was a pawn in the Great Game of Mr. and Mrs. Amidov. And as is often the case in politics, it was already too late to be neutral.

JODY MCAULIFFE

BOZO'S CIRCUS

What day is today, I hear him ask, my father, who is called Bill: the dreaded question. I've just woken up. Last night I stayed up late watching *The Yearling* on my portable TV with the rabbit ears antennae—the one my mother let me buy with the fifty dollars I made dancing in *Sleeping Beauty* with the Leningrad Kirov Ballet. It sits on my desk so I can watch it from my bed. White gloves keep me from biting my nails to a pulp before I finally surrender, peel them off, and tear nails and flesh till I draw blood. That Jody boy in the movie loses his pet deer, Flag, but my beagle Star sleeps curled around my big feet on my parents' old double bed with the caning on the corners chewed out. My cousin Mary-Jo and I like to jump on it till the box spring crashes and my mother comes in screaming at us and pulls my hair. Late last night in the screen's flickering glow, I thought I saw Mr. McD, with his poodle Jo-Jo in tow, peering in my window trying to look at me—my room is just off the front porch—but I can't be certain. My dog will protect me.

What day is today? It's a simple question, simple enough to answer once, but not simple to have to answer a hundred times in the same day. Maybe if I answer it right away the word Saturday will be the be-all and the end-all right here, right now. I mumble to him, Saturday, thinking if I don't make a big deal out of the question this will all go away, and then I head for the bathroom before he can ask me again. I'm afraid to look at his face to see if his eyes look strange the way they get when he's what we like to call "confused," without knowing the word used to mean "covered in shame." He works all week, then on the weekends he sometimes falls apart. He's not confused every Saturday, but, lately, he's confused on more Saturdays than not. Usually, by Sunday he's not confused anymore; he returns to himself.

Do you want to have a cup of coffee with me, he says somewhat mechanically through the bathroom door. I detect a hint of desperation in his demeanor when I come out, even though the question seems normal enough. Maybe he's still okay. Sure, I say, even though fifteen is too young to be drinking coffee. It's something we can do together. I pour us each a cup and sit at the kitchen table, but I notice his place is empty. He's not sitting down; instead he's shifting his weight from one foot to the other in front of me.

Your mother's not here, he says. I don't know where she is.

I can tell he's afraid even if he can't articulate the fear.

I don't know how I got in this get-up, he says, tugging at his maroon velour zip jacket.

Why don't you drink your coffee, I say.

Okay, then, Jody, he says, all right then…

Now I know he's on the downward spiral. I get some Frosted Flakes and milk and try to eat. Everything tastes like paper and I start wondering where my mother is because I can't deal with him alone when he's like this. I'd like to get out of here, escape like she did, before it happens, but I don't know where to go. He disappears into the living room and I hear the TV playing low. I bolt the rest of the cardboard cereal and head back to my room to get dressed and hide out.

I hear him outside my door tapping. Jo, Jo—all I'm asking for is a little reassurance. Just a little reassurance. I open the door and he's holding the dreaded TV guide. Oh, well then, Jody… Come and see. We head down the hall for the living room, me following him. He shows me the TV guide and points at the TV. It's not the same, he says.

What's not the same?

What the TV guide says and what's on the TV.

I don't know, I say, and he looks at me as if the house is being lifted up by a tornado and spun around. I take the TV guide and look at it. I can see that the listing and what's on are indeed not the same. *Bozo's Circus* with Ringmaster Ned is not supposed to be on channel nine, but it is: the Prohut family of tumblers today. The father calls out for a round-off flip-flop and the littlest girl cries, I'll try, Daddy, and she does it.

They're not the same, I say. I point at the current listing and at the TV, confirming the channel. I sit on the sofa and he tries to sit down in his armchair, but he can't do it. He can't sit still even for a moment. Obsessing over the guide, he stands in front of the TV, looking back and forth between the TV, the guide, his watch, and me. He comes over to me and asks me again why they're not the same. I don't know, I say, starting to get short with him. When the TV guide and what's on TV don't match, he can't prove what day it is. I tell him it's Saturday; why doesn't he just believe me? Why does he keep asking me the same thing over and over? I'll try, Daddy, I hear one of the tumblers cry.

I have to do my homework, I say, as I brush past him heading for my room. My door doesn't lock, but he won't come in even though I can feel him hovering in the hallway. I just want him to go away or snap out of it and come back to himself. I hear him go into my brother's room. He tickles Jack's feet to wake him up. Thank God, I think, now I don't have to deal with him on my own. I hear him ask Jack the question, What day is today? I'm doing math homework and I don't understand how to do the problems. I'm getting really frustrated because I don't understand. First I start pulling my hair and then I start kicking the wall under my desk, but I keep trying to do the problems even though I don't understand them. The harder they are, the more I try to do them, the harder I kick the wall. After about an hour of this fun, fun, fun, I go to the kitchen and by now Dad is standing on the rug just outside the kitchen doorway. I'm experiencing difficulty in articulation, he says. How can somebody who's experiencing difficulty in articulation put together a sentence like that? That's why I half don't believe he can't control this breakdown. I'm having trouble swallowing, too, he says, but he keeps trying to do it—dry swallow—and struggles over and over till I yell at him to just stop doing it.

My brother is in the kitchen. He's three years younger than me. Dad tells both of us that all he wants is a little reassurance and asks us over and over what day it is. Sometimes we say it's Saturday calmly and sometimes we yell: IT'S SATURDAY! Either way it never gets through. I show him the TV guide and point at the TV, gesticulating wildly that there is a discrepancy between the two. I feel like a psycho salesman hawking television sets. There's a knock at the door. My brother and I panic. We don't want anybody to see our father like this. We have to get rid of whoever it is. Jack goes to the front door and I try to hustle my father into his room and out of sight. He resists with some force, though not yet all the strength he can muster. I have a few more hours before that starts. I push him back down the hallway and he starts moaning.

All right then, Jody, okay then Jody, over and over. It's hard for me to keep him in his room because he's pulling on the door to open it and I'm pulling from my side to close it. Jack is at the front door with his friend Dave. The kids on the block want to play softball in the street out front and they want Jack to come out and play. Jack gets rid of him.

Jack's friend gone, I let my father out and he's more agitated than ever. I tell Jack to go ahead and join the game. There's no reason both of us should be stuck in here. He leaves and at long last my mother comes home from Great Lakes Naval Base where she's been shopping. My father is retired Navy. She takes one look at my father and knows exactly where things stand. I leave him to her and go back to my room to study. I hear him ask her the same questions over and over and over. She yells at him and he moves down the hall to their room. I think maybe he'll go to sleep now. It's always better after he goes to sleep, even though (or because?) he can never remember what he said or did.

I put a record on my phonograph—*Rubber Soul* by the Beatles—snap on a pair of goggles, and sit under the sun lamp to try to burn off some of my zits. By the time I come out of my room, my eyes looking like sunny-side-up eggs floating in a sea of pink skin, Dad's in what we call his track suit—stripped down to his athletic tee and boxers and black socks. I don't know how he got in that get-up. Midafternoon and the boys are still out in the street playing ball. Dad's extremely agitated, looking like a rabid whirling dervish on the rug in front of the kitchen. He's beyond a place where any answers from me or my mother, in tones ranging from quiet to screaming, can reach him. She tries to move him from the rug and convince him to lie down. He wails in protest. I just want him to shut up, and all of a sudden he's on the phone dialing 911. He says he needs "outside help," whatever that is. My mother is trying to pry the phone out of his hands and hang it up before he gets the police over here. She roughts him up enough to make him drop the phone. I don't hold it against her. Then he starts crying and spinning in circles. He's on his way down now and he heads for the front door and out into the street in his underwear in front of my brother and his friends. He's running around in the street and the kids are all afraid of him but I can tell they think it's funny, too. My brother blanches. I don't know what to do, but I run after my father and try to pull him back into the house. I want to run away but there's nowhere to go.

My mother puts something on the table and we manage to force it down. I'm still hungry so I start eyeing my brother's plate. When he looks finished, I ask if I can take what's left. He nods and I eat that, too. It's Saturday night and I'm performing in *How to Succeed in Business Without Really Trying* at the boys' high school. I'm playing Smitty and even though Miss Adrienne, the choreographer, told me not to sing Goddammit, voila in my song, *This Irresistible Paris Original*, I decide I'm going to do it anyway. Fuck her and the horse she rode in on. It's a Catholic school so she doesn't want me to sing Goddammit, but oh, dammit instead. There's a cast party afterwards and I've secured a bottle of champagne ahead of time and planted it in the backyard for safekeeping. My friend, Marian, and I have been planning for weeks to get drunk at the party. It will be my first time. After the show, I spend the evening at this party in somebody's basement next to the dryer, leaning against a post, drinking the entire bottle by myself, getting dizzier and dizzier. At the end of the night, we get a ride home from two guys on the swim team a year ahead of me, one of whom will turn out to be my friend for life (the boy my father names the mythical Dan, because he never actually lays eyes on him), but I don't know that at the time. They drive us to my house and I have to stop the car several times on the way home to open the door in order to puke. On one of these numerous pukings, my wallet falls out of the car and into the gutter, along with all the money I've collected from schoolmates for tickets to see American Ballet Theater downtown. I don't notice a thing. They drop me off after midnight.

Did you lose something, my mother says, waking me up with a knowing smile. I decide to play it cool—I have no idea if I lost something because I can't remember much of what happened last night. She laughs as if it's all some kind of in-joke, a rite of passage, and tells me a lady from Oak Park called to say she found my wallet in a gutter in front of her house with a hundred and fifty dollars in it. I must have a guardian angel. I believe in God even though I've stopped going to church, because I'm sick of those nuns telling me how bad we all are and giving us the silent treatment. My head is splitting and my mouth tastes of vomit.

I stumble out of bed and catch sight of my father lying on the bed in his room. He's neatly dressed and holding a rosary in his hands. I stick my head in the door and he looks at me with sad eyes, his real eyes. He says, I know something terrible went on yesterday, but I can't for the life of me remember what.

Are you okay, he says.

No, I say. I don't know. Yeah. I have a matinee today.

Knock 'em dead, he says.

I'll try, Daddy.

MICHAEL MEJIA

TO VISIT A PLACE FOR THE FIRST TIME IS THEREBY TO BEGIN TO WRITE IT

I had hoped to call on you immediately upon returning to Tokyo. I was in love with a young woman, a slender horse, a paid hag, a terribly jealous piece of black bamboo in patent-leather shoes who might have wounded me deeply if we assume that she is no different from a normal Japanese. She works part-time for this gourmet food place in Yokohama and is very well compensated for a number of added expedients that the daimyo dislikes. As soon as I come here I start feeling drunk. But what is it? Something has happened to the old capital. Manners have changed. A man came along, naked, his face almost entirely covered with blood. A girl of six or seven was struck repeatedly and brutally by someone she had thrust off the train. Everyone was saying *Open the windows! It stinks!* Petals began to rain down, then all the soldiers had been scared away, and the sudden appearance of a wall of air on the shore at Chiba portended future disorders. I do not often see old friends these days, and it is tempting to break the law. I'm risking my life on this project, so there is no one else in the city I trust as much as you. Swear to keep it a secret!

The buying and selling of fetuses all over Tokyo is really induced by the air pistol in my pocket. I suppose it is only natural that their parents would dote on them, worship the whole narrative of school gear, the fiction of a life other than this. It happens a lot these days, as in the reign of Emperor Sujin. They're kept in numbered bamboo vases by a tea master of the Ura Senke School, in a unique underground structure, extensive as a city and so cold you just put up with the smell. The fluctuation of their aquatic hearts, like rows of ringing pachinko machines, is more subdued, tired, and lonely day by day. So, this is the Palace of Eternal Youth! The fact is, I spoke to Natsume and would like to sell them at a low price, but I do not have the confidence. Of course, it's only a hypothesis, but here every wish can seem intense and fragile, like tears of sympathy or the name of the author. In the United States, however, such merchandise is only undone by a baser sense of shame. I know those beastly Americans from Western films. Actually, if we compare present conditions in Tokyo with those of ancient times, the release from the sense of shame seems to overlap with the recent tendency to give a *chanoyu* entertainment using tables and chairs. Various acquaintances who might be expected to let one know that the thick tea is served rarely have good hearts anymore. The worried, slightly embarrassed housewife stands there in the void of the bedroom, staring at you, her eyes flashing, and men all feel as uncertain as drifting clouds, just like in a science fiction movie. The tea ceremony, strongly signifying identity, is also spiritually empty these days, a speck of melody from another life, almost erased, terminated beneath blocks of pure noise. Now my head was spinning. Altogether it is as if a youthful luster does not constitute an important part of whatever makes one comfortable, so that you tend to be looked down upon by those thousands around you at the station, the crowds fleeing to the far western provinces, the sea of humanity in canvas shoes, exactly following customs, lost in contemplation of the lines at American home improvement centers and the many duties to come, which prevent pressing on toward the annual pileup on the eastern sea road. And then the lower part of your body moves in this way that gives an account of even worse misfortunes. Everything was wrapped in darkness. As they went past, a warm fragrance escaped and I heard the announcement: *Next stop, Roppongi.*

So I went into the grove with him. He was a friendly man who had had some sorrow. At first, he would turn around after each step and wipe away the footprint, which left no other way than to go the roundabout road. Taxis avoid the circle, but off we went, sweaty, fearful, tired. He talked about the Emperor, oak walking stick in hand, no longer a living, seeing creature, wealthy and relatively free of questions of art and history. A warm fragrance escaped. This feeling of release was very comforting, he thought, only his longing to have Yoko there in the shade was so intense—the ground moved up and down! "Someone has given me the address," he murmured. If the German scientists got to Fuji before it started, they would cut the tow rope! So I held onto him about the waist for a very long time. The man groaned. When he came, right on the scrap of paper, the rather empty map of a different town, I was listening for the light step of the Gosechi dancer, gloves edged with black fur, drawing the Kōriyama figure in the rocks and trees. "Good bye." He clutched his chest. She buried her face in his neck. The body rose gently into the air. Then a radiant moon came out and the capital was engulfed by a sudden wave.

This day, the tenth of the fourth month, I decided to go dancing in one neighborhood or another. But for the furious sound of a koto, all was quiet. There were no cars or trains along the edges of the snow-covered parade ground. There was no crowd of refugees drinking coffee together, only ruined house foundations, empty bars, huge steaming basins. The town hall was on fire. There was no one, or almost no one, just the son-in-law—the company's president—and his four guards—much more factual than legal employees of different races—conserving remains in numbered bamboo vases. That's what research is all about these days: blackmail, extortion, robbery. It seems a great exploit to me! Kazuki, a short sword on his hip, undiluted by that English perfume of his, ran down the stairs of the ruined Industrial Promotion Hall to give me an address among other things: brand-new clothes, paper cherry blossoms, the air pistol in my pocket. The sensation of it was something like holding a plump newborn baby. Even in this trivial action it was natural that I should remember Yoko was gone. Oh, Yoko! Men do stupid things sometimes! "How sad for you." Kazuki spread his arms and flapped them eleven times, the Japanese way. He felt nothing whatsoever, yet he told his girl to be gentle with me. Eventually I came. Until then, feeling the weight of the liquid upon my palms, I had no awareness at all. I hadn't realized that my senses had declined so far, hadn't connected my anemia with the smell and feel of the maidens who live in Kazuki's bath houses, those red-hot stones, some still bleeding, who ooze into the city from the hills on muddy swirls for our purposes, such efficient conductors of a heat which really cannot be differentiated from the moderate radiation I encounter daily on my journey between the stations at Ohira and Kōriyama. My attempts to calculate the months I spent without those women were accordingly frustrated, and if we assume that each of them produces a particular artifact—some dark lines, say, or pee, or ashes, or a toy horse—I must be a miserable bricolage of error, a hill of nothingness that is really disliked by others, a glowing dreamlike barrier to time and work. This is especially true when I crash into cities and absorb people—apparently over two million a year!—in the cool light of a comely gaze. I am huge. You must be worried. But I can't very well go looking for that chin on the telephone, can't listen for the murmur of that voice, a broken noise, a musical offering to being that has to be heard to be believed. What's the comfort of tomorrow morning? Oh, Yoko! She's changed! I want to sleep for three days. I walked, then, from street to street, a ceramic dish, no lid, filled with the most intense feelings of sorrow and regret. A little line of neon lights flowed once more toward the phone at the station. If I'd been a bit more sound of body I would have picked it up, but there can no longer be any doubt: it, too, had changed. Changed how? I didn't know. Though they say beautiful women are so cold, one feels them to be the source of all wanting.

As was observed long ago of Kyoto, Tokyo, too, can be light and soft to the touch in the ninth month, giving forth hardly a sound within its lacquerware atomic dome. The Commodore, a jewel of perfect health and strength, crept into her room wearing the uniform of a Tokyo Imperial University student and fell upon me, asking in a coquettish voice: "Who would not be happy to go to his death?" A man on the screen said, "The complexity and added profundity of this city can be known only by an activity worth the expenditure of freedom." Was the remark addressed to someone else? I lifted my *keshō-mawashi*, laying bare the air pistol and the heavenly grandson, Profit and Loss, as happily intermingled as two young wrestlers in a cozy little condo. Dazzling! Didn't he know that they heard the melodies of the floor, that they would sense someone descending the stairway, so he couldn't just burst in? A moth was still for a very long time. "When the officer comes, he had better bring a present!" That reined in his horse. Now the President of the United States was on, a fine performer of Japanese ancestry. I administered the ten commandments according to *Nihongi* tradition, fiercely raining down on the Commodore's inkstone for about thirty minutes, correcting my facial expressions in the mirror as necessary. Naturally, for fear of upsetting the serenity of the old pond frog or Tenazuchi, the arrogant neighbor, the rhythm of these pious acts was altogether in consonance with his tender objections. A pure style is such a rare thing! It made me proud knowing that not one hint of this would be heard above the sound of a koto. After a time, he repented and rose gently into the air, choked with tears, lamenting the fact that he had not been born Japanese. "Excuse me." It was so moving to see this exhibition of the man's feelings! I reflected on the effect they might have on the crowds milling around outside, worrying about the life to come, but *Hagakure* says don't go into personal luggage. Now they were interviewing Yoshimitsu about the removal of a hundred eggs from a certain well-known woman in Switzerland. It was time to turn in. The next day was Sunday and I had to get up at four to accompany the Middle Captain to Sendai to return the scorn of someone who hated him.

That same evening, within the private confines of a Japanese room, under strict orders from Captain Adams, Hitachiyama touched a razor ten times to Kiyomori's fourth son, a young man who never would be faithful to the Commodore. It is sad to imagine. Such a clever face! That cat was cute, a man of education, the finest chanter in this shabby *kusemai*. The fresh down on his arms recalled a mystic realm without morality, holy writ, or Confucian intellectuals. In other words: total freedom! With obvious reluctance Kyoko buried her face in his neck, and then, once his body rose gently into the air, the two of them were able to make more extensive observations. "Oh!" They began weeping. "You can see it! It's…it's…such a beautiful thing!" Indeed, that little inkstone of his sent and received love letters constantly. In fact, it's a major reason there is such a large population of Grand Champions in Izumo Province. If only he'd decided not to make further inquiries! Particularly since the Middle Captain turned out to be such a pitiful coward. To have been laid by him in the morning dew—in reply to his written request!—was apparently of no importance to anyone. I heard it from Hōnen that he told a friend he did it to impress Kurō and the other *shin-nageire* club members. Oh, Yoko! It appears that, these days, all the good ones truly have been taken and that a man must more closely regulate admission to the upper floors of his virtue in order to keep from becoming another purely colorless quantity lost upon the taste buds of Japan's great overseas enemy. The next morning, when he hadn't returned, I showed up with Kajiwara and found the two of them crouched together on the kitchen floor making a feast of that gentle autumn fowl. They were using his retainer as an alcove decoration! "You again?" At first we hesitated, unable to reply because the scene was precisely as Amida said it would be: an exhibition of such evil changes to the human form that we were about to give up and go home in tears. But I recalled the divinity of my teacher, Mikoto, pressed to my lips long ago at a different place, far from this floating world in which I'd been born a man, the scented stream from her proud *fushi* offering protection from death for as long as Matsukage remains Japanese. Then a warm fragrance escaped from the disposal—a fighting spirit, the Kōriyama figure in person, its armor edged with black fur—to conduct the sacred rite of their departure! If they had anything to say, it was concealed in the sound of a koto. The negotiations of commerce make no clear-cut distinctions about the various efficacies of the serpent or the bee, even for the Japanese of today. One may always entertain a doubt, that is, even if, in the interim, an ambassador one happens to meet in the toilet reverently praises one's sword and other accouterments before showing his own and his willingness to perform the very favor one requires. To summarize: They were mulched.

"Well, back to work!" As soon as the lieutenant had drained his sake cup, I cried out in triumph. What! I have tried calm dignity, but just looking and saying nothing could do me no good. If my kick did not quite connect, it built my confidence. The way the man staggered back, protecting his face with both hands, as a married woman might! His daughter dropped the phone, wrapped a towel around herself, and knelt down to bury her face in his neck. Petals began to rain down. From the floral art exhibition outside came the faint sound of a koto. Dreadful work, painful to think upon, these young sumo wrestlers performed the humiliations, emphasizing how one stuck in the shallows should evaluate the final evanescent section of green melon, the hour of death. "Why hide the address?" It was impossible, though. There would be no reply. Lying on the study floor between Komako and the baby carriage, the abandoned lieutenant only looked in the mirror and harmonized his gills with the total freedom of the city: the buying and selling of fetuses, the Kōriyama figure, the Serizawa Research Laboratory, the numbered bamboo vases. The air pistol in my pocket! For such a tiny death, the empty eight-mat room seemed enormous. A moth was still for a very long time. The phone rang. It was you, remember? "Did you find it?" A man's laugh echoed through the hotel. So unlucky! We inquired at the Kobe country club, yet no word ever came. Oh, Yoko! When a party breaks up, my heart is like a ship in the sea near Okinawa on a certain day and month: a moment of sharp intensity—and then vanished without a trace!

You've got nothing to worry about. It's all over. Now the Commodore has transferred his broad black pennant to the *Powhatan* and the Western mode of living will prevail everywhere in Japan. People will be heard through the endless winds having a fine, noisy time. You will have forgotten the sacred name. To wind up the failure, a white object will reappear where the sun should be. Only an astonishingly long darkness beyond this. And Yoko, clapping, gloves edged with black fur. Yoko unknowing. Yoko unknown.

MIRANDA MELLIS

DEMYSTIFICATIONS #1-37

1.
Getting up early is the cause of a long day.

2.
She didn't know what was about to be said.
She had to find out after it came out.

She knew what was about to be said.
Was she hearing faster?
How can you hear in advance?

Hearing what's already been said.

Getrude Stein said *Many words spoken to me have seemed English.*

3.
What happened to that giant building? Why is it empty, its walls, soft and green?
It's turned back into a forest.

After that, they never could think of architecture without thinking of water.

4.
After the landslide, a sheer wall of dirt, flat and punctuated by stones.
I refuse to attribute my sudden and unwelcome feelings to anything at all.

5.
When ambition rises up it is fuel. Happiness depletes it.

6.
The trees slide up hill greenly
Layered and lineated
Go back to your roots; write only to know yourself.

7.
We can't congratulate you on your success; it's the first time we've heard from you in a year or two.
Write with bad news first.
Then we might be more receptive.

8.
Wear a suit: dressing for politics is not magical thinking.
Then it's your fault for wearing ribbons in your hair on Election Day.
You confused poll with the May Pole.
You'll wear your dunce cap to the voting booth from now on!

9.
William Carlos Williams said *War is the first and only thing in the world today. The arts generally are not, nor is this writing a diversion from that for relief, a turning away. It is the war or part of it, merely a different sector of the field.*

10.
The economists haven't learned that politics is made of language.

11.
"Epic fail"; "novel fail"; "haiku fail"; "microscopic fail."
Like when an ant loses control of its mandible. And drops the torso of a wasp.

12.
Resentment is the dried blood of wounded virtue. The Utah of emotions.

13.
Would you like to know my secrets?
I don't have any.
My secrets are feelings.
I have a secret, but I don't know what it is yet.

14.
On *House of Cards*, a show about the normalcy of criminality in politics, a

lying, back-stabbing, immoral murderer becomes president. Hannah Arendt warned in the early 70s against the normalization of crime in government. She also warned, in the 60s, against the dangerous stupidity of those in power.

On *Orange Is The New Black*, an incarcerated mother tells her incarcerated daughter, "Lots of stupid people go on to become great successes."

15.
Milan Kundera said *Totalitarian society, especially in its more extreme versions, tends to abolish the boundary between the public and the private; power, as it grows ever more opaque, requires the lives of its citizens to be entirely transparent. The ideal of life without secrets corresponds to the ideal of the exemplary family: a citizen does not have the right to hide anything at all from the Party or the State, just as a child has no right to keep a secret from his father or his mother. In their propaganda, totalitarian societies project an idyllic smile: they want to be seen as "one big family."*

16.
Walking on eggshells in a forest.
Don't want to wake up the trees, or kill them.

Seeing a bird you've never seen and having a sinking feeling: what if it's the last one?

Worrying about nature, like holding a sick newborn in the Intensive Care Unit.
"Maybe my love will make a difference."
"That's not falsifiable."

Babies thrive when they are loved.
Is nature similar?
Am I projecting on nature, or am I nature?
Am I history's ventriloquist, or nature's dummy?

17.
Phillipe Descola said *Between the effacement of humans in the virginity of a practical world without rules or representations and the preponderance of the human in the definition of that which makes sense on the earth, the middle path of being-in-the-world lurches through numerous zigzags.*

18.
Passion for a stranger.
Who isn't a stranger?

19.
Feelings, especially the feelings of others, are enigmatic and soldiers are young.
"You killed people!"
"Nobody told me they were *real*!"

What if the norm was to send bourgeois over fifty to war?
"Come on, let's not kill ourselves here, life's too short!"

He rubs his elbows.
"Where can I find a decent cappuccino?"

20.
In Errol Morris's documentary about him, Donald Rumsfeld exclaimed, "It would have been *wonderful* if we had killed Saddam Hussein at Dora Farms!"

"I'll have the pie a la mode."
"*Wonderful*!"

Allen Ginsberg said, "Almost all our language has been taxed by war."

The last question Errol Morris asks is, "Why are you talking to me?"
Rumsfeld answers, "That's a *vicious* question.... I don't know."

Unknown, unknown....

21.
Extemporizing: it doesn't always end well.

iMouth.

"Did I really just say that?"

22.
Knowing the answers in advance, that's ideology.
Ignore contradictions, like an unwanted Christmas present.

23.
Canned laughter, rubber chicken, dead snake, trigger-happy, false alarm.

24.
In the early 60s when a bill to protect women against discrimination would come before the Senate it was considered hilarious. The bill would come up, and the mood would turn jocular. One senator joked, "When I argue with my wife I always get the last two words: Yes dear." Ha ha! A man pretending to be stupid.

Dude, you think your submission is a farce.

25.
Steven Zultanski said *Why can't I come in peace?*

26.
If you came on to you, would you want yourself?
Would you know exactly what to say?
Would you confidently seduce yourself?

Or would you be like,
"Look, I'm not a mind reader."

"Fuck it, this is too much work."

27.
My neighbor casually mentions that he is in the Special Forces. "Don't worry," he says, "I've turned off my web monitoring, so I'm not monitoring the websites you visit." A few minutes later his wife says that every morning, after she reads her Bible and prays, she scans craigslist. I quickly ask, apropos of nothing,
"Do you look at the free stuff on craigslist?" She says, "I look at everything."
I say, heartily, "That's *amazing!*"

Grinning. Eyes cantilevering.

Can they tell I'm nervous?

28.
Phobias:
Religious people

Military people
Narcissists
Politicians
Intellectuals
People who hug
People who don't hug
People who give me a present and when I thank them, tell me they stole it
People whose legend precedes them
Barking dogs on country roads
Surveillance
Tourists
Truck stops
Cell phones
Email
Indoor parking lots
Off gassing
Cougars
Bleach
Most foods
Drones
Subtlety
Lack of subtlety

Liliana Mizrahi said *I am, for myself, a hypothesis....*

29.
With soil depletion due to capitalist genetics, food becomes representation, just a chewy sign. "Food" becomes the epitaph for food, nutrients an extinct language, lost in translation.

30.
"If everyone has their basic needs met, I'll lose business."

But time is not a fish, waiting to be caught.

31.
Mahmoud Darwish said

The myths refuse to adjust their plot.
They may suffer a sudden malfunction

and some of the ships may drift to a dry
unpopulated land
where the imaginary becomes afflicted with the real….

Milan Kundera said

The psychological mechanisms that function in great (apparently incredible and inhuman) historical events are the same as those that regulate private (quite ordinary and very human) situations.

Staretz Silouan said

Keep your mind in hell,
and despair not.

32.
Sometimes you arbitrarily encounter a piece of writing that makes you feel,
"*This* is the key to my whole existence."
It makes sense that someone's mind gave you access to yours.
Someone else's body gave you your body, too.
But about this text that has unlocked you, what if you had never come across it?
Why does it happen repeatedly, with really different texts?

How many such "keys" are there to your whole existence?
Three? Ninety? Seven thousand? A Billion? Countless?

33.
Can I see that which I am outside of?
Can I see that which I am not outside of?

Liliana Lukin said

there is a silence here

that has nothing to do with silence

34.
Rae Armantrout said

Find the place

in silence
that is a person

or like a person
or like not
needing a person.

35.
"The spirit is willing."

What about the flesh?

"The flesh is too."

How about history?

36.
We have a fight about
…. ferns.
A bee angrily chases me away from the lavender.
I fall: break nothing.

That's my run-in with the law
of nature, today.

37.
Invitation to a pop-up
pops up at
Greener Commons. Theme:
Space Cholo is the new Sea Punk.

LAURA MORIARTY

from *VOLCANIK*

Movement generates SPACE
Catastrophic terrane disruption
A way to name the time
Holo or ANTRHOPOcene
EPOCH
Longer than an age
Quaternary (now)
Shorter than a period
Names of times
Including the present
ACCELERATION
Stilled life lay
Awake the last
2.6 million (or 60) years
This time different
ECONOMIK
As we change
TERRANE TERRAIN

Current volcanic alert level the same
"Terrane" a fragment of earth's crust broken off from one
and attached to another TECTONIC PLATE.
"Terrain" the vertical and horizontal of land surface, so-called relief/I was relieved
Saying to myself "this time doesn't exist" though I knew I was caught in it.
Time not existing meant only that I was not available for the next hour.
And not at work or being otherwise made or paid or observed
Mount Konocti, the nearest volcano to my present location
part of the Clear Lake Volcanic Field
whose more or less active
composite dacitic lava dome produced an ashfall 10,000 years ago
Unknown things go off unknowably
And change the EARTH
Cretaceous Inland Sea
Mount Shasta erupted in 1786
Lassen Peak from 1914 to 1921
No things without time
Without warning and in spite of scrutiny and expectation
They take shape

"To illustrate how attitudes toward nature can change…
consider the mountain." Yi-Fu Tuan, *Topophilia*

Temple MOUNTAIN continuum

Ash crafted series of calderas
Today we live in a giddily active volcanic regime
Crumbs from which LAYER CAKE
Taste like memory

"Volcanoes of passion" mentioned by my lover during the
open relationship we were attempting to have then.
Gets in eyes and mouth producing TEARS,
coughing and unbearable sadness.

The Antler and Sonoma Orogenies
Forces and events associated with MOUNTAIN building
Preparation for the TRIP includes choosing a date and
itinerary, researching places to stay, making reservations
deciding what to do there, getting maps.

A seamount in the northwestern Pacific Ocean, the largest volcano
on Earth, could rival the largest in the solar system—the mighty Olympus Mons on
Mars
whose gradual rise might not however excite much interest if you were there.

Beyond being on MARS
Happy again

The artist experiences the LIGHT and speaks about it in the library he
built
A tectonic and temporal analog

Fragments less than a tenth of an inch across of minerals and ASH
along with gas ascend forming a huge, billowing eruption column and,
eventually, cloud.

"And roll'd along the ground"

HOLLOW EARTH

No permanence meaning no Eternalls but time everywhere going in the same direction
Lead melting in hollowed out clouds and other theories of lightning that proved
In 1335 Petrach climbed Mount Vesuvius
The invisible hand appears originally
meaning the ECONOMY or here NATURE or even GOD
to be false

An exploration of what can happen next
nuées ardentes
Alterative temporality
Human-relevant timescale
How To Build a Volcano

If ROCK is like BONE or one becomes the other over time
These ossuaries
"Seismic scream portends volcanic activity"

These orogenies
Whose forces include much that
Begins and ends

From the tip of your nose to the top of the Transamerica PYRAMID
A system whose time is short but seems long

But where are we in all this stone?
Time stretching out behind
And before meaning ahead into
Interval, period, personal history, ecstatic
Hour, rate of marching, mood, existence or job
To mention the worst and best of duration as experience
For a specific contract with reference to
Prevailing conditions seeming endless
END

Peak of wonder
a new thing for the eyes but old also
reading applied to rocks, minerals stuck together we stick
together FLEXURE occurs below and among us travelling variously to
places where objects, this pebble, saved by me gets in everything as for example
ash or hot wind blows into and around us when leaving Mount Pelé explodes
in 1902 you and I not there then but later looking back and chose that moment

pictured by me

                              as memorial
to yourself on your book
                              not dead yet
                              then dead
doors where mourning occurs in those shots shown also as open to the sea
crockery, columns, items smashed   suspended
in earth

The disaster table
in our house on Jackson Street
another house another Jackson Street
another HOUR spent walking through
the forest on the upper reaches of the mountain
another mountain covered with ASH as if
ASH meant nothing

Mineralized pages bound or
forged forced to dig through
loose GRAVEL to the thing destroyed
take away this earth the artist said or
"author" of this book that it was too late
Good bye sadness cried out as one monumentally
difficult though not called that in his PLACE

    THERE in Oakland where now
We talk about your FACE
    "for wind is air"

Or FLAME years since
Oakland Fire at the Oakland Museum
    of a traffic jam
    wind driving flames
    around those who presumably got out
    but did they?

From across the bay we saw the ASH CLOUD
    familiar now
    maculated dark
    pine tree column as younger Pliny wrote
    his uncle went into it forever
    fire raining down

first letter
disaster itself
not OMEN

Is this a geological cataclysm
Or one of the spirit?

Or body whose
Throat and mouth as word for entrance hall
fauces term given by Vitruvius to
narrow passages on either of the
tablinum through which access would be
obtained from the atrium to the peristylar

Earth or MOUNTAIN as house: old idea
Body as plant i.e. throat of calyx, portion
of spiral shell you look into and hear

Your FACE fair not as light but
Lit like Moses with his God on
full of grace or space

Everyone looks away

LAURA MULLEN

PAPER CROWN

WHO SEES THIS AND NAMES IT

Who negotiates a way through what is
Saying what ought to be

In a colorless room
The camera angle

Who calls the shot*

The experience of seeing

That which appears to deny
The existence
Of the audience

I have the experience of raising
My hand to my eye

Covered in glass

Just watch+

---

* Bolt gun cuffs protagonist
I call the shots around here—
Sweetheart.

\+ Windows *admit* light

Note: the body (more or less desperately) "honest"
And I, I…
Caught up in the effort to be anything but

I SPY WITH MY LITTLE EYE

The colorless room
The bird in its cage
"Fluttered"[*]

In a sense
Innocence

Nothing seen by me except what I saw why is it so hard to believe that—why is the sense of having "seen it" (from someone else's point of view) of having entered another's visual field (as the subject) so strong I start "No *no* I perceived all this saw so much I never…" (as through my sleeve the dark seep of)[•] then (hearing myself)

Stopped

Bridge[+] station accident

What I remember

The camera not
The tracks

One of the two
Inspectors hangs the receiver up behind the curtain
Thinks
Then
Replaces it with the transmitter

"'I am the vessel of life'"

This conveys something to the one
Who said it

---

* Distressed (in that sense)

• Evidence

\+ Also car and embankment what

MEASURED AGAINST

Not a character

But both

Camera and watch-
Dog or canary
In this case
(*Sing*) frantic
To be at once

On both sides of
The apparatus*

Noisily making a
Record+
Of what
Of what

---

* Aperture

\+ A racket

PEEP PEEP PEEP

A sense of having been in rooms
When those who should have been there were not

"I meant my mind"*
Tracked+

Down
("I meant my mind but could only point to it via my body")

The light
Beating of these
Spread wings
Against the bars

That shot

(Confined space) (and the train
Of associations)

I point to it you get
My (drift) I indicate
The POV

One might take
As if living it

Out

But the wad of blood-soaked gauze
Tossed in the gutter

I didn't choose this

(Hand to) mouth

---

* *Windows we never gaze out of*
Take it from me

\+ Across the newspaper
Lining the bottom of that cage
Grey fluff stirred by the frantic activity
Drifts and gently rises up

HAVING BEEN SHOT

Having taken the shot*

Having been hit and also
The one who struck
And also

The one who left
Without a mark+

Shut off

Already beginning to think
Of something else

A kind of alarm
System

My breath *my ha*
Art

---

* The train the chance the hint the point what else

+ What does it mean that I can imagine the world without

SHEILA E. MURPHY

[UNTITLED]

A spindly and
transparent winter
parts from

lake
the color snow,
foreground

of sticks
alongside
evening's pale

sky parted
from shared
place.

THEN

I wanted to
be locked in
to the music

store, no heat
on, jazz through
bells of horns,

the reeds' sweet
taste, those
unheard songs.

I owned them

all, talked
back by heart.

TEND NEED

Tend need
not be
probable.

Relax into
the white
blush

open to
continuo
carved sounding

accident
astride
a practice.

BEFORE

All the pretty men, now old,
pantomime
with panache
return of serve,
heft extra weight,
walk gingerly, draw
lovers in and of
shared history,
divide their time
between living and
embellishing
the story,
source dust
chalking sidewalks
prior to
inevitable rain.

ADAGIO

A pavanne of lace and shadow
lights the snow
apart from a crescendo,
toward plush rest.

Winter tenders
conversation amid
thin branches, mood
made crèche.

Young crystals touch each tree,
protractedly, as winter forms
retreat from
the harsh friction of next steps.

[UNTITLED]

in the middle seat
beside me, a woman sleeps
in another language

LISTLESS

Small keep
sakes rounded
form
the gist.

Who needs clefs
when seeing
one's own
music?

Breath marks
longed for
take their rest,
in the meantime,

driving toward

tone codes
to a quiet,
placed just so.

[UNTITLED]

In a little less than an hour, it will be now.

A. L. NIELSEN

VIEW FROM THE SCREAMED IN PORCH

The God of lost things was gone
And so the narrator found her place
There between the irrepressible object
And the immobile force

Memoirs were in the air that year

TESTAMENTARY

Cry
O genesis

Overgrown with firs
Enjambed with fog

A vocabulary argues
With itself

Are not all attractors
Strange

A congruence between
A vowel and avowal

Is there some form of
Ennui we
Can agree on

The best "of"
Of both worlds

CLARENCE FARMER'S COMPLAINT
(with apologies to Clarence Carter)

Didn't have but one meatball left
So you know how I felt
When it tipped out the spoon and
Rolled off the table

Dog got that
Used to be a good dog too
But he'd known he was wrong
And that's why
Soon as he got that meatball
He scudded out the door and
Into the street

Too bad about that
Car that ran him over
Only had that one car all those years
Till the wife drove off with it
And over my dog

Which wouldn't have been too bad
Either if she hadn't phoned
My girlfriend who she'd just found
Out about so there I was
Suddenly
No wife
No dog
No girlfriend

Which wouldn't have been too bad
Except it was the girlfriend
Used to cook the meatballs

TOY STORY

In a town with no edge
With no other side
No tracks at all

The bad toys gather
Bright shapes flitting by
Broken bus stands

The silly putty that smothered its child
Melted Gumby who forced my hand
The G.I. Joe who ran amuck
Wiping out an entire ant farm
The wind-up mouse that tore the little girl's hair

And always on their way
To the compulsory dance
Blighted Barbie and crippled Ken
Leading their battalion of skunk cabbage
Patch dolls in desultory steps

WITHOUT A SONG

Soul looks back in Wonder
Wonder wonder wonder who

Wrote the book who
Can I turn to

When you turn away
Way over yonder

Look over Yonder's
Wall all in all

It's just another brick
Thick as

LANCE OLSEN

from *DREAMLIVES OF DEBRIS*

Someone, I tell you, in another time will remember us, but never as who we were.
Sappho

:::: debris
I have my doll and the screamings behind my eyelids. The screamings look like fluttery lights. The fluttery lights believe they live inside me, but I live inside them, too.

My doll's name is Catastrophe.

:::: debris
Daddy once made his ideas purer than King Aegeus's. Now every year King Aegeus sends seven of his bravest young men and seven of his most beautiful young women from Athens to Crete to visit me. I let them wander the passages of my heart for hours—or maybe it is days, or weeks—I do not know what any of these words mean—before I step out of their frothy panic to welcome them.

:::: debris
The liquid architecture will not hold still. Sometimes I cannot locate the walls. I shuffle forward, hands outstretched in the grainy charcoal air, breathing mold, must, fungus, sulfur, damp dirt, wet rock, waiting for the gritty touch ushering me onto the far shore. Sometimes so many walls erupt around me I am forced to crab sideways to make any progress at all.

Sometimes the walls become a whirlwind of hands or dying alphabets.

The ceiling sinks without warning and I discover myself crawling on my belly across the chalky floor, Catastrophe clutched tight to my chest.

:::: debris
Despite my height, I should mention, my strength is not negligible.

Last month—no, last year—next—I am not sure—I am never sure—no surprises there—one always knows a sliver less than one did a flinch ago—at some point in timelessness mommy and daddy gave me a little sister to play with.

Our wrestling match persisted the length of one short startled bleat.

Since then I have been an only child again.

:::: debris

Apis the Healer tells me I am thirty-three years old. I cannot remember. He tells me nobody believed I would live past thirty-three months.

This, he says, is why mommy calls me Her Little Duration.

Why daddy calls me The Minotaur.

I call myself Debris.

:::: debris

When I set out to greet my new guests, I tuck my doll beneath my arm and carry a torch. This is not so I can see them. It is so they can see me.

The brave young men, unarmed, unnerved, usually shit or piss themselves a little when I step into the open. I think they are expecting someone else. It is not unamusing to watch their secretions trickling down their legs as they blunder into blank walls trying to unsee me.

All I have to do is stand there clearing my throat.

Matters usually take care of themselves.

I follow the women like their own shadows, torchless. They cannot hear me, have no sense of my presence, until they feel me clambering up their backs, hands searching for necks, teeth for arteries.

:::: debris

What I am telling you, I want to say, is a love story.

:::: debris

And then mommy brought around Lady Tiresias.

Calling my name, listening for my response, she zeroed in on her princess.

Soon the three of us were sitting cross-legged in a chamber I had never seen before. It stank of language.

Vowels, mostly.

The blind bony seer with wrinkled female dugs has known life as both man and woman. He had my pity. She reached for my hand. He wanted to read my palm. I hissed at her. He drew back.

Mommy stroked my scruff.

Be nice, button, she said.

Lady Tiresias tried again. She discovered my palm bloated smooth as a baboon's ass: no bumps, lumps, fissures, figures, failures, futures.

You are born, she said, of a very special race. The Minotaur belongs to a people old as the earth itself. Beneath the skin of your shoulders grow wings. Someday they will break out and carry you far away from here.
I reached back, felt nothing.
Give yourself time, she said. The number thirty-three controls your life. You are concerned not with personal ambition but with uplifting the loving energy of humankind.
Out the corner of my eye I saw mommy shift.
Lady Tiresias's bald head reminded me of an enormous gland.
You are a born leader, he said. This is what I see. You will achieve great fame through kindness, tenderness, compassion. Remember: whosoever is delighted in solitude is a god. Lady Tiresias has spoken.

:::: debris
That afternoon mommy led the unsuspecting blind man to the Brazen Bull. The hollow bronze beast hulked on a raised platform in our central courtyard at the edge of the shallow pool swarming with eels, each fitted with a pair of tiny gold earrings. Two Athenian slaves helped him through the hatch in its side. Lady Tiresias ordered them to be careful. They obeyed. Crouching here in the darkness I watched them light the fire. It quickly crackled into consciousness. Soon clouds of incense were shooting from the bull's nostrils. The complex system of tubes and stops inside its skull translated the soothsayer's shrieks into infuriated bovine bellows.

:::: debris
First *comes pain*, whispers mommy, rocking, *then knowledge*.

:::: debris
Next day they opened the hatch and extracted what was left of Lady Tiresias. Mommy asked the most delicate bits be fashioned into my beautiful new bracelet.

Mommy loves Her Little Duration.

:::: debris
Before that and after that I watched many wars. Or maybe it was the same war many times. Before that and after that I watched the slow wreckage of my city bog into the earth. I watched Daedalus's boy attempt to scrabble up a hidden ladder above a seascape like hammered silver, his wax wings reducing to air around him. My sister Ariadne, whom I have never met,

hands something I could not make out to a muscular young man I could not recognize standing in front of a gate I could not place. I watched daddy, whom I have never met, reclining in a silver bathtub decorated with octopi and anemones. Watched the daughter of Cocalus, King of Camicus, signal her slave to empty a pot not of warm water but of boiling oil over his head and chest and groin. Me hanging weightless in mommy's womb, strangling my almost-brother with his own umbilical cord, preparing to bestow upon my parents' my first gift, which they would in turn mummify and boon back to me, a mutual sign of our abiding affection.

:::: debris
There are the stories that make sense. These are called lies. There are the stories that maze you. These are called the world.

I should mention your body is a haunted house you cannot escape.

:::: debris
Which is to say the worst is still to come, was still to come, will still be to come, has come, had come, is coming, has been coming, might come, is going to come, will have come, would have come, but not yet, and already.

:::: debris
Because, outraged once, daddy set off to Athens. Revenge seared through his veins for my brother's death at the games. On the way he invaded Megara, whose King Nisos' power derived from a single magic lock of purple hair. Nisos' daughter Scylla saw daddy from the battlements, tumbled into love with him in the beat of a hurt, and that very night sheared her own sleeping father like a feebleminded sheep.

:::: debris
Because, appalled by Scylla's lack of filial devotion, daddy departed at once, leaving Nisos' daughter keening on the dock.

Each star in the sky a pinprick upon her skin.

:::: debris
Because the screamings say I will never have heard enough.

:::: debris
The voices just keep on arriving.

:::: pasiphaë chorus
and when the midwife pulled the steaming godshit from between my legs

I took one glance and commanded her *kill it kill it kill the inaccuracy* but my husband chuckled and said *this bounty is yours sunshine a reward from the gods for how you have lived your life* and with that he ordered the wet nurse to deliver my living failure into the labyrinth's flections deep beneath our bed and Minos strode out of the birthing chamber and out of my love and before that day drowned itself in the wine-dark sea the godshit had been tucked away from our citizens' eyes and ears forever while I had discovered just how lavishly a woman can hate a man how much you think this blistering affliction is all the white-hot loathing you can fist inside you only to learn there can always be more and after that more still and

:::: debris

And before that and after that I watched Paris steal Helen away from her husband and black flames burn through a decade. I watched beautiful, broken Cassandra—pale skin, blue eyes, red hair kept in curls; raped repeatedly by Ajax the Lesser on the floor of Athena's temple where she fled in search of refuge—I watched beautiful, broken Cassandra babble from the post to which she had been tied before the gates of junked Troy, disinterested pedestrians passing her by. I watched a nation suffer toward truth, believing it was sharing something important, something lasting that would unite it, even as it already knew all its beliefs had been nothing but bluffs, its politicians best at organizing human weakness. Hell to ships, hell to men, hell to cities, and Clytemnestra clawing a dagger across Cassandra's bared throat because Agamemnon had taken the disbelieved seer as war spoil. An arrow pierce swift-footed Achilles' heel and his body pitch forward into death. And before that and after that I watched him, Achilles—no trace of his own ruin shadowing his features—slit the heels of Hector's corpse, pass Ajax's belt through them, and drag the breaker of horses around the fortress walls until Hector's body effaced itself into the rocky earth.

:::: pasiphaë chorus

and still Minos makes a daily art of amnesia refusing to mention the mistake barking up at us into our sleep every night or consider the boundless perplexity webbing below our feet and so it is that every day hating him I have a greater and greater sense I have how to say it have begun to approximate myself yes a greater and greater sense I am gradually becoming the how do you say it the imprecision of Pasiphaë a for example cousin yes or perhaps friend who stopped writing decades ago

:::: catastrophe chorus

accuse me

It is

true

but it is also true

Shall I repeat

The sun

of a child

gathered stones.

nothing

is communicable by the art of writing.

for the nights and days are long.

I let myself

fall until I am bloody.

But of all the games, I prefer the one about the other . I pretend

that comes to visit me and that I

The house is the same size as the world;

Perhaps I have created the stars

my redeemer
my redeemer

my redeemer

MAUREEN OWEN

noir came in from the night   warmed itself
by our fire

of the river   of the water
working its way through   our tilting geometry

for Sasha Steensen

"holiness that is a condition   independent
of deity"

We want to light a candle in a holy place   as we did when
We were younger   but we no longer believe in god

rowing through clutter   what's left of the path   as if this
morning light   crammed itself into a prank   uncrowded disarray   framed
into evaporate   our arms   strapless   tho any
string may be a yoke   We were hello   nudged
by the nose   of nature   nodding to wearable signs
putting that mood until   orbit layers played inference
It's been enough to shift   I cannot kneel
Kneel down!   Kneel Down!   But

I can not kneel

the "theatre of war"   is not   theatre
not   a play

or
a chorus from behind a grillwork

to not to want to put   a meaning to it   so much invisible
the war's invisible   summer's community of raspy hummers
full throated chorus under the billowing gauze curtain   invisible

August always makes me think of Faulkner   the leaning long slow
weight of the heat   the heaviness of bodies great expanses of thigh
languid locust and catalpa   rustling   motion whispering to herself

as tho that detail of Rembrandt's red slippers   in *Susanna und die beiden alten*
breathed at the dark ochre of their placement

but into the very core   needing like herding
above blue skies white clouds

warbling conversing from the barbeque next door
heads bob and pulse the fence top

late summer floating breezes trees

Just Another Day on Mars or let's look at the map later

the shadow of the ant moves at exactly the same speed as the ant
(does) only a little to her right levitating over the terra cotta almost
skimming almost
sailing on a salt tile sea

the wars have ruined the palace powdered interiors sprawling wigs
the pure flat surface of the land turned
into a source of mockery it winds along
only as a kind of release waiting for them to arrive back

it starts with in the distance of the egg tempera a dense grove of (trees)
quickening then ominous so ending up completely

it starts with being pushed aside above the surface of the water
simply too many mountains to acquire

it begins pliable a red red sand a red red sand

Popped

Or

A cat so black it had only eyes
A patch of high grass at the edge of
our confidence

on the floor of the brain the hippocampus reclines an odalisque with raised arms
clothes not bothering (fragrances) spicy amber Somehow inhale it now bergamot
our night catapults way up & under her vision a mirror

metropolis eyes sleeping in a dish the only ones not looking at the camera

and this all about how she meant to stay a maquette without being done or having not
been done eliciting how many and just as much by the next subtraction

did looks got in her way? holding the breaths that
flat reveals lined in rubber without closure the Balm wasn't seamless

she had scrambled her directions and now she was rambling

in an aura of replicas she circled herself

like private moonlight on a beach just passing through

MICHELLE NAKA PIERCE

from *CONTINUOUS FRIEZE BORDERING RED*

As you sleep metaphorically, you try to understand the dorsal aspect of the body. Though not your first crossing, you are on the outside, inside this once removed zone, just beyond the city. Underground you hear languages not easily recognized, and the sounds are muffled, as though submerged. Hold yourself underwater, placed ever so gently in the hand, like an uncompromising narrative. Much of your time is spent examining little movements, between center and cinder, for instance. For the first time, you begin to feel your age in the arch, Achilles, and left fin. In the unexamined clinamen. You meet everyone you know in letters or at the long syllable's edge: to foreground the aspirated consonants, the dripping vowels. The page is wet and moisture distorts meaning and vision. If objects contain the infinite, then you are only a shade of red. You are in place and displaced simultaneously. As the daughter of an immigrant, you've had barriers established for you. Not by your mother, but the union. Not the union exactly, but the war and the occupation that followed. How to be eastern when due west, in a city that sets in burnt orange. Your skin, in the end, is a similar shade of foreign. You are other overcoming otherness. You are different in the corners under the same shade, under a protested focus. Your self-exam reveals a macula, which may be the result of age or the result of crisis. Winter glides along the force of sacrifice. All room in shadow. The immigrant is seen as exotic, but the offspring ugly and deformed, except when a child. Then neighborhood teenage girls want to walk you around the block in a stroller, as though you were a doll, which gives you reoccurring nightmares about being kidnapped. They want to strip you of your clothes where no one will see. In this unkempt sentence, in this lattice of vagueness, lies violence. Stain upon stain upon tender withering letter. You are an ordinary color. A neglected Tuesday. You are not that which is not white. But then again, maybe you are: fucking hyphen. Your "struggle is to see [and be seen] from both perspectives at once." Color peeling off its object. Separation is difficult under any degree of order. A clot occurs in the temporal lobe, and you seep into that sticky mass. You desire to soothe the discoloration, the wall of red, the lack of breathing room. Single color in an arrangement of equation, not ordinary. There were no rooms but room and a limit. There was an occupation, and the space within was a space within. You unthread the hem: reconfigure the shades between reds. White walls surround you. Your presence in this absence complicates the sensation of emptiness: o n c e a b o r d e r h e r e.

PATRICK PRITCHETT

THE FAMINE ELEGIES

1.

The famine is not of spirit.
We are drowning in spirit.
The famine is not a lack of anything
but its lack stains everything.

The famine runs us out
to the bitter end.
Carnal bodies heated by
unremitting sorrow.

Or is it dust for bread
and for a time
no more time?
The inconstant beauty

of these sparrows
on the porch.
The flowers, too,
dandled over the edge.

2.

The basics of light.
A bloom looms
in a well of shadow.
Last blue blur

of sundown
measuring its own decay.
A day and its arc
sputter. Faith, but no cure.

3.

How to read the signs
and will they guide us
or make us go blind?
Whose fire I can see

white limbs running down
and whose fissure blazes
to make a bear dance
or melt a star?

4.

Beings, plighted.
Without respite even under
the sky the entire field
is made to weep. For what?

Ground unfinds again
the turmoil of belonging
to one fixed site.
Amenities of passage.

The famine is what
opens the granaries.
The trees unsuspended
in their flight.

5.

At the stroke of downfall
you lift your head.
This is your life
come at you in slices.

Could I say what
spoke me
if I ever knew?
Rather cast the crumbs

of this manual back
into the sea
and the sea's
casuistries, too.

6.

Creeley
says everything—

We know
it's true.

We've been there
and we're lost

inside a black frame
on a white wall

it may rescue
or destroy us.

Emptiness
is a form of
thinking

the poem testing itself
against
the real.

An echo
of what was heard
once

and still
distantly
remembered.

7.

The care of
this world
is given

to fools

and it is by
their happiness
we lose our way.

8.

I dreamt
Saint Emily
came to me late one night

all crinoline
and dark air

and further into summer
she was beyond
its ghost

a glass of sherry
murmuring
sweet apocalypse

and thunder

She tendered
her hand

furious
like the day

when August
and everything

burned down low

She said:
dear boy
we are not saved.

CHRIS PUSATERI

from *THE LIBERTIES*

ARNOS GROVE

It's said North London is bucolic.
Its thought process sounds like a slowly approaching train.

There are birds and there are birds.

        Bucolic
      yet still
    in need of
barbed wire

We say *proximity to London* when there is no London anywhere.

The train now approaching is for Uxbridge.

RUSLIP

He is going to Uxbridge.

The announcement on the train says
    This train is for Uxbridge, but when it reaches Acton Town, it says
    This train is for Ruslip. There are
      no accentless voices. *Good service is*
    operating on all London Underground lines. Like real travel & not
        a simulation, it has its variables.

What is the unattended article? Who will attend it?

This is not
        illegible script: its vehicle is motion. Take only taxis on the rank.

At Ruslip, they announce this train is going straight through
to Uxbridge (which the train conductor
pronounces *Ux*-bridge).

He gets off at Ruslip.

We'll pause here a short while to even out gaps in the service.

REGENT'S PARK

will turn his attention to other projects entirely
as long as I'm talking to my ability's best
he would kill for an invitation, jealous of the attention the animal
received from his wife
but I feel like it's a little clichéd to say
I hate it when my lips get dry, especially on the plane
I feel like I have a mask
Just lying on my bed, listening to tunes,
I never loved a star so much
Wished on it, lying on my bed, listening,
Buy them lip balm, but don't wear makeup,
I think I'm being natural, having confidence, you know
When I created disco, I founded friendship, I have sixty bests,
Sincerely, yours, close the line, time to climb,
text the word to 8-doubleone-doublenine for your chance to win

WATERLOO

Sometimes, you can tell
by how the feet hit the pavement
that it'll be a beautiful woman there
when you look up.

Let's now upload the previous shift's data. The oblique sound of a nose
being blown.

At one stop: *This is a service update: the Victoria line is suspended because of* **strike action**. This remark, two stations down: *Victoria line is suspended because of* ***industrial actions.*** Language is
only standard
when circumstances are routine.
A woman with red hair & turquoise socks

sucks on a limegreen lollipop.

And at the all-change: *Victoria line is suspended because of* **labor negotiations**.
So much to learn
about the speaker and his sympathies,
just by
hearing what passes.

GREEN PARK

The air is dank in the deeper tunnels,
the brick wall as old as the woods.
Ration mortar, you might guess.

A delay coming into Green Park (*an incident*, they say, so as to tell you
pro forma, without letting anything slip). This
is an art form, an exercised awareness.

There are whole days when it might as well be night. Tanned bodies
on holiday in Tunisia are not the measure of trauma. The trains run
oblivious to any but their own schedules and life again imitates
the automatic where
it's a split difference—nothing ventured; poetry, accidentally.

HIGHBURY & ISLINGTON

If you're not comfortable in public spaces, you won't be comfortable
in private. What serves our changing notions is chiming in your pocket.
Tweets—'a society of strangers,' natter, natch.

And sometimes,
the observations are as plain as
the seats are uncomfortable.

Then, you conceal your *r*'s
under your vowels. This nicety
has just departed your generalized nervousness and become part of your
rarified other

another's
other will
sit beside.

There are days
            & there are paintings of days
                        that occur before your computer
            as it shows you life
as it might be (could have been) elsewhere.

There are days
            & there are photos
                        & there are afternoons of you,
                                    the dumbed-down cousin of texting.

What has just been recorded for posterity
            is unfathomable even
                                    if you
                        were you. The Greeks and their privacy,
            the Romans and their porticos   & me
                        with my shaking black grip

standing before the aperture.

GREAT PORTLAND STREET

Biometrical information like a print from a boot you bought. Snowflakes
            less unique
when they cover you by the thousands—it's just a sensation: cold

but use is as use does

its value
places you at the scene

tells us not what you did

the evidence physical, the circumstances circum-
            scribe you.

CHESHAM

You can tell a lot
about a village by
its prevalent forms of rebellion

funded largely
by mother's labor

how like life
the many aspects of Plato's cave
are everywhere apparent
one is surprised to find there again
so fast, so little time,
where could truth lie but exactly where we're looking

in cuttings, edited footage, the very leavings

JED RASULA

RECTIFYING THE EVENTUAL

The adventure of a family of kangaroos, of course, is an extremely clear example of a comic interpretation of the formula of ecstasy.
Sergei Eisenstein

that was then
this is now

as now now
as it was then

when then
was a former now

known in nouns
and sometimes verbs

as if "y" and "sometimes w"
were vowels, & vowels were owls

*

the string navigates itself into a contortion
and then the shoe is tied

if you can't persuade the string to do it
you'll have to do it yourself

it could be you you :
know it could be you

it could be you you

it could be you you :

know know

*

the paper clip of cognition
still springs eternal in the out box

where the next you
denudes the me that used to be

(I used to be you, you know
 but got used to being me instead

 until nothing was left
 but density & snag)

*

a door ajar
a tooth or two
a smiling faucet
& all at once
the mind is like a clown act

comparing a cow with a worm
a norm with an arm
an absolute
        with modesty or crumbs

meanwhile
a piece of meat tries to make the scene

two drops of saliva go down the street
fetching the arrow of time
from the quiver of space

& suddenly there you are

all night long
stooped over the burner
steaming the postage stamp of the concept
off the envelope of representation

watching words bubble up
to captivate experience

*

there's a mountain of pacing about
that wears a trench of you
down to sprung plush
gulp on gulp

there's also a mountain
of meaningless Hercules
where dowel pins owl
hour by horrible hour

there's an estuary
where meaning doesn't mix
with matter—what's the matter
with that estuary? what's it mean?

instead of beginning, middle & end:
beginning the middle again
& again, end to end

as though As If were a cage
in which birds were stuck to the sky
& feathers were weather

*

ooooooh, looky here
here's an experimental flesh they want you to wear
so you don't wake up
you wake *down*

wondering
what did god the goad   learn to think
to make matter   talk back with?

Mr. Blank is out there Bossing the Universe
                    on your behalf

this is it, Land of the Knowing Look:
everywhere you go
the fecund minimum
stares you down

so there must be a "self" that correlates to all this
rubble of experience
[—shall I (de)posit one?]

what's up? what's down? & *what's it to you ?*

does the hound of the Baskervilles bark at the Owl of Minerva?

Let's have that again, does the…. No,
never you mind.

A sentence and a worm are *stupid animals.*
The dusk is in *French.*
Danger is *one new word.*
A rap on the door is an index.
Why do *cinders* grumble?
Call it The Average Itch of the Phantom Rider.
The ball gown reverts to mystical mud.
No universal ego, just an *ash-pit.*

It's only a technical maelstrom, so let it go.

Doctor Because might know who you are.
Let's give him a ring, shall we?

His feet are webbed, his neck is long,
his iridescent demeanor will astound you.

He's the sole survivor of four of his kind.
But he's not what you think.

His intentions suffuse you with gravity
and yet you float. His happy children
smear about like a slick paste
until dawn breaks.

He is used to you by now.
His pivot is a legend
raised on happy food.

Bring me a glass of water
he says to the spark.

Like an oiled axle
he shines in the watery light.

He's a bubble
pleading at your door.

*

Or is it pulling?
Pulling or purring
it purrs. He purrs.
It's a person
enabled to appear:
a fast poison singular
relieving itself
in the dis-
continuous ex-
tremities
of the subject.

*

It would have been a zero day in County Whiteout
a squirrel imploded with the force of a bull
or was it you?
& if I wonder was it you
do you wonder it too?

It was a very old hour in the math of afternoon
a kangaroo peaceably bullies an owl
it will be a very old owl

I was an odd duck, wasn't I
but where was I sitting?

He could move a ballerina with his mountain
to make ends meet
until someone blinks first
then yesterday is over

It might as well be a day off
to hear you tell it:
what else did you tell it to do?
"Go home, little mouse," the bayonet says
to the friend or maybe cousin of the voice
voiceless in an anecdote
the speech therapist knows
who gives you measles over the phone

which is not at all the same as saying
less & less of the same thing over & over
until less is more, more or less, unless you let that
cat out of the bag, & more and more of "less is more"
is more than you can take—& what's more,
it's there for the taking

("take it or leave it
 but where does taking it leave it?")

how else would you know
what Mr. Sugar does after dark

but it's still a neat trick how it all came back tomorrow

MARTHE REED

AWAKENING: GRAND ISLE

After Kate Chopin

could hear again
the water
the hot south
passed through her
making her eyes burn

the reeds
the saltwater pools
little gray weather—
among the orange
low, drowsy

solitude
flushed and
muddled like wine
a first breath of
the beach

sporadic
acres of chamomile reaching
away still
and lemon trees
the gaunt

water-oaks
the stretch of yellow
melting hazily
blue
water of

the sun
clamoring, murmuring
along the white
up and down
a broken wing

circling
it had no beginning
the sycamore tree
the hum of bees
pinks filled the air

THE OLD CITY

unrecognizable good this
pure magenta
its lush
roses

populate the old city
recreates it
more mystical
more matter

-of-fact
a glittering wheel turning us
inside out
a fabric of abandoned gestures

"Will you be there?"
perilous and not that
somewhere in this mess
a river

being the future
a set of words spelling numerous
attracts her
such vivid exhaustion

"Hurry up!"
coastal geometries

sinking into the air
a fundamental circumstance

the bushes flowering furiously
"Well, I—"
sleep's impossible meat

PLAQUEMINE AQUIFER REPORT (EPA, 10/7/04)

It was a beautiful spring morning—warm & quiet with mists.
Dorothy Wordsworth

it was a beautiful contaminant transport
a beautiful original source area
beautiful probable source

& quiet solid phases eroded
quiet turbulent river flow
quiet cutbank

its was a beautiful turn in the stream
a beautiful channel each
beautiful shift to the outside turn

& quiet any contaminant
quiet any released at or
quiet near site 13

it was a beautiful fluvial process
a beautiful site 13
beautiful facilitated the movement

& quiet cutting tends to be
quiet prominent at the likely
quiet significant source

it was a beautiful direct ((in direct)) contact
a beautiful upper sand aquifer
beautiful once contaminants moved

& quiet Plaquemine Aquifer
quiet aquifer
quiet upper sand

it was a beautiful transport
a beautiful Mississippi River transport
beautiful dispersed away

& quiet processes ((advection and
quiet dispersion)) contribute to
quiet plume growth ((feather

it was a beautiful headdress ornament
a beautiful funeral sheath)) likely not
beautiful like as

& quiet not
quiet described in this report
quiet lateral stream cutting

it was a beautiful preferential pathway
a beautiful pipeline
beautiful accelerated descent

& quiet cutting there
quiet vinyl chloride
quiet cis-1,2 Dichloreothene

it was a beautiful order of magnitude
a beautiful contaminant reach
beautiful Myrtle Grove wells

& quiet 20–40 year
quiet time frame
quiet 1964 Dow dioxin

it was a beautiful [formerly Morrisonville] spill
a beautiful racial
beautiful profiling of chemical

& quiet plant placement

quiet likely significant source
quiet area in black

it was a beautiful ((color line
a beautiful color line)) does not rule out
beautiful does not

& quiet rule out
quiet 1993 release
quiet the contaminated material

it was a beautiful no longer identifiable on the surface
a beautiful vinyl—
beautiful chloride in ground water

& quiet 97 ppb
quiet drinking water
quiet Myrtle Grove water supply

MATTHEW ROBERSON

THIS PLACED

DOWNTOWN

A counter covered in pink slips and white. A pen and a mechanical plaque announcing the date: June XX. Outside, air conditioners drip.

And the drugstore slash soda fountain. The florist's shop. The dance studio filled with girls in leotards and black and pink shoes.

There he stands.

His socks have gone damp with sweat, and he takes off his cap.

He knows that woman.

She's turned in the other direction. She doesn't see him. Her shoulders roll down on her frame. Her hips are opened. A knee bent.

She talks to a man he doesn't know. She smiles. Smiles. She lays a hand on the man's forearm and then gestures down the block. Is she laughing?

He steps to them, walking in the wake of a car the color of smashed plum. It has a bag taped over one window.

The car has a small trophy jutting from its hood. It might be called a medallion.

He stops to watch the car.

Then she moves, turning to leave, so he gets onto the sidewalk behind her.

She walks splayed, turning out first one foot and then other.

She's had her hair cut and colored. Her bra strap shows at the edge of her collar.

Her purse tugs the shirt up her hip. For a second, he sees the brown of her skin and thinks of bumps lit with fine hair and the wrinkles a waistband makes in flesh.

He closes his eyes to concentrate on the black of his eyelids. When he opens them, she's gone.

THE PARK

They paved the path along the river. On either side, flowering bushes. Beyond, a depth of trees.

He steps over places where the blacktop has melted in weather.

At every turn, benches overlook water.

A footbridge ahead, its pilings sunk. Beyond it, more path, more bushes, more woods. He hears birds and sees squirrels.

Men and women walk by and run, and boys and girls pass on skateboards, bikes. They sit by the river, stripped down on the sand.

Dogs strung on leashes.

How many times has he walked this path? How many times? Mornings and just before dusk? Past dark, with the moon. With his wife. With his children. He has, he knows, often.

But they don't live here. They never have.

And the path once ran past a park. It once looped a pond.

Didn't he bring a blanket here on that first night? Didn't that happen long ago?

He knows this: His hair is hot from the sun. It's the middle of the day.

He has no trouble walking or breathing. His body feels fine.

Goldenrod grows in every open space.

He knows the boy skating by, he thinks. That boy there.

The brown hair, the thin edge of the boy's jaw. No more than nine, and happy.

He knows how the boy holds his shoulders above his chest, and the curve of his back. The way he pushes with his legs and turns his head to shout at friends.

How he lives in what he does.

He thinks he could see the boy skating in winter, in a rink, in hockey pads and a helmet, and he'd still know this boy from the others.

The way the boy uses his arms to balance.

The boy is waving. The boy is waving at him.

He waves back. He says, Oh.

Oh.

Maybe the boy didn't wave, or not at him.

He holds his own hand in the air, and the boy has gone away around a turn.

He doesn't think he'll see the boy again.

He turns himself and starts to walk.

STRIP MALL

Rusted cars fill the lot. Trucks on their high tires, and minivans rounded like links of sausage.

One car leaves, out into traffic, and one replaces it. And again.

He stands and sees an older couple emerge from a car, and from one a younger pair, and then a man who shuts his door unlocked.

Stains and trash on the pavement.

Storefronts of glass in painted metal. The sidewalk fronting them stretches a half-mile. Small squares of gravel shelter saplings fixed by wires.

A bicycle rack. A garbage can. Parking signs.

He walks, looking in each window, wondering why he's here.

Not to buy a cell phone. Or a sandwich. Or a haircut. He's not here to frame a painting or a photo.

Not to buy a book. Not to buy computer parts.

He doesn't need to mail a package. He does not want a cold drink.

A woman walks to the parking lot with a package she sets down before opening her car door.

He hasn't seen this woman before.

Blue veins mark her legs. She has white skin on her heels. Long shorts with pockets. A purse on a strap. Thin, stiff hair he can't imagine touching.

She pulls the purse off her shoulder, lifts the package, which isn't a package, at all. It's a little girl, maybe five, with long, light brown hair—a little girl with baby fat arms.

She shouldn't need lifting into the car, but she won't go on her own. She doesn't want to, he thinks.

The face she makes. Her folded arms.

She has red juice around her mouth.

She wears dirty pants a size too small and a necklace of plastic beads over her shirt.

How beautiful she is.

She can't belong to this woman who shuts the car door too hard.

He should say something. He wonders why they don't see him watching?

He wonders if he could open the passenger's door and ask to go.

STORE

The scuffed linoleum floors. The carts on bad wheels.

Managers in the elevated office.

The gumball machines by the automatic doors.

Racks of candy and toenail clippers in the checkout aisles.

The produce. The meat cases.

Shelves and shelves of eggs.

Old people at tables by the bakery, drinking coffee. The men wear ironed pants. The women watch the shoppers.

Workers in matching clothes, and workers in smocks behind counters, and workers fixing flowers.

The pharmacist has a white coat.

Swinging doors that open onto the back rooms.

The dirty bathrooms up front.

Chickens rotating on spits at the deli. That smell.

Freezer after freezer on the floor, open like trenches. Others upright behind fogging glass.

Aisles with cereal. Aisles with cans of tomatoes. Aisles with birdseed and bleach.

The customers trolling the shelves, picking items for their carts.

That man the next aisle over. That bearded man in his sweater, handling cans. That man doesn't seem to have a thought. Look at him relax into his shoes, humming. He can't imagine someone watching him. He doesn't seem worried or sad or guilty.

He's never done a thing wrong.

He's never cheated on a test. Never stolen a pack of gum. Never walked on a bill.

Not him. Not that man.

He never emptied out another man's life.

Well then who did?

He uncurls an index finger into a pistol and thinks. Then he points.

Maybe it is that guy.

THE BARBER'S SHOP

Like every other Barber's shop ever, chairs spinning on fat poles alongside a counter with jars of blue fluid and combs and clippers and dryers for hair.

The TV showing reruns. Seats filled with men reading magazines.

The snap of the capes. Hair on the floor. Talcum.

When he steps in, the room goes still.

They seem to know him here.

How?

The barber nods and the pace of the place catches again.

What do they know?

THE RESTAURANT

The table has one short leg. The red and white plastic tablecloth. A plate with a rolled napkin on top. A fork, a knife, a spoon. Slatted blinds over the window.

A counter by the back, its bell and spinning ring of slips.

That woman again. That woman who walks splayed. Maybe he knows her from here.

Maybe he comes here because he knows her.

She's a waitress, but not his. She doesn't look his way.

He wants her to look. He wants to see how her teeth sit forward to catch her lip.

He wants to see the hair touching her neck.

She has the smallest wrinkles in the skin by her eyes.

He thinks she must smell of food, and clothes that have been worn all day.

He imagines folding her to him with one arm as he sits. He imagines resting his head on the round of her stomach.

He remembers doing this. He remembers crying.

To the man who comes to the table, he says he's here to eat supper. He says he'll have some of this, and a piece of that, and a drink.

The woman walks through a door to the rear and doesn't come back.

OUTSIDE TOWN

He drives and drives past houses stretched like lights along the road. He passes fields filled with mud and cows. He passes stands of trees. He smells wood smoke and thinks he could go on like this, slipping out of one place into another. He can barely steer for the sun in his eyes.

HOME

A room. A yellow sofa on casters. Carpeting.

And another room, its table covered in mail still sealed and circulars and plastic cups.

In the kitchen, a full glass under the dripping tap.

A new mouse in a trap he puts gently in the trash.

The bathroom with black and white checkered tile. A rusted medicine cabinet with a slot for razor blades. A shower stall, its plastic floor sunk like the peeled end of an egg.

He goes to the bedroom and lays down.

On the dresser two belts. In the closet, shirts. A pair of boots on the floor.

Above his head a window with one sheer curtain. The window is closed.

He lays on the bed on his back in his clothes.

He doesn't have a book to read. The clock by the bed is only a clock.

There's no TV.

He folds his hands on his chest. He feels his heart turn.

He feels the solid wall of his ribs. The unbroken bones of his fingers. The covering skin.

He's uninjured.

Healthy.

Some would say lucky.

People have said it.

That he lives.

Without a scratch.

Only he doesn't feel it.

He doesn't feel lucky.

Not lucky.

He only feels awake.

And he can leave his eyes open.

Or he can close them.

Open.

Closed.

It won't make a difference.

There's nothing to see here.

LASANTHA RODRIGO

MOVING LANTERNS

After monsoon rain subsided, after darkness seeped into the suburban neighborhood, after Mrs. Perera plucked star-shaped white blossoms to offer Buddha, a host of quiet fireflies invaded our garden. They dotted every corner with moving lanterns of life: above the yellow orchids hiding in darkness, near the Chinese guava tree, over the light-reflecting brilliance of the patio floor. Dad watched Crown Court on the television, so we had to maintain pin-drop silence. Mom took Sha and me out of the house and sat on a fading red patio chair, closing the door behind her, leaving Crown Court within, escaping the unpredictable wrath of the house. The moon tried to expose the contours of her aging face, and Sha and I collected fireflies. We got them to land on our palms until they got tired of us and flew away. In the buttery moonlight, Mom couldn't hide her eyes, glistening in their moistness.

"Mom, is there a rabbit on the moon?" I asked her.

"Yes, there is. Can you see the outline? Look! Can you see the ears?"

"Are they ears? Is he listening to us, then?"

"He is, so you have to be a good boy."

Sha had three fireflies on her palm, and she was oblivious to us. I could catch a glimpse of her brown eyes full of wonder.

"Then he probably heard Dad shouting at you," I said.

Mom hesitated before replying, "Perhaps."

* * *

I remember very vividly how fireflies arrived in abundance after a monsoon rain. They seemed to know when it was time to come out and not get their flimsy wings wet. After a cool rain, the air smelled fresh and invigorating. When fireflies were out, Sha and I came out, too. Our tender minds were elated to see the little lights all over the garden. Such a miracle it was, to us. Our eyes full of marvel in the darkness of the night, we wanted to find out where they came from, where they went. We never could, but we could always find joy in those little lights. In those flying lanterns. We knew that in a few hours, they'd be gone to a place we didn't know about. A beautiful mystery. An enigma.

"Where do you think they come from?" I asked Sha.

"I'm not sure, but maybe we can find out. Shall we follow them?"

"Yeah. What if we get lost?"

"Don't be a girl! I know the way."

"I don't think you do."

"I always do. You know I do."

"All right, then. You go first. I'll follow."

So we went in search of their elusive homes. We never found them. We didn't give up, though. Every now and then, when the garden was dotted with those moving lanterns, we followed them. But they were always gone like in a fairy tale. Sha and I made a pact.

"When we grow up, we'd be faster and smarter. Shall we try then?" Sha asked.

"That's a good idea."

"Don't tell anyone, though. It's our secret."

"All right."

"Promise?"

"Yes."

"Cross your heart?"

"Cross my heart."

It's been decades since I was fascinated by those moving lanterns. Here in Illinois, I have rarely seen fireflies. Just the other night, though, I saw two of them near the back entrance of my apartment. They brought me Chinese guavas, yellow orchids, and a bit of home. I thought of Mom's eyes, glistening in the moonlight.

My life was a song. Some parts were dissonant. Some mellifluous. Decorated foreign aunties on my windowsill. Mom's piping hot black tea with sliced ginger root in it. My pink room. Playing Rapunzel. Combing my strawberry blond wig, waiting for Prince Charming. Dad's arms around me on the orange belly of the motorbike. Benji's ears standing up when he heard my footsteps. His moist, black nose. Pausing in the mild drizzle to smell a pure white coffee blossom on the way to the bus stop. My long, black, silk kurta flying in the wind at the Puget Sound Waterfront. Fireflies. Their tiny lanterns of light against the dark night. That tiny hope. I will remember these, the happy, the beautiful, the exotic, the compassionate. Tomorrow, I might be left with nothing but these memories. Then I will close my eyes and imagine those moving lanterns.

JOHN RUSSELL

THE MAN WHO ARRIVED HOME AFTER A TRIP TO LONDON AND WAS GREETED BY HIS WIFE (OR LOVER) AT O'HARE

When I arrived home from an otherwise uneventful trip to London (there had been a disturbance of some kind between one of those air marshals and an elderly gentleman who insisted that smoking was indeed allowed on international flights), my young wife—at least I think we were married at the time, if I'm thinking of the right woman here, so many of these things have become confused in my mind, though I'm quite sure that there was an age difference involved—told me what a man most fears: "I'm in love with someone else and am leaving." I had just come through Customs at O'Hare, and we had begun walking towards the car when she told me. It was a bright spring day with a slight chill in the air. My first thought was, "Couldn't she have picked a less-perfect day for her announcement?" My second thought was: "Well, now what!" We had a long drive ahead of us to our home out in the country in Central Illinois, what Chicagoans mistakenly refer to as "Downstate." What had gotten into her? Why now? What had happened? Who was she?

We drove mostly in silence. What was there to say? Her decision seemed both sudden and final. As we came up the long driveway to the house, she said I should put the dogs away for the night (I could hear them barking as I got out of the car), and then we might want to spend time tying up "loose ends" (her words). After all this time together, we just had to tie up some loose ends?

I was hesitant to ask her who the man was. A mutual friend? Some complete stranger? A neighbor? An old boyfriend? One of my colleagues? Had she perhaps fallen in love with more than one of them? When I finally did ask who it was, she said it was none of my business, that it was a private matter, and that my asking was just another example of how much I had always tried to control her. Later, almost as an afterthought, she said that it was the handyman who'd been doing odd jobs around the house. When I asked her whether a handyman was the answer to her dreams, she said, "He's not just a handyman, as you call him. He's an artist. He has ambitions. He's going to start a rock band or make movies, or even become a painter, and he writes poems." I thought, He's already a painter, of houses and garages! She said the man loved her and accepted her in a way that I never had or could. I thought this strange because, as far as I knew, he'd been doing his "odd jobs" at our house for only a few weeks, and so how much love and acceptance could there be?

Before leaving that night, she came over to where I was sitting, kissed me gently on the forehead, and said, "I hope you won't be too upset. You're strong. You'll be fine." I had already been thinking of the ways in which I could kill myself that evening. I said, "Well then, have a nice life." She said, "I'm sure I will, and you have a nice life too! Let's stay in touch." In a minute or so, she came back inside the house and said, "That doctor's office called and said something about your tests. I forget. Better call them. Bye!" And off she went.

After she left, and long after her handyman's pick-up truck or car had disappeared down the driveway and out onto the country road, I went into her room. Scattered on her bed were dozens of what could only be called obscene photographs that the man must have taken of her, and she of him, as well as photographs of her with what seemed like old boyfriends. I didn't know whether I should be feeling envious or disgusted. I then threw up on the bed and photographs. She had turned out to be someone I hardly knew, even after all this time. My future wasn't looking very good. And now I had one hell of a mess to clean up in the morning.

The next day, I found the journal that she'd been keeping for a very long time. Most of it was filled with lists of "things to do," and most of these things related to what she'd planned to accomplish in her life in years to come. It didn't appear that I had figured into those plans very much, if at all. Many of the entries concerned former boyfriends and gave rather detailed descriptions of their sexual adventures together and her hopes for what she'd do with them in the future. I'd known nothing of these things. Who was she? Who had she been? Was it possible to have known so little about her? One entry indicated that she wanted to sleep with as many men as possible and that, after her, they'd never again be satisfied with any other woman. This is a goal for one's life? Another entry read: "We had one of our 'talks' last night. I tried not to listen to a word he said." This was one of the few mentions of me.

The last entry was quite confusing: "I'll miss him. He understood me better than anyone else ever has. I know he loves me, but this just isn't fun. I need more fun in my life." Fun?

What had it all been about? What had any of my relationships with women been about?

2.

My wife at the time had always been somewhat unstable. She used to take several (what she called) "naps" each day. One therapist after another, but always concluding in more endless "naps." We often argued whether getting out of bed at nine in the morning and then returning an hour later for a "nap" could possibly count as a "nap." She said I "shamed" her by saying this ("shame" was one of her favorite words). Later, she'd say she was thinking of all the ways she could kill herself. When she wasn't napping, she was often eating, and this frequently led to various gastrointestinal problems, the forms of which she would describe in great detail to me. And when she wasn't eating, she was dieting and buying books on dieting. What she rarely did was clean the house. Three entire rooms were filled with her "things," usually her "projects" that would get half-completed and then put into one of the rooms. We had separate bedrooms because I couldn't make it to the bed at night without tripping over stacks of old newspapers (unread), piles of catalogs and magazines (usually unread), dishes, knives, forks, and other kitchen utensils, shoes, piles of dirty laundry, two broken rocking chairs, dead plants, empty bottles of anti-depressants, and a series of electrical chords that were somehow intricately connected. She said that she liked a house that felt "lived in." I had a somewhat different view on the subject.

Despite our occasional disagreements, I hadn't expected to find her note that night when I returned from my trip to London. Unexplained delays at Heathrow, an eight-hour flight, a woman on the plane who rather insistently told me her life story (or that part of it that involved sordid matters related to her relationships with men), the usual long line at passports at O'Hare, my wife's failure to meet me at the International Terminal as she almost always did as I emerged from Customs, the three-hour bus ride to Downstate (as Chicagoans always call it), and then this note that inelegantly read: "I'm outta hear. Don't forget to feed the dogs. Life is about change. Water the plants." There was a P. S.: "I found someone else." She might have at least checked her spelling.

Well, that was that. The end. Years (was it years?) of what I had thought of as a good marriage. Bills usually paid on time, a cleaning lady to put things in somewhat recognizable order, but then the unusual number of naps, which in part explained the need for a cleaning lady. But a great deal of mutual caring, I thought, if not always expressed very well.

My last memory of her was that of a smiling face, as she waved goodbye to me when I boarded the bus for O'Hare a week before. She had a remarkable smile. Not a hint that she must have already been composing in her head that heart-felt letter.

Because of an argument we had had the night before I left for London—which I won't go into here—I hadn't called her while away. The basis for the argument is too embarrassing for me to describe. I knew that we were approaching that time for yet-another soul-searching talk when I came home, the shedding of tears, mutual pleas for forgiveness, my asking her whether she had any plans for killing me, and then a few long yawns that signaled she was exhausted and ready for (what else?) bed. In retrospect, I find it strange that I would, on occasion, feel as though I must ask her whether she had any plans for killing me. Perhaps those fears arose because of her inclination towards violence.

Instead of the much-repeated talk, there was just the silence of an empty house, with the dogs barking out back, and her rather cold note. Wasn't there some other way of saying, "I'm outta hear"? Was her misspelling just another way of showing how utterly indifferent to and careless about anything related to me? I was in a state of shock.

There was nothing to be done except to find the cleaning lady's phone number and see when she could make it out here to the country to our (or rather now, my) house. We'd had good years (was it really years?) together, more than good; I thought we had been secure with each other, that the world had seemed a safe place. At times I had thought we had even been content, if not always enchantingly happy. I knew that I had loved her. But one can never even imagine what is going on in the mind of another. Here today, gone tomorrow, as the saying goes. Life moves on. You never know what's coming next. I soon got tired of hearing these clichés rolling around in my head. They were of no comfort. Perhaps one day I'd figure out what had happened and why. But this seemed rather unlikely.

SELAH SATERSTROM

ON WRITING FROM THE EXCLUSION ZONE

Graphite is an important material for the construction of both historical and modern nuclear reactors as it is one of the purest materials manufactured at industrial scale and it retains its properties at high temperatures.
Gareth B. Neighbour, Management of Ageing in Graphite Reactor Cores; 2007

We saw graphite scattered about. Misha asked: "Is that graphite?" I kicked it away. But one of the fighters on the other truck picked it up. "It's hot," he said.... Then those boys...they went up to the roof, they went up the ladder...and I never saw them again.
Grigori Khmel, first responder, Chernobyl

It's like throwing a handful of fine graphite dust on a piece of paper to see where the hidden indentations are. It lets you see the words that were written on the piece of paper above it that's now been taken away and hidden.
Douglas Adams

PART I

Graphite, aerial, swaths down
and sticks to the crossroads. This lumen blooms
in fundamental pitch, slides sheen into the slip, towards a
gentle slope, in a field, the effervescent lumen transmigrating.

Accrual becomes mattered:
stitches congregate into the line. Above,
a jagged edge calibrated to past and future ruptures. And inside
the area thus created, a smaller version of itself. A memory
hardened into future fuels, emanation's proof, both.
Meanwhile a Biwa Lake Tree matures to fruition.

Perfect for animating the winds. Its bouquet is resilient.
If pressed upon, it springs back.

The abysmal lip: eroded as an old hung fang. Walking the plank, the abyss is less dense than imagined. At the edge of its Cadillac wide-assed swerving toward the vanishing point we could do as others have done. We could work this lip into land. We could settle the territory. A voice from somewhere, we don't know where, *says ancient history the story of the twelve tribes I'm bored tell me something I don't know don't let the door hit you where the good lord split you*, this goddamned screwball comedy in which our births map the thirty-eight slots of a roulette wheel. The story of a tomb-keeper heir to a kingdom though she doesn't know it. In which Odin hung from an Ash tree. The laborious opera concerning how we came to name the eternal. The glitch in the episodic situating the theme. The exquisite cold of being disregarded. The disgust of things feral. The shining hatred.

The line emits frequency. Vibrational waves that appear, in some dimensions, as humming chevron patterns. The frequency's edge, feathered through by ten thousand horizontal eyes en-gridding, as if ten thousand glass plates were stacked and everything was seen through this lens. There is only frequency. And the patterns it creates. A dust mote footnoting the invisible. *Here is what a fetal heartbeat looks like on a monitor in a county hospital in 1986.*

The line curves as a sweetheart neckline curves. It remembers that a reclining woman breathes. The larger shape is also that of a folding fan, if slightly open. In the bottom of each fold, a deep ravine. From one such ravine, a gray emergence, a graphite mound. The reclining woman posits the exquisite fan over her navel, shielding the passage that leads to the text. In the other world everything also exists. But in versions complicated by the softness that dissolution makes. Graphite writes its likeness. The portrait reaches into another hole inside of the one we are in. Erasure saturation is the line lining itself over. The portrait's hand makes shadow shapes behind the backlit sheet: here is a crow and here is a murder.

Failed punctums as recognized in the old-timey valley of death feeling. Proof that when conditions are conducive, expression unfurls, fern like. Accidents constitute the small town in the Hospitality State. On top of a botched remain, an ecosystem thrives. Surrounded by white space, shredded and whipped, clouds loom as if in a sticky photograph removed from a crime scene. Can I live here? Is there room for one more? Punctum, one in each eyelid, puncta lacrimalia.

A line, plucked, throws up a quivering bouquet.

A line lies next to another made of entirely different material. Connecting these, an illuminated string. All around, the remains of previous lines. One such hovers above the luminous string, its phantom paws touching all the surfaces. What was written there? Dark clouds slide in. How many times can one be consumed? More than once inside the original.

Inside the graphite mound, steaming remains in an array of contrary textures. Above the mound's toothy opening, weather or angels. They hold moisture and indicate hidden activity. Within the mound's cavernous chambers, the old passion plays slinging on a loop. Everything that has ever been. Is there as guts. Without regard to formal invention.

Outside, standing on the slope, we admire its silver, handsome qualities. We do not recall that it was this medium that caught the people's mouths in their final terror shapes. To be under the blinding light of the hand moving back and forth, back and forth. The atmosphere sounds: *we are voices speaking from the multi-path spectrum stream.*

The line has broken into nine parts, which correspond to the nine conditions. The line, broken, lifts its gentle necks to the morning. Emerging from the depthing spot, smeary swans constellating in orchestral precision. Come noon, the lines appear as needles floating in still water. Migration. Down. Silt. There is no advancing.

There is a sheet of paper so far away that we see it on the big screen, emergent and hemorrhaging, broadcasting star patterns and birth charts.

A raw garnet dug up from earth appears as a piece of burned glass and smells of warm dirt. How did this garnet come to rest here, pinned between sky and sea, a mineral between the here and hereafter? Lines made through the absenting of lines suggest their specter shapes into calligraphy. And someone arrives. A dead poet, she writes in an elegant script a melancholic poem featuring geese, a landscape, and reflections about death. How do the deceased live within the blurred calligraphic strokes dependent upon whatever it was we erased? Who was here first? The process of being read, truly read. One day our lines appear in some other's erasure. The garnet speck poised between sea and sky, the unpolished mineral of previous earths. In those earths there was vegetation, humidity,nakedness.

Finally night appears. As a black veil worn in August heat, a wax tablet written upon with an iron nail, a slate for punching out the dots. This is my favorite form of night. Below, a silver lake. In its natal and deathful surface, the whole process in a cloud-sea of parts. During the darkest nights what we have erased appears more luminous. What we have erased has power restored. There are times when everything deserves rest and it is given. There are times when graphite dreams and what has been erased passes its cool hand across a forehead and the fevered child within all things sleeps.

On April 26, 1986, explosions at a reactor at Chernobyl produced radiation effects almost fourteen times greater than the 2011 Fukushima Daiichi disaster in Japan and was four hundred times more powerful than the 1945 atomic bomb dropped on Hiroshima.

This essay was greatly energized by the photographs of Michael Kenna and his series Japan (2003) and Ratcliffe Power Station (2004). I looked at these photographs, as a meditative practice, for one hour each day for six weeks after being denied entry (twice within five years) to the Exclusion Zone in Pripyat, Ukraine (Chernobyl) where I hoped to do eco-poetic research. When applying for special research clearance in Chernobyl, in janky script, ghost-webbed over by many ancestral photocopies, it states: YOUR APPLICATION TO BE EXCLUDED.

DAVID SCHNEIDERMAN

13 THINGS WIKIPEDIA TELLS US ABOUT JOSEF MENGELE'S EXPERIMENTS AT AUSCHWITZ

1. Mengele used Auschwitz as an opportunity to continue his research on heredity, using inmates for human experimentation.

2. He was particularly interested in identical twins; they would be selected and placed in special barracks. He recruited Berthold Epstein, a Jewish pediatrician, and Miklós Nyiszli, a Hungarian Jewish pathologist, to assist with his experiments.

3. Mengele took an interest in physical abnormalities discovered among the arrivals at the concentration camp. These included dwarfs, notably the Ovitz family—the children of a Romanian artist, seven of whom were dwarfs. Prior to their deportation, they toured in Eastern Europe as the Lilliput Troupe.

4. Mengele's experiments also included attempts to change eye colour by injecting chemicals into children's eyes, various amputations of limbs, and other surgeries. Rena Gelissen's account of her time in Auschwitz details certain experiments performed on female prisoners around October 1943. Mengele would experiment on the chosen girls, performing sterilization and shock treatments. Most of the victims died, because of either the experiments or later infections.

5. "Once Mengele's assistant rounded up fourteen pairs of Roma twins during the night. Mengele placed them on his polished marble dissection table and put them to sleep. He then injected chloroform into their hearts, killing them instantly. Mengele then began dissecting and meticulously noting each piece of the twins' bodies."[13]

6. At Auschwitz, Mengele did a number of studies on twins. After an experiment was over, the twins were usually killed and their bodies

dissected. He supervised an operation by which two Roma children were sewn together to create conjoined twins; the hands of the children became badly infected where the veins had been resected; this also caused gangrene.[13]

7. The subjects of Mengele's research were better fed and housed than ordinary prisoners and were, for the time being, safe from the gas chambers, although many experiments resulted in more painful deaths. [17]

8. When visiting his child subjects, he introduced himself as "Uncle Mengele" and offered them sweets. Some survivors remember that despite his grim acts, he was also called "Mengele the Protector."[18]

9. Mengele also sought out pregnant women, on whom he would perform vivisections before sending them to the gas chambers.[19]

10. Auschwitz prisoner Alex Dekel has said:

    > I have never accepted the fact that Mengele himself believed he was doing serious work—not from the slipshod way he went about it. He was only exercising his power. Mengele ran a butcher shop—major surgeries were performed without anesthesia. Once, I witnessed a stomach operation—Mengele was removing pieces from the stomach, but without any anesthetic. Another time, it was a heart that was removed, again without anesthesia. It was horrifying. Mengele was a doctor who became mad because of the power he was given. Nobody ever questioned him—why did this one die? Why did that one perish? The patients did not count. He professed to do what he did in the name of science, but it was a madness on his part.[20]

11. An Auschwitz Prison Doctor has said:

    > He was capable of being so kind to the children, to have them become fond of him, to bring them sugar, to think of small details in their daily lives, and to do things we would genuinely admire…. And then, next to that,… the crematoria smoke, and these children, tomorrow or in a half-hour, he is going to send them there. Well, that is where the anomaly lay.[21]

12. The book *Children of the Flames*, by Lucette Matalon Lagnado and Sheila Cohn Dekel, chronicles Mengele's medical experimental activities on approximately 1,500 pairs of twins who passed through the Auschwitz death camp during World War II until its liberation at the end of the war. By the 1980s only 100 sets of these twins could be found. Many recalled his friendly manner towards them, and his gifts of chocolates. The older ones "recognized his kindness as a deception—yet another of his perverse experiments to test (our) mental endurance."[22] He would also kill them without hesitation, sometimes administering injections to the children or shooting them himself, and would dissect them immediately afterwards. On one evening alone he killed fourteen twins.[12]

13. In 1960 Hans Sedlmeier returned from Asuncion, Paraguay with a statement from Mengele that said, "I personally have not killed, injured or caused bodily harm to anyone." Mengele repeatedly insisted that he had not committed any crime, and that instead he had become a victim of a great injustice.[23][24]

SUSAN M. SCHULTZ

A MEDITATION ON MEDITATION

Define "meditation." The workings of the mind; a thinking through of issues, ideas; what introverts do. Redefine "meditation." Sitting, letting thoughts go, detaching from one's emotions. Write a sentence in which you use both meanings of the word. The sentence will fall apart in your hands, like wet drywall, refusing to wall in or wall out. White dust on a bathroom floor.

Malaika King Albrecht, whom I know from her exquisite writing on Alzheimer's, quoted Pema Chödrön yesterday on her Facebook wall: "You can cruise through life not letting anything touch you, but if you really want to live fully, if you want to enter into life, enter into genuine relationships with other people, with animals, with the world situation, you're definitely going to have the experience of feeling provoked, of getting hooked, of shenpa. You're not just going to feel bliss. The message is that when those feelings emerge, this is not a failure. This is the chance to cultivate maitri, unconditional friendliness toward your perfect and imperfect self."

Define "shenpa": usually translated as "attachment," Chodron calls it a "hook," a "sticky feeling," a "tightening." (Good teachers translate translations into literal feelings, those that work inside the body rather than on or in a cloud.) "We never get at the root, which last night I was calling the scabies. The root in this case is that we have to really experience unease. We have to experience the itch. We have to experience the shenpa and then not act it out."

When we adopted our daughter from a Kathmandu orphanage, she had scabies. She scratched and scratched, legs, arms, body. We had to apply poison to her skin to kill the insect intruders. So one of our first acts of parenting was to poison our daughter. The better for her to "attach" to us, in the positive way that word is used in parenting. "Attachment parenting" is considered a good thing in the magazines, while "attachment" causes suffering, according to Buddhist teachings. The sentence falls apart.

Early this summer, I did some Buddhist shopping (meditation and capitalism are eerily aligned) and purchased a meditation cushion and a mat. They are a lovely maroon color that my cat loves; some days we meditate together, he and I. Equilibrium was what I sought, but equilibrium was not what my sitting brought. At the Diamond Sangha in Palolo, where I went for a refresher in meditation technique, I had an intense urge to run screaming from the zendo. On my own cushion, I find my meditations punctuated by grief, by scheduling, by Tinfish ad copy, by compositions like this one. Intruders all.

What surprised me most, however, was that these meditations freed up anger. It is not *my* anger, I know, but an emotional field. I do not feel that yet! Anger is energy. Anger rides on waves of energy like a Carlos Beltran 400-foot home run into the body's upper deck. Anger does not answer to no. Anger fills the chest and means to explode, plasticity to everyday flexibility. (See Catherine Malabou.) I've found myself acting out, announcing my anger to colleagues, my husband. My mind has roiled with the usual poet-editor-angers, the no-one-notices-my-good-work self-pity festival. My feelings have not hurtled with such speed since my depression/anxiety disorder were successfully treated and my mind slowed to a liveable pace, a walk instead of a jetpack.

But as Chödrön points out, "We have to experience the shenpa and then not act it out." As Malaika writes, "It's called practice for a reason." Define "practice." The OED has it as: "The actual application or use of an idea, belief, or method, as opposed to the theory or principles of it; performance, execution, achievement; working, operation; (*Philos.*) activity or action considered as being the realization of or in contrast to theory." And I love how this sentence also crumbles, a broken tower of babel, as it juxtaposes the application of belief or theory with the contrast to theory. It is the operation of theory when theory falls away. It is the rain that comes after the clouds, as in Mānoa Valley, when the rainbows borrow a ride on the mist.

There is so much at which to be angry. I'm pissed off that everyone else is angry, too, the BMW drivers, the entire species of lone gunmen, radio shock jocks, my kids. Twenty-TWO new condo towers in Kaka`ako, really? Our neighbor loudly curses her kids mornings and evenings. I'm angry at Ralph Waldo Emerson for telling us in "Self-Reliance" that we are powerful, that we should never conform, that "nothing can bring you peace but yourself. Nothing can bring you peace but the triumph of principles," so that when we discover we are without power or control, we get angry. I'm angry at the notion that "the triumph of principles" is where we need to go. Then again, if Emerson had one more sentence, he might well undo this one.

MEDITATION: ON MY MOTHER'S ASHES

Life is a pure flame, and we live by an invisible Sun within us.
Sir Thomas Browne, "Urn-Burial"

I picked up my mother's ashes from the post office the other day; they came in a priority mail box, certified (not registered, as the post office employee told me was mandatory). "It's because they need to be under lock and key at all times," my own mail carrier told me later. The man at Georgetown University's Anatomical Donor section told me on the phone that UPS and FedEx do not deliver cremains. He was checking my address, which he (like everyone who calls from another time zone) could not pronounce. According to a certificate, which came in a plain envelope, my mother's body—she died on June 14, 2011—was cremated on September 2, 2012. Her remains arrived, then, a full year later to the Kāne`ohe Post Office.

The lead story in the *Honolulu Star-Advertiser* on September 16 was, "Rights clash amid dispute over mural." The mural, "Forgotten Inheritance," by Hans Ladislaus, was installed at the Convention Center 16 years ago. Since the 4th of September of this year, it's been covered over by a black cloth. Native Hawaiians, including those who protect bones against construction, asserted that "they were offended by the depiction of bones in the sand [left exposed to the elements] at the edge of the mural." According to Native American Legal Corporation lawyer, Moses Haia, "iwi [bones] of our ancestors provide us with our foundation. It's what makes us who we are."

A few weeks ago, an artist at Na Mea Hawai`i (a store at Ward Warehouse in Honolulu) told me about a group of native Hawaiians who very secretly bury the iwi in isolated locations on the Islands. In the old days, the person who hid the bones was killed, so that his secret could never be revealed. Many of these iwi are repatriated from museums, others from sites where rampant development is taking place—hotels, highrises, highways. In his law review essay on the iwi, Matthew Kekoa Keiley describes the burial of a young man's bones, and explains that "Na iwi ku puna represent the immortality of our ancestors. After the flesh decays, the bones remain. The bones of our Native Hawaiian ancestors symbolize an important link between our past, present, and future." From the sublime to the ridiculous, my google search also locates an episode of the new Hawaii Five-0 called "Ka Iwi Kapu (The Sacred Bones).

When my friend Charmaine Crockett saw the date on my mother's ashes, she said that the delay is grounds to sue, that disrespect was paid to my mother's remains. When I tell a non-native colleague that my mother's ashes arrived, he says most people apparently never pick them up. Never could there be a starker difference between cultural notions of human remains and the way they represent (or fail to) our connections to the past, and to each other. Charmaine notes that I do not sound upset by this, but reminds me that remains are sacred to native Hawaiians. I respond that I'm not upset by the delay, that what is sacred in these remains is my memory of my mother. My sense of ancestry resonates not in a larger community, but inside the small unit of daughter and mother.

My mother was never one to hold anything sacred; she would not have had much interest in her own remains, or anyone else's for that matter. A vicious combination of cynicism and fear, along with a healthier dose of realism, governed her notion of death, though occasionally she'd let on that she believed in reincarnation. That belief, such as it might have been, came divorced from any spiritual tradition and seemed to be the least of what she could take from traditions she otherwise admired not. "Can Martha go to heaven?" her Catholic school friends had asked of their one proto-Protestant classmate. I gather the answer had been no, and that no had decided her against that spiritual path.

*

My mother's ashes. There's pathos in the apostrophe. She's no longer in possession of them. She never was in possession of them. "How the bulk of a man should sink into so few pounds of bones and ashes, may seem strange unto any who considers not its constitution, and how slender a masse will remain upon an open and urging fire of the carnall composition": Sir Thomas Browne. Their weight is literal; there appears to be no spiritual heft to these ashes as they sit on the floor beside my computer desk. Proust describes the world of Celtic belief as one where material objects hide spirits that escape when someone walks by later. He shifts that magic to memory in his study of how the past emerges (like new life) from odd encounters with the material world (a tea cup, a madeleine). So I might say that these ashes, sitting as quietly as my mother did in the years before she died, contain memories yet to be dislodged.

Her ashes sit beside me, not in the suburban chair she sat in at Arden Courts Alzheimer's home, her elbow slipping off the arm rest, right shoulder slumped lower than her left, but in a black box inside which a plastic bag holds visible gray ash. The box's label tells me where the remains were cremated (Beltsville, MD), when (9/2/12), her name (Martha J. Schultz) and includes a "cremation ID": 026518. The last line reads "Georgetown University School of Medicine." This is her epitaph.

My husband wonders why I did not have the ashes sent to Arlington National Cemetery, where my father's ashes are interred (after quite a fight between my mother and me). That would have been more practical, I admit. But to have them here, not quite knowing how to feel about them; not yet summoning involuntary memories; unsure of what to do with the undifferentiated material that was my mother's body; this means something. Meaning must await its unfolding. Perhaps it will be stored in a warehouse with other boxes of latent memory, or maybe it will never unfold. But these ashes, if not quite sacred to me, if not quite the Christian "dust to dust," sit still as possibility, containing a future not of their own making, but of ours.

If we begin to die when we live, and long life be but a prolongation of death, our life is a sad composition; We live with death, and die not in a moment.
Sir Thomas Browne

Firewood becomes ash. Ash cannot turn back into firewood again. However, we should not view ash as after and firewood as before. We should know that firewood dwells in the dharma position of firewood and it has its own before and after. Although there is before and after, past and future are cut off. Ash stays at the position of ash and it has its own before and after. As firewood never becomes firewood again after it is burned and becomes ash, after person dies, there is no return to living. However, in buddha dharma, it is a never-changing tradition not to say that life becomes death. Therefore we call it no-arising. It is the laid-down way of buddha's turning the dharma wheel not to say that death becomes life. Therefore, we call it no-perishing. Life is a position at one time; death is also a position at one time. For instance, this is like winter and spring. We don't think that winter becomes spring, and we don't say that spring becomes summer.
Dogen

MARK SCROGGINS

GOOD FRIDAY

Say it, it looks so easy.
The night is black, with
a chill. Half an hour ago,
two raccoons passed my chair,
a rust-red moth settled
on the desk, refused to mount
my finger. Tell it plain.
There is no silence
here. No silence.
Scratch, and breathe,
and hear the little animals'
high chitterings over the tires
on pavements. Over sand and
water. Over shards of stone
and chemicals and unfamiliar
bones.
          The palms, bushes
wrap around them, tense, push
up into the air. We cut
them back. Her sister's snoring,
breathy, faint, almost illegible,
keeps her awake she says. Machine-
hum of the cat, satisfied.

Easy. Plain. I hear animals
and mechanisms in the night.

FORCE FEED, FORCE FIELD

Whatever comes up, gets drawn
in. See it here, shaped and trimmed
to manicure.

That two of three meanings come down
to *force*, energy, force to beat us
about the shoulders in the small
of the back, tack us like a crow
to the barn-door.

Force and erosion, resistance.
Moral.

That jaunty Herakles would cauterize
the harmless lizards' heads, throw
a lion's mandible over his own skanky
mane.

The mucus membranes tender against
the tubes, cold or chafing. Stripped
and straps. This air, look you, not good
for wild flowers.

A lawgiver from parts unknown, or parts
known. Club and nail, key
and rudder. Keys in massy bunches
bulging the jeans.

POST-TROPICAL

Consent to buckle, consent to rhyme.
Concretion stares the terminus
of unrepentent waverers, miniature
boskage tangled, vine and tenthrils.
Skyvine, grapevine, bacchic and grand,
the soil as sandy as the shingle.
off the dial and aft
the charts full moon
lŏwering an angry lover

heavenly judgment v.
inept earthly remuneration
Raise or raze the roofbeam, stilt
those homes beyond my parents' reach.
Tongue-and-groove ceiling and walls,
tongue thrust—on the bed—into
emptiness, emptiness clutched. My restless
heart, careening imagination, straining after
vees of Canada geese. What rood to read.

THE ROUÉ

If you were, then, like a snake
or some other animal to turn
on me. If you could
like an animal only speak
through mimes and gestures
and movements. If we all laid
down our cocktails and agreed,
this was where the line must
be drawn, no day without
a line drawn. I could dis-ply
myself along those lines,
but have no more desire
to be spectator to that display,
given the flaccidity, mushroom
pallor, general mopishness
and lack of spine, than
you. Your eyes are not
topaz, half-turning in the half-
light. Like a snake
rotating, cold scales
measured out across the room.
Is one always *helplessly* in love,
or is there such a thing
as calculated entrapment, half-
love in the half-light, love lite?
Writhe like a snake, turn
on me, flip me like
a switch. Off and on.

[UNTITLED]

What do you mean, I asked the poem,
its gears for a moment at rest, steam
leaking from its boiler. Who
are you to ask, it replied, touching

my cheek with a human hand.
Where do you come from, I asked
the poem, marvelling at the shining
grooves behind it, which seemed

to vanish into the forest, but might
be snaking out across the plain
or climbing into the amber hills.
Who are you to ask, it murmured,

nodding its stiff mane, so like
the plume on Hektor's blinding helmet.
What are you for, I asked the poem,
but the poem had nodded off, drive-

shaft disengaged, bowels a muted
mechanical hum, carapace bright and impassive.
So I lay full length on the grass beside,
moistened by the poem's breath, acrid, hot.

THE HEIGHTS AND THE GRANGE

It was only when the credits started to climb the screen
that we realized the show was really over, that the blond
boy would remain forever on the shore against
the sunset, his true love always out of reach. For my part
I wanted a simpler ending, one more conventionally "happy"—
a wedding even, though I know you snort
with a kind of superior contempt at those things.
It was time for dinner anyway, light dishes
for a warm July evening: asparagus and trout,
perhaps, and of course a salad. Watching a lover
move around the kitchen in the twilight,
before one turns on the lights, is comfortable,

like settling into a favorite chair with a book—
a novel maybe, just on the verge of trashy—
you've read a couple of times before. The protagonist
is darkly handsome, he has trouble keeping his hair
out of his eyes, doesn't know which of the women
throwing themselves his way actually loves him
for who he is, rather than for his unaccountable millions,
houses and steam-yachts and so forth.
He likes the red-haired one, but worries her pre-Raphaelite
mane is the sign of some kind of wildness—know,
the sort of woman who'll break dishes in a rage,
maybe even slash the tires of his car. For her part
she doesn't know who her parents were, grew up
in an orphanage with stern but kindly nurses,
tried to keep out of the way of the priest
with the suspicious gleam in his little piggy eyes.
The twilight is all salmon behind the picture window
which frames the trees, the lawn, the street and a couple
of street-lamps into—well—a picture. I considered the relation
of landscape painting, the *seeing* requisite to paint
a landscape, or rather, to *frame* it rightly, to the art
of landscaping, moving all those trucks and wheelbarrows
of earth, planting and mulching and nurturing shrubs
and trees, hedges and an occasional flower. All behind glass,
the vast incline of the lawn. We can't see Catherine, Linton,
or even the gormless Hareton; perhaps they're behind
the ha-ha, fumbling at each other's drawers in the gloaming.

STEPHEN SPOTTE

INVISIBLE

I don't wonder what I am or where I might be headed, and I never look back. That's seeing yourself too clearly, the mistakes and trouble everywhere. Better to leave it behind.

It's nice in the barn watching sunlight slip through cracks in the old boards, throwing imaginary animals onto shadow. About head high, there's a knot hole shaped like a rabbit. When I was little—eight or nine—I'd come out here on summer afternoons and sit in the hay with my back against the splinters waiting for that rabbit to show itself. I'd stare and stare at the far wall, not once looking up at the knot hole, and suddenly, like magic, there was the rabbit.

As the sun moved lower, the rabbit dimmed and faded away. They all laughed at me, but I could never shoot a rabbit. Squirrels are different. The light glows purple and fades as another day goes by. Through board cracks the trunks of the trees turn soft.

I'm grown now with no time for shadow rabbits. Starting in fall there's heifers to feed, and the mules need their hay pitched, too. They work all the seasons, these mules, but in fall and winter there's nothing for them except pulling logs out of the woods. Not a bad life if you ask me. I can think of worse things than being born a mule. Being born invisible is a lot worse.

Outside the leaves are turning colors. It's their time. I like watching them through the big doors we keep propped open to let in air. I like it when the wind hurries them down, leaving behind a space where a leaf once grew. Not an empty space, but a space filled with emptiness. Tunnels. Every leaf hole connected to another, the bunch of them twisting and turning away like memories.

I dip into the sweet grain and give each mule a taste. They see me head for the bag and perk up their ears, stamp a heavy sound.

Can they know what's underneath? Their hooves leave flat places on the floors of the stalls. The hoof prints cover up others already there, making them disappear at the edges like days layering on.

With time the floors slope to the middle. Then I rake out the stalls and fetch the wheelbarrow. I fill in the depressions with fresh clay, dusty pale as dry cement. I breathe in its lightness as I shovel. My snot turns white. The stuff blows against me, mats my hair, turns me into a different kind of invisible. So big, and all that happiness in a handful of sweet grain. There's worse things to be born than a mule.

The heifers look up as I fork their hay, eyes big and trusting like Mary Louise's. Hers were blue. Big as a heifer's and blue.

She cried last time and told me love is all two people need. We could see it through, the bunch of us, her kin and mine. She pressed her face against my neck. Tears trickled down my skin like hot sweat.

Love can do that, mix the hard with the easy until problems seem harmless. I know better. I come out of the shadows, trouble starts. It always did and always will. Stay in the greenbriers like a rabbit, that's what I say. Mary Louise never understood, and I couldn't tell her. Now it's over and done. Never look back...but it's hard sometimes.

Pap hobbles through the big doors looking dark against the last light. I can't see his face at first and think how he could be anybody, even a scarecrow with that old straw hat and coveralls. He drags one leg; the arm on the same side hangs flopping with every step. He's got a cane now. I made it for him out of hickory. The bottom is brown from manure, the top brown from the sweat and dirt of his hand, but the middle still shines gray.

He nods and heads for the tractor where his parts and tools are spread out on the seat and on the empty hay cart hooked up behind. Pap hasn't done farm work since the stroke, but he intends to tune that tractor engine before spring. He can't talk now. He's got one arm and one leg for a job that needs two of both. I nod back.

Pap gets mad if we talk to him now that he can't answer. It bothers the others. Not me. I'd rather not talk anyway. Pap has made it plain we're to stay the hell away from the tractor.

Pap's invisible, too. We all are. Our births aren't recorded, so it's as if we were never born. Sometimes I see my reflection in a store window and think, there goes a ghost, but ghosts were somebody once. A ghost leaves behind a record of a life. Paperwork filed with a name and address, next of kin, accomplishments.

I finish up the heifers, get the milk buckets, and go to the end of the barn to milk the two cows. The barn cats hear the buckets clang and come tumbling out of the haymow. I empty some ants and bits of hay from their bowl. They live on milk and mice and whatever else they catch, a bird or a chipmunk. I sometimes find the evidence: feathers and bits of fur mixed in with the hay. Our cats are born and grow up here. Some stay. Others go off and don't come back. When one leaves another takes its place. We're never without cats. As I stoop to pet them I think how they're invisible, too. They have no history either, like the leaves and the light, a different light today than yesterday, a different light every day since the world started.

Nobody knows our situation except kin and people who marry in. I tried explaining it to Mary Louise. Now that's over and done. We barter produce and make some cash cutting wood. We don't pay taxes or Social Security. There's no electric bill. None of us has ever set foot inside a schoolhouse or had a driver's license, but we drive our pickup over every inch of road in this county because Pap's third cousin is sheriff. The county is plenty big enough for me. I never had the urge to go anyplace else, until now. Now I've got no choice.

The spiders are starting to hide away for winter. Maybe they live under boards or in hay. I don't know. I see those brown spiders come out in spring, each to its own corner. A spider lays a big ball of eggs and hangs there, never moving. More patience than I'll ever have. Sometimes I drop in a fly and watch while the spider kills it and wraps it up in spider silk, a little blanket of death. Not quite the same situation, I'm thinking, but the dead are still dead.

The mules stamp. If I was superstitious I might think they could read my mind. They can't. They're just mules wanting sweet grain and wondering what I'm doing down here at the other end of the barn.

Pap is hammering on that rusty engine casing. I hear him breathing long and hoarse. I can tell he's mad; the hammer's heavy. His mechanic's light throws a bright circle on the floor. Maybe his lungs will bust open. I don't think he cares anymore, now that he can't talk. Only he and I know the truth. Not even his third cousin knows. Kin are kin, but close kin count more.

I tried explaining things to Mary Louise. I asked her to sit down and watch the rabbit come up on the wall, but she was yelling at me and crying. All I said was we couldn't get married. She kept asking why and hitting me with her fists. I couldn't tell her why: invisible is forever. She wanted something else. She said we could go to Charleston where people don't know us. I could find work. Be among strangers? When you're invisible, it's the strangers who are dangerous. They might tell, and suddenly your picture's in the paper. Picture. I'll never stop seeing that one blaze up behind my eyes, a red desert of washboard dunes. A picture memorized out of a magazine when I lay with a fever long ago. After I got well I went looking. I found it, crumpled up and smeared with ashes. Pap smoothed it out. The land of Egypt, he said, where Pharaoh persecuted the Israelites, and when he opened the coal stove the flames licked it out of his fingers.

Why that came to mind just then I couldn't say, but I felt the purity of fire again. White heat behind my eyes. God's anger. When my eyesight came back everything was like before. The same but somehow different. There were boards all around, stalls with their dug floors, light coming in through the big doors. The rabbit.

Who died in anger?

To be consumed in fire when the leaves are turning makes a certain sense: red leaves, red desert, no green anywhere. Then the chill of the hollows, of darkness out beyond. The valley of the shadow of death. I saw what I'd done. Shadows without walls. The sudden stillness was God's whispered forgiveness. In the desert everything moves with the wind, dunes gliding over dunes. Pharaoh's army lies buried under sand. Pap told us so. Here the boards resist. I'm safe from being covered over. The mules hear something. They stop and listen, ears toggling. Mules can tell what's down there compacting slowly in the quiet. I'm glad those stalls are done. Someday I can stop thinking about it. Never look back, that's the secret. Pap came in just as I was finishing up, but he knew. He stopped and looked at me, and his eyes didn't say a thing.

In summer the daylight slides into evening. Time is gradual; there's a softness. Now the difference is a thin pale sheet. Mary Louise's kin will wonder. When the moon comes up I'll start walking toward it. There won't be anything behind me, not even a shadow.

STEPHANIE STRICKLAND

from *DRAGON LOGIC*

ALGORITHM

Recipe

Ingredients

instructions

Instructions

map a metaphor or more
to computational processes (not
to *compositional*
capiche?)

twiddle (de dee) tweak (de dum)
execute / run repeat
till well (enough)

done oh
will this one
halt

MEASURABLE pleasures
30 seconds or so of a non-changing environment
are enough to relax *Octofungi*

inorganic anemone
electro-sensitive to light
whose small arms tip and reach extend and rock

a plug-in neural net—
its ingredients *mass : atoms* whereas
bit packet life

can transit the solar system in hours its ingredients
instructions—
(only who to receive?
what storage-and-expression system?)

Whale ancestor coming ashore air-breather mammal
after an eon returned to the ocean—

Digital biotics well-adapted to space : is this life
going *back* or moving *on* escaping
earth and the coils of DNA as the algorist asserts—

Cross it! Jump the bitomic / atomic barrier declared frontier
the airy cages hacked
reconfigured felled unspared— are we clear?

THE SAME interaction the same charge and enormous

speed my brother Finn my virtual my transient

twin seething with energy some

or none or any at all

except that one

number that makes me

real and not

him he the ghostly the free

loader the thief exuberant slid in under the bell

UNTIL recently considered not writing
not reading the readme
when all else fails the assailed grid goes down data congeals

>The housekeeper arrives to remove Eryk
>The housekeeper arrives to remove Eryk

canned instructions are not what you (written) need you need
connection type-chat upgrade feeds ping simulate engage
find Easter eggs work the layering zoom

to global and back spun *z* plied *s* or
as in ancient
fiber foundry repositories *also binarized* the reverse—

>Everdeen wraps][*.mez][in electric blanket telepathic controls

positively 3-D
until recently considered not writing (khipu / quipu)
(ascii)(C)

>][*.mez][says, "Sue, 4 1nce I managed 2 sit back & ab.sorb rather
>than prattle on :)"

BIRGITTA the Healer

and *Graugans* the gray lag goose *Anser*

anser and Babalu-Aye

(Bab-ilu) gate of God

and the man who listened all the time

Nijinski (Vaslav) and

orisha Oya with that bit of buffalo

on her shin yet

and Simone who did "Fall, gall…

and gash gold-vermilion" as Father

Hopkins saw

—and Mister Rogers quiet

butt of slurs who knew childhood grit

broadcast engineering nit-

pick knew the only neighborhood we'd

know was mediated magic

knew how knew

why we had to be *inside* it

COLE SWENSEN

from *ON WALKING ON*

STEVENSON

The happiness that in the end is man   only as luminous as alone
walks one by one   opposed to reason   R. L. Stevenson   found
an abandoned loom   of equable stride   in the evening rising
in which we dwell   in rhythm held   streaming through the trees
Stevenson claimed   that the walker becomes the landscape by
the end of the day and the view, a living thing with no sense of time.

DEBORD

à la dérive de la Bièvre de Guy Debord who could sweep through any city
on a curve   could river aloft   even an old river knotted   in the middle
of the night   can be traced by its heat   Debord who refused to follow
the meticulous scent nly a city could in such debt   could a city disarticulate
its imprecate grid   in walking is   the destruction of city planning   the de-
Haussmannization of the mind on an October afternoon   filtered light
fingering
a break in the seal   cast aside   decades later a group of young people
got into the habit of walking a straight line across Paris   no matter what
buildings
rivers or other obstacles happened   to refuse the pattern   they unlocked
the genetic sequence   and not without effect   on the English Inclosure
Acts of
the 18th and 19th centuries though this is difficult to document which is one
of its principal strengths.

SINCLAIR

To sail around London as dreamed by Madox Ford 100 years later
Iain Sinclair, seeing the rage of it, or walking as interactive cartography
take any major city, take every single inch of it, make of it this intricate
and then make it orchestrate, or (again Sinclair) just an endless attempt
to forget (Quinn tracing the Tower of Babel all over New York) of the
ritual in which one forgets one by one the faces caused a fugue—
the psychological imperative to walk straight ahead without stopping—
it's a rare form of amnesia—the person is usually eventually found
hundreds of miles away living a new life under a different name, invisible
ceremonies, such as the blindman's stitch: the conviction (Sinclair again)
that one can orbit London on the M25.

Sinclair says that it is in the fugue that writing and walking fuse, which
implies, as has been proved, that writing is the erasure of memory, and
as such, annihilates the past, as does walking—i.e., you can't walk
backward without hurting yourself, and most likely also somebody else.

SELF

i.e. to walk is to forward. Will Self
upon the metronome, this history

of pacing, paced the earth
in 4:4 time, the opposite of the fugue

as we turn the verse on the station platform,
carve a furrow in a worried room. The step

is an animal music, though at times
an airplane intervenes, though Self insists

and no doubt rightly, that he was only
going out for a walk.

JODY SWILKY

ANIMATION

A man walks through a district
of perfume and dress shops,
and wherever he turns,
whatever his eye might spot

through the sunlight, shadow,
and damp odor of traffic,
he sees only the cold beauty
of women in windows.

If a mannequin leans,
offering her perfect hand,
or the woman sitting in bed
whispers a few words,

he knows, as the body absorbs
sight and sound, they're calling him.
And if they stand as stiff as plaster,
he thinks each inviting gesture

is saved until the streets empty,
until his fingers touch luminous glass,
leaving a handful of kisses
on their billboard smiles.

TENANTS

The woman sunbathing on the roof
knows men are sighing at windows.
Sometimes she turns over,
staring back through dark glasses.

She has seen them all summer—
the unemployed who drink
in the steam, who offer sad smiles
as her arms reach toward the sun—
so she spends the day oiling her legs,
yawning like a banker's daughter.

But many nights when these men
lounge on fire escapes
or fall asleep before old movies end,
she gazes from her terrace
towards the corner cafe,
where couples lean across tables.

Once, looking for stars and air,
I found her crying.
I wanted to talk, but I left her alone.
The sky sagged, a tar roof,
and a haze of heat rose between us.
The wild-eyed tenant who passed me,
later, on the staircase—
was he sweating from love or murder?

I can't forget his face,
nor how the next morning,
opening the lobby door,
I smiled like an anxious child,
and she brushed by, not even nodding,
as if we were still strangers.

A SMALL GATHERING

They crowded on a corner
while a steel ball crashed brick.
The silent men wore suits
and the women stood like mannequins,
looking calmly towards the sky.

Through the air they followed
the slow fall of stone and dust.
Each swing, the pendulum's arc,

brought them closer to a distant day
when the body, like gravity,
seemed to pull them down.

Perhaps someone saw a sign.
Perhaps some remembered the chill
the night their fathers fell.
But all hearing the blast
of a morning work whistle,

turned from the grind
of loss and stern machinery.
They brushed the grit
from their suits and dresses,
and one woman, before walking away,
wiped a man's watery eyes.

CARNATIONS

They're everywhere on this city street,
except in the earth around trees,
long-stemmed flowers
picked from an aluminum barrel
and passed from the flower girl's fingers
into the hands of Sunday shoppers.

And they're broken into parts,
stems cut from flowers,
kicked and crushed by the crowd,
petals scattered where the girl walks,
back and forth, along the avenue,
waving a perfect carnation
in the faces of summer tourists,

her face wavering in the heat,
drifting above a dress
embroidered with flowers,
in the sunlight that blurs and forms
a smile or a wince
and flower after flower after flower.

SHARED MUSIC

They shared music for years,
across a continent,
sometimes staying
awake until dawn,
humming to a frosted
or foggy window.

It wasn't until years later
that they danced
to ballads in a dark room,
careless of stepping
on each other's toes.

The trumpet lingered
and something burned their faces—
the remains of
an incredible embrace,
what stays after
the heartache of healing,

the body speaking
a startling language,
the way the woman
who just left her lover
and now arrives home
suddenly stops smiling,
then smiles again,
surprised by her daughter's laughter.

CHALK

A shining face hovers
above a windowless house
surrounded by huge teardrops
hanging in the air.

Chalk filled my small hands
before I could draw a body,
so I connected straight lines
to a thicker stroke,
attached them to an awkward circle.

No title, no signature,
until someone asked,
What do you call it?
and I began to scrawl letters
and utter drawn-out syllables,
filling still air with my name,
saying something
like the marks I was making.

CATHERINE TAYLOR

from *APART*

After it is over, after the shooting stops, after the blood bath, after things change, after democracy, after reconciliation, after redistribution, after understanding, maybe then it will begin.

See how the periodic sentence uses parallel phrases to withhold its essential element; marked by suspended syntax, it places its final revelation right before the concluding period.

Like the sentence, the people move forward, want resolution, seek conclusions, note parallels, but they, of course, reach no final revelations, no concluding periods—no time with an end, no discrete clause of history, no full stop.

A period is an interval of time in a cyclic motion; a period is determined by recurring phenomena.

(Listen.) Even a sentence can seem like a pendulum.

A period is an interval of time in a cyclic motion; a period is determined by recurring phenomena.

To start with this or that. Oscillation, vacillation. Once, my children and I made a science project: Foucault's pendulum. A squirt-bottle of black paint hung upside down from a rafter on a long string. Un-stopper the bottle, set the paint-bob swinging, watch the trail of paint inscribe the motion of the earth beneath you. In my notebooks from this time there are endless meditations on oscillation, on going back and forth in approaches to a topic, in modes of representation, in love. On being pulled between poles. Back and forth the notes swing between prose and verse, narrative and rupture, hope and despair, faith and doubt, black and white, change and stasis, self and other, amnesty and retribution, sound and silence, remembering and forgetting, colonialism and independence, poverty and wealth, belonging and alienation, alien and citizen, positivist documentary historiography and radical performative constructivism, sick with desire and sick of it. Back and forth.

But look at the line the world traces. The revelation of the system, of course, is that the pendulum doesn't just swing back and forth, between this or that, inscribing simple opposites. Instead, it leaves a trail of ever-shifting ellipses, each arc overlapping the last, but also moving on—all a single line that loops into a flower, describing, ultimately, in its center, a circle. Inside the circle flower words that trouble simple oppositions, the frustrations of impossible choices, words like discourse, ideology, blood, race, family, nation, history.

A complete swing of a pendulum is a period. What is periodic repeats itself.

A pendulum keeps time.

A pendulum is a harmonic oscillator. So is the human voice and some stars. Usually, we cannot hear harmonics as separate notes; instead, they appear to be the timbre of the tone.

A pendulum exhibits resonance. It vibrates easily at particular frequencies, less so at others. An acoustically resonant object filters out all frequencies other than its resonance. In the telling of histories, what if nothing is filtered? Will we hear only noise or everything resonating at once?

Resonance is produced by sympathetic vibrations. Resonance evokes associations and emotions.

Resonance can result in catastrophic failure of the vibrating structure. This is known as "resonance disaster." (Soldiers, break step.) Look how we have learned to love the wreckage.

*

A jet-lag dreaminess. White arum lilies twist above their three-foot stalks. Bunches, circumferences big as tree trunks. Papery red poppies with bent hairy stems. Irises. Sick visual abundance. Colored women man the stalls. Across the sidewalk, a single black man sells knit caps and radios.

One flower seller asks, *Did you come to see the new South Africa?* Some mocking sound in her voice. Yes, my mother grew up here, was briefly a social worker in a black township, emigrated. I visited as a child, until '76, Soweto. I haven't been back since then. A laugh. *Coming for some "truth and reconciliation?" Huh. Truth is it's much worse now. At least for us coloreds. More crime, worse schools, no jobs. There's no "liberation."*

Don't listen to her! The guy across the way yells. We have democracy now! *Hah! Democracy. Good for the blacks. Used to be whites on top, us in the middle, and blacks on the bottom. Now black's on top and we're on the bottom.* No. He says no. We are all black.

I nod my head. This seems like a good anti-racist slogan. I'm getting ready to raise my little white black power fist in the air when, without hesitating, she says, *Oh. How about we're all colored?* A gesture at the three of us: black, white, colored. *We are all colored.* Even better. The mix, the creole, "mestiza consciousness." He looks away and hesitates. She says, No? *How about we're all white?* He closes his mouth and frowns. Doesn't respond. *See. We can all be black, but not all colored or all white.*

I nod more slowly as the categories unravel and resolidify. The power of claiming black clear for him and maybe for her, but troubling when it comes to white me. The compromise of all of us assuming the middle place of "colored," seems more possible. And yet, if I were him…

He says, No. All black. *Because he doesn't want to give up the power. It's about power.* He shakes his head, no. *They're just switching apartheid.* Okay, okay. We are all the same. *Okay. All the same. All colored.* He shakes his head, no.

They are at an impasse.

He says to me, She's crazy. It's much better now, he says, and backs away from the questions of race, nation, power, and identity she has so cogently raised. When he calls her crazy, I feel my allegiance shifting away from him, a gendered history tugging me to her.

She hands me my flowers wrapped in white paper and I think she is a brilliant political philosopher and rhetorician. But then, his insistence on both his and "our" blackness, his refusal to take in any whiteness, and his ultimate backing away from our mutual search for a common name make sense in terms of power and a politics of difference. Still, confusion blooms.

STEVE TOMASULA

MEM

So then I was downtown, right? Trying to remember the street they renamed in honor of that hometown kid who was killed in our last war, when I found myself in front of this granite pillar rising from a pedestal, a tidy pyramid of bowling balls at each corner, a huge stone Eagle at the top, even a poem:

Till the Years of Earth are Over
And the Skies Gathered like a Scroll

(or some such)

. . .

We Remember The Union Army
Erected, Chamber of Commerce, 1939.

Words cast in bronze (now green). And I'm thinking, that that's like 1939 minus 1862 = 72, 71 years after the Civil War. So what did they know about it? Them and their bowling balls. Or maybe they were supposed to be cannonballs. Did any of them, the artist, poet, or businessmen who made the memorial, fight in the Civil War? Was anyone from the Civil War even alive in 1939? A matter of representation. Or knew the difference between a bowling ball and a cannon ball? It's not impossible. Some squirt, a drummer boy say, 15, 16, mans-up in 1865 just as the war ends, and so survives to make memories another day. That means he'd be like 94 in 1939, which is possible. But then you gotta wonder, how much did this squirt see? How sharp's this geezer's recall? Not that some of the kids aren't wide-eyed, not that some of our geezers aren't sharp as tacks at 94, or even 100. Even good bowlers. But still, you see the point. This granite memorial isn't at all like those memorials to victims of highway crashes, or drive-by or schoolyard shootings where the photos, flowers, and teddy bears pile up before the bodies are cold. The wounds still fresh. Too fresh. An outrush of emotion. Too much to bear. Can't have that. Can you imagine? A forty-foot granite teddy bear in our town square? No, better to wait. 7,000 corpses scattered across the fields of

Pennsylvania, blackening in the summer heat. Better granite bowling balls. That's what makes history history. And not journalism, or memoir. The forgetting. The not being there. Dear Diary, I'll get back to you... .72 years later. That's like farther from the Civil War than we are from WWII. Dear Diary, (Voila! Instant history)—Are there eagles in Pennsylvania? I remember it as pretty flat, flat enough for fields and armies, anyway: 3,000 swollen horses and mules mixed in with those 7,000 soldiers. Six million pounds of rotting flesh if my math is right. Quite a stench. Vultures, more likely. Maybe that's what that drummer boy saw. Doesn't take long. Vultures, lots of them. And mistook them for eagles. Doesn't last long. That's why you got to write it down. Even then, people forget. Or get confused. I mean, maybe the squirt saw vultures and the geezer remembered eagles. It happens. Or maybe he saw it wrong and remembered it right. Just as common. Or saw it wrong and remembered it wrong or saw it right and remembered it right to the artist of the memorial who heard it wrong. Haven't you ever played telephone? How many historians does it take to screw in a light bulb? Shed a little light. Illuminate a subject so everyone can see. "One"—me—at least that's what they seem to think when every historian before them (obviously) got it wrong. I mean, history is a special kind of memory, right? What I leave out is as important as what I put in, Hemingway wrote about his war. Still, makes you wonder why historians have such faith in things written down: birth certificates, letters, memoirs, laws, deeds, treaties, documents, agreements, vows—*Till Death do us part*—histories (obviously) all flawed (obviously), speeches, memorials, all given meaning by the absences. The silence. The way sound without silence is just noise. Or print without gaps is just solid black—not the marbled page, not letters of the alphabet, which are important to poems, memoirs, histories, novels about wars, etc. Hemingway's war was the Great War. The War to End All Wars as they called it before Wars to End All War had sequels—37 million killed—and needed numbers to tell them apart. Like Superbowls. 60 million in WWII. You can look it up: 263 tons of ammunition fired by U.S. soldiers each day. 42,500 aircraft destroyed; 5,151 warships sunk by U-Boats alone; 767 U-Boats alone (crew of 54 each) sunk in reply; 603,400 civilian deaths from air raids; 12,000 heavy bombers destroyed, but not before they dropped 3.4 million tons of bombs, obliterating 197 towns, too many pounds of rotting—or evaporated—flesh to even guestimate—and that's just some numbers from our side, the victors, the good guys whose records were written in places like here instead of places like Dresden or Hiroshima, the Great Cornucopia of America replacing all of those lost ships and planes, uniforms, helmets, shoes, canteens, playing cards, bullets—also chandeliers, chess sets, kitchen tables, board games, wallets, dog tags, filing cabinets, radios, cigarettes, boots, shaving kits, pots and pans and pens, libraries, churches, railroads, beer steins, schools, desks, dolls, bugles, clip boards, grenades, pogo sticks, pencils, typewriters, erasers.... Bowling balls too, no doubt. But not people. Not even family photos. In 1954 there were still six soldiers from the Civil War still alive, the last of them dying in 1956. On his 100th birthday they gave him a tee-shirt: I Survived the Civil War. The photo of him in that shirt in his obituary is what set off the war over who should have gotten the tee-shirt, a Confederate solider claiming in 1957 that he was the last civil warrior standing, until he died in 1958, whereupon a Union soldier piped up from his nursing home to claim the shirt. Then he died. And a different Confederate soldier pressed *The South Will Rise Again!* button on the hospital bed. A pride thing, etc. And so it went, Union, Confederate, Union, one old geezer after another claiming he was the last. The winner. None able to prove it. There not being any written records. No one ever wrote it down. Or they lived but their records didn't. Sherman's March to the Sea. Who can say? Maybe some of these geezers were just confused. Brain fade. Memory as roadkill along the march of time. Thought they were at Bull Run when they'd really been at Iwo Jima. And that's not counting those who were there but didn't want to talk about it. Didn't want the tee-shirt. Remembered vultures not eagles. Like my uncle. 77 Years—as far from the Civil War as we are from The War to End All Wars II—got a Silver Star, my uncle did. In Okinawa. Or maybe it was Normandy. Hard to say since he never wanted to talk about it: how his entire unit was being mowed down by machinegun fire. Uncle Cab rushed right at the pillbox with a flame thrower strapped to his back, a weapon sort of like the bowling balls full of napalm that his son dropped on Vietnam (if you want a more recent reference), with dozens of Germans or Japanese shooting at him the whole time as he dodged and danced his way to the pillbox, just like in movies, and sprayed in his liquid fire—what I put in is as important as what I leave out—burnt alive a bunch of guys. Saved a bunch of guys. Depending on your point of view. Stench of burning hair and flesh. Not what they show us in the movies. At least according to my other uncle, Cab's brother, who loved to tell the story. Of course I was only a squirt then. And he was pretty old—a geezer actually. Who liked to embellish things, gild his words, leave out details, too, or arrange facts to make a better story. Not so unlike historians, though sometimes he'd confuse things with movies he'd seen.

When the sublime celestial bugler
Rings our heroes' reveille...

Too bad no one was there to take a photo. Like the photo of those guys raising a flag on Okinawa. Or those Civil War photos that Mathew Brady took of corpse-strewn battlefields. Not that words can't be memorials.

Remember the Alamo!
Never Again!

Till the Skies Unroll like Scrolls, etched (by businessmen) in bronze (now green) to last forever. Like the plaque erected just south of here, on the Little Bear River where troops, fresh from their victory in the Civil War, were sent to join the war to end all wars with the Indians. *The Battle for The Little Bear River*, the plaque reads. The troops sent to The Little Bear River being hardened military men. Maybe even the same guys immortalized in bronze poems back east. Used to the stench of burnt bacon. Strategists. Savy enough to wait until winter, when most of the Indian warriors would be away hunting. And the snow so deep that army horses could charge but the women and children camping at the Little Bear River wouldn't be able to run away. When they attacked at dawn.

I wonder… Why don't holocausts have numbers? Wouldn't that make them easier to remember? Like Superbowls? It's complicated, of course. One man's genocide being another man's Battle for the Little Bear River. Like when my uncle asked me what I wanted to be when I grew up, and I told him I wanted to be a vet, meaning I wanted to take care of sick animals, and he thought I meant a 'vet' the way everyone who'd been in The War to End All Wars II meant a 'vet,' and he just misted up, shook his head and walked away. What I leave out… Lots of rapes at The Little Bear River, some say. Not the Indians, of course. Nor photos, like Mathew Brady took, and the camera doesn't lie, as people say. Of course, the people who say that obviously never took a picture of someone trying to kick them. Have you ever noticed how enormous the foot in one of those photos looks? Still, people say things like that. Meaning, the person had to be there for you to take a picture of them, the way a vase of flowers had to be there for you to take a picture of it, or a teddy bear, your uncle, or a Civil War memorial had to be there for you to take a picture of it. Of course that isn't strictly true either, or means that just because you *were* there someone would take your picture, but whatever. The point being, 9 times out of 10 the thing that a picture was of had been in the world at a particular place (in front of the camera), at a particular time (shutter snap), and that's what's so mesmerizing: proof of existence. That's what makes a picture a memorial. Even if it's a memorial of a memorial. It's the reason old photos of the dead have such power over us. Sepia-toned stares. Or those washed-out colors in photos from the 50's, when everyone was digging bomb shelters and Kodak was king—*4th of July!*—but the kings of photo-as-memento-mori are daguerreotypes like those carried by Civil War soldiers of their wives, sweethearts, mothers. Or those daguerreotypes soldiers left behind of themselves in uniform. Poignant. The way they had to sit still as a corpse (instead of waving flags—*4th of July!*—or having a squirt-gun fight in a backyard pool). Because of the long exposures. Open, dead-eyed stares at the camera. Couldn't duck-and-cover like we used to in grade school, or even smile, or blink because a blink would blur the picture, not at all like that famous photo of soldiers raising a flag at Iwo Jima, a victory, an instant memorial to the taking of the island, though afterwards the story gets a little fuzzy, with some soldiers who were there saying that the shot was faked, if by fake you mean staged the way some people say Mathew Brady faked his shots: put one dead soldier's hand on his heart, or slump two together as though they passed away in their sleep, rearranging them into more moving postures. Makes a better story that way, though the Iwo Jima photographer denied doing any such thing. Said it was spontaneous—the photo, not the flag raising which everyone knew was staged by a general—until a second, different, negative was discovered (the camera doesn't lie) at which point he remembered that he'd shot a spontaneous one, then asked them to raise it again so he could have a do-over, but couldn't remember which was which. Whatever. Anyway, our Representative sponsored a bill in Congress to make a statue of the photo, and came up with a really great line that he used in his speech at the unveiling—"Those who forget the past are doomed to repeat it"—which even made it into the movie that Hollywood made about the statue of the staged or rehearsed or spontaneous photo of the raising of the flag, and seems to be even more true today, given all the talk about "The death of photography," photographers laying teddy bears and wreaths on what the creators of those Civil War daguerreotypes meant by "a picture" when their subjects couldn't even blink, let alone run around with squirt guns or raise flags. And photographers couldn't change the hairstyle of their subjects, or airbrush out their acne, or Photoshop my wife's Ex out of their wedding photo in which she looked so hot, and her parents were still healthy (the last picture of them that way), and it was really a simple thing to erase Asshole (bad memories) and add in her old college Roommate (good memories) who couldn't make the party. That day. My wife has a photographic memory, everyone says. Anyway, the movie was very popular here in town. When it came out, our son's history teacher took him to see it, along with the rest of his class—including the kid they renamed that street after, come to think of it—'lest they forget. He even wrote a paper about it. The movie still plays down at the Biograph, I think, on a loop.

ANNE WALDMAN

CLIMBING THE HYBRID: NOTES FOR A PANEL

Naropa University 2011

We have the recent example of "Amina"—the Arab/America lesbian character purported to be writing her blog from the frontlines of the Syrian Revolution, bringing attention to the struggle for gender rights in that difficult place. Tom MacMaster now living in Turkey has admitted the hoax but also felt it drew necessary attention & support to a critical issue in Arab countries. & it just ran away with itself. The blog caught on; he felt the responsibility to keep it going & so on. He is working on a novel. What kind of hybridity is this; what are the ethical bounds? Does he profit from the very critical issue he raises? In a way he is drawing on the actual use of the term. Syncretic layers of cultural realities, conditioning.

New mixes of the socio-political; environmental occupy memes; racial ideological possibilities. Maybe the real Amina is lurking nearby?

The term "hybrid" has been a critical term widely used in postcolonial theory to describe the newness of many disparate forms of migrant or minority discourses that flourish in the diasporas of the Modern & Postmod periods. This rhetoric examines the creation of new transcultural forces within the contact zone produced by colonization. Examples would be Pidgin English or Creole. Spanglish. Homi Bhabha, one of the main theorists in this field, speaks of "The Third Space of Enuciation," not unlike William Burroughs & Brian Gysin's "Third Mind," which emerges as a result of collaboration, appropriation, cannibalizing of text, the bending of genres, or the meeting of two minds. & Burroughs himself conjured in his work the ultimate hybrid fantasy of a super-being with the eyes of a hawk, the ability of reptiles to grow back limbs, the sonar power of bats & more. He also invoked the transplanting of organs, used to best advantage. I am most interested in a Being—a consciousness that still smells of human—that will survive our ongoing holocausts.

That isn't a machine.

In my lifetime it was fascinating to see Viet Nam come to the west, & if you visit Viet Nam now you see the huge cultural changes the war brought there, as well as the devastation of the ecology & the psyche. & rebuilding. What emerges from horrific tragedy? New generations of intermixed gene pools, terms of societal discourse, new cuisine, etc. See also the extraordinary world-wide influence of Hip Hop. White Rap. Chinese Rap. When I visited Muslim schools Kerela in India recently, the students wanted to know what I thought of the French government banning the headscarf, & the continual racial profiling—as they see it—of the Obama administration—although Obama himself is a "hybrid," & why can't he close Guantanamo?

"&, Professor Waldman, what were the agrarian policies of Franklin Delano Roosevelt?"

This question stumped me as I realized this was relevant to India today. Is this a sign of a more progressive outlook?

Hybridity has taken hold in poetry's experimental zones. We have Cole Swensen & David St. John's anthology *American Hybrid, A Norton Anthology of New Poetry*.

From Cole Swensen:

"This anthology springs from the conviction that the model of binary opposition is no longer the most accurate one...& everywhere we find complex aesthetic & ideological differences, as the contemporary moment is dominated by rich writings that cannot be categorized & that hybridize core attributes of previous 'camps' in diverse & unprecedented ways."

She goes on to describe how the hybrid shares qualities with Ron Silliman's third wave poetics. & with what is increasingly known as the post-avant work. (I prefer avant derriere!). The term elliptical poetry is also summoned.

Today's hybrid might engage such conventional approaches as narrative that presumes a stable first person, yet complicates it by disrupting the linear temporal path or by scrambling the normal syntactical sequence. Illogicality, fragmentation, erasure.

She talks about the ability of the hybrid to renew the forms & expand the boundaries of writing—the expressive potential of language itself.

But I want to prioritize the hybrid of animal/human. & of past/future. Arche/techne. I want us to save & cultivate our humanity & morph with other beings so threatened &.... I falter...is it too late? Imagination's other place.

Finally this: an image from the Chauvet Caves in the Ardeche region of France. A cave believed to go back 32 thousand years that is filled with some of the most exquisite & sublime rock art in the history of the world. Extraordinary lion & horse, & leopards & bison & ibex. I highly recommend Werner Herzog's documentary CAVE OF FORGOTTEN DREAMS, which provides a meditation on the psychic liminal hybridity of cro-magnon consciousness, & images of shadow plays & virtual performance. How the open horse mouth seems to be neighing, how the bison etched with the contours of the cave walls, engaged in combat sound, their antlers butting at each other.

The image is of a female vulva—similar to the various Venuses (of Willendorf, etc.) hybridized with the head of a bison. What are we to make of that? What is that forgotten dream in that cave? Is it over? Will it come back? That insures perhaps a continuity of our imagination & link to our co-inhabitants.

The Buddhist view is that we are all related below the level of sub-atomic particles. We share the planet with many non-human elementals...Om mani padme humanity hum,

Om mani padme manatee hum....

ABDOMEN

ancestors go nameless til you ask
three thousand years in the floods
& bust a few pyramids
they're vagabonds too

stole the argument of asphodel
climbed Mt. Athos
a stag no longer hiding behind a fig leaf

& see the thrush hop onto a branch
deer stepping shade to shade
insects again will buzz into the 21st & a half century

    away from Mars or be swallowed up?

in this document search a comet a common a "connect"
such is the force of illusion waiting for the hurricane
in blind democracy

abdomen: *solid citizen*
stomach: *vulnerable on the Occupy! Battlefield*
cheek: *a definition that raises itself & some to be "cheeky"*

MARK WALLACE

from *THE END OF AMERICA, BOOK 13*

City capped by a flight
path close above

houses and shaking

apartment closets in its final

descent across
the San Diego hills

There is nothing
inside us

that isn't out
side also

skins, bones, guts

bought up by

men at the
docks behind wire

gates I don't

want to be only

that, only some flogged

money launderer pissing

into his own feed bowl just south

of the freeway clover-leafed clove foot

in some heaven myth

of nothing to be

done about what
happens, what lives

following the worn trade

lanes with plastic

crates by truck and boat

I want to have
some love left in my

shaky fingers

One cannot
be documentary only—

it doesn't touch
my hand to your

arm before dawn—

Still I cannot say

me anymore and stop

just there
tired

on the buckled
sidewalk
*

What comes up out

of the bay?

Wedding rings, syringes, bullet casings

In the picnic, on the grass

the talk of weddings and
babies and new
eating spots

people with rubber mat

swords in the distance

There's always so
much world to be

in and on the edges of

that people
mat it down

some portion of vastness

for quick removal

Time, a storage shed

among many in the industrial park

maze that rings
the highway-ringed city

To remember who

visited me and left and
visited again

the shape of small

instances in
an aching hollow

and cries to keep the pace intact

cranes rising
high beside the curling

bridge that cruises

along in the flat

blue that people
dreamed of,

of being outside

their own mortality

gin and tonics on the balcony

now and in

the picture of

a time made quaint

by its lengthening

absence
*

Balconies serving

as ashtrays for upstairs

neighbors sending cigarettes glowing

into the void
they think stands

outside their dreams

or their cubicles, their stalled

vehicle nightmares

Who has imagined

the world as a safe place must

still also die there

Is it living to be

shut away

in the All Rules Guidebook

straddled
by a long row of numbers

counting and counting

checking in
for updates on figuring

the proper row

in the overall Big Bubble Meltdown

borders made in mind
claiming

to describe whole

bodies and their histories

o slavering textile

and landscape dreams

fertile with anything

done to them

old dredged harbors
and refurbished

military barracks

longed for like love
*

The only army down

the street here

is the ripped-up

men, missing

an arm or leg or both or

leaning

against a cane less than thirty

years old mostly they

laugh in the

Warrior Foundation Freedom Station

courtyard, look

from wheel chairs

with shaded eyes against

the long afternoon
sun that drivers

drive past in, not seeing

between the video store, the Starbucks,

Sandwiches to Go

the courtyard built

around what
remains of people

I
walk past alone and leg-sore and

full in my limbs

any metal casing only

what my

mind can't rid

itself of, remains of people

oh I know

dreams I know images "we

have learned so

little of care"

like these box

apartments where

the dismembered live

bartering, joking, got a cigarette

staring

at the sun hot street

*

MARK WEISS

DIFFERENT STORIES

1

The man who lives in boring times
bucket by bucket moves a mountain.

Wedded to the trajectory,
a collection of shattered lenses,
a matrix of rituals.

Man, or machete.
A catalogue of expectations.
Cutlass, for instance,
the brute violence of the toolshed
become a scimitar in the hands of pirates.

2

On the subway platform the girl sways
to invisible music.
Maybe she's gone to the islands.

Different stories.
I knew a girl whose childhood
was her mother's experiment
in elective surgeries to make her
"beautiful," new nose, new eyelids,
as the world sees it.
Except that she'd refused the last experiment.
A different story. And what became

of all that perfection,
that one defiance,
that vote for symmetry.

3
Failure to make circles.

Old age, as the young man assured me,
is a state of mind.

In the order of things
there will be fire.

Ownership of islands will be swept by the sound
and all these wetlands.

This has been home
and this has been home
and this has been home.
Much of what you plan for
won't happen, and what does
you'll be unprepared for.

Following beasts,
elk and elephant providing wisdom.
"Where grass is good
there will be meat."
"Salt is aggressive
and rises to water."

4
Mist
and mystery
in the English
idiom, math

and mastery
in the physics of war.

5
A nice day,
flaxen girl in flat sandals licks
a cone of white ice cream
and strides through the park.

Strides through the park in flat sandals
licking a cone of white ice cream.
So nice a day. She eats
white ice cream.

Oh custard.
Oh sugarplum.

6
A Mayan woman with her Mayan children
at the Delacort fountain.
Hard to imagine a beauty more divorced
from that belle époque fragility, she
recalling blood and viscera.
But her children
will speak the local dialect.

7
A tendency to swallow whole when excited
(a tendency to excitement)
but masticate, grind,
that the chestnut not
become the death of you. Chew
as if your life
depended on it.
Time enough for the visible world
beyond the restaurant.

8
In his will he endowed a fund
to feed a homeless person once a year
the finest, most expensive,
and record
the recipient's despair
thereafter.

9
Gleaning the last of an insufficient harvest, he
chops down the final bit of scrub so that his child
will have warm food. Who knows
what luck might bring
to keep them for another day.

First worry,
then despair.

Maybe the last
of insect or mammal
will descend upon them.

Where blond means enough to eat
and brunette not so much.

10
So it turns out
that we're not the answer
to the dreams of centuries.

Lope of the hunter from field to forest.

"We have adapted wheat to grow on clouds
and grain to fall like rain."
Laughed, then died, and the living
guess at the joke.

HISTORY

The imposition of metal shoes
is the least of the horse's hardships.

The sweet disposition of geldings. As a leather bag
testifies to the mortality of cows.

Once by the shape of a hand
you could say which tribe,
which not.

Let us proceed to the emptying of all things.

Scrape of blade on toast,
each teacup carefully chosen.

Take personally the affronts of the past.

Above, dark water.
Below, dark water.
Rises.
Falls.

Once by the shape of the hand
you could tell the land.

NATIONHOOD

1
We wear the same clothes differently.

Death as a boundary disturbance.

The sway of her hips against the gothic.

Man with man
beast with beast
house of blood.

Explaining perspective to the blind.

The occasion of necessity between ping and pong
as tentative as blossoms.

Not to have been shot at or starved
would seem amazing luck
in the world as it's been.

It's this complex engineering called beauty in motion.
A kinship with cows.
The disguise of the native.

The intelligence of a dog
applied indifferently to landscape.

As useful as feet.

Your body's quick intelligence.
All praise for instinctual virtue.

The language of sorrow has an Irish accent
a Jewish accent
a Scottish accent et cetera.

2
Yellow haze of mustard
among cactus and thorn. Salad
for the border-crossers.

Hand to mouth
as easy as

"...and given the times,"
he said...

Noise and predation.

Become accustomed to muscle and bone
where before
skin
and a skein of nerves.

Sticks his finger in his ear
shakes vigorously
clears his throat.

The unknown codes of the law of twos and sevens.

In considering the greatness of this or that ruler
include the accomplishment of questionable goals.

ROSS WHEELER

TREMBLAY

The couple sat opposite me at dinner. A man and a woman in their late twenties, reading the menu together as if it were a pleasant riddle posed to them as a way of passing the time. The woman seemed to know some French and would hazard comments such as, this is duck in some type of sauce, or this comes with vegetables. They ordered wine, shared the tasting, and relaxed in anticipation of courses the fixed menu provided. The man's chair faced me and as I ate I felt his gaze drift across the room to my table. Did he wonder if I was also taking the tour?

From the hotel matron I had learned that three bicycles were deposited in the garage, and when I'd inspected mine, I noticed the names of the couple on yellow cards slid into the map sleeves between the handlebars. I took no notice of the names. There was no hurry—the names would take care of themselves.

The couple came in to breakfast as I was finishing my second coffee. The room was filled with families, older couples, and a large group of German retirees eating with an urgency imposed on those under schedule. I was the only single person in the room. I felt the man and woman scan the tables for seats, but finding the only open setting to be opposite me, they slid back the chairs and sat. There was in their faces a recognition from the night before. They must have guessed that I was the other cyclist.

They were wholly together, brushing each other in a kind of caress as they reached out for the breads and fruits and cheeses on the buffet. Sitting, they spoke with a secrecy that suggested they feared being overheard, as if this would dilute their intimacy like a sweet steam in a cold room. They invited no approach. I left without acknowledging them. I would be underway before they came down for their bikes. They needed to know that they were under no obligation to me. We were not a group. I understood this. We were three people traveling the same direction. I needed to assure them that they could trust me not to burden myself on them. I started off from the hotel, backpack strapped on, tour map in sleeve.

To train for the tour I had purchased a new bicycle and for several months had ridden every other day between ten and twenty miles. Though past forty, I was not in bad shape. Still, the ride was difficult—the sun cut like a brand on my neck; the pack's dead weight dragged at every hill. I lost the route, found myself on a high promontory overlooking a wide bay. Across the water white and yellow sails bulged as the wind tugged small boats out to sea, and up from the shore white villas rose in steep, gardened terraces toward a sky smudged with clouds. The couple, I thought, would enjoy the view. When I introduced myself, I could perhaps share the experience with them.

I started off, down dead-end streets and found myself on a route trafficked with heavy trucks and fast-moving cars but finally recovered my direction. The ride was dreadful, and I felt—in a sense—relieved that no one else was with me.

The first day's destination proved a city set high on a hill behind battlements. The approach to the town followed the course of a narrow river along which houseboats with blue and red hulls lay tied in succession. Fat men in suspenders and coveralls talked together along the quay as they polished bronze portholes and scrubbed spotless prows. At quay-side cafes, under umbrellas of bright yellow cloth, men in white slacks and women in sundresses sipped iced drinks and ate plates of golden steak and frites. Hot and sweaty, I rode past them, into a row of shops selling cheeses and pastries and preserves covered with linens, and ceramic bowls stenciled in blue arabesques that wove themselves into names like Kate or Clair or Felicity.

The tour had arranged for my luggage to be delivered to the hotel and it lay beside a red and a black bag which I gathered belonged to the couple. I bathed, sat on the bed and scanned the television stations. They were all in French. I checked my watch—three thirty. Dinner was at seven. I dressed and set out into the town. Along the narrow streets, British retirees walked in clusters, or emerged from shops holding open plastic bags into which they peered. I walked in the narrow ribbon of shade that fell from the roofs behind an orderly group of elderly German women wearing long full dresses. I passed with them through the cathedral portal into the cool, dark aisles and stood at a back pillar as their guide directed their attention to the right or the left or overhead. I knew no German. I emerged on the battlements, stared through arrow slots onto the cobbled streets below, surveyed the tiled rooftops, descending in sharp angles to the river along which I had ridden two hours earlier. I accumulated the experiences which one should have on such a tour. I would be held accountable for these experiences, would need to refer to them when I returned to my job and my life.

At five thirty, returning to the hotel, I saw the young couple emerge from the glass doors. The woman carried a camera from a strap on her wrist. She and the man were laughing as she directed him to stand just so on the street leading to the cathedral square. She stepped back, raised her camera, and motioned him slightly to the right. I would have to walk past them. But now was not the time to meet them. They were as much together as if they sat alone in an empty room speaking in whispers. I would not intrude. I averted my eyes and walked along the street toward them. The woman lowered the camera and wound the film and I saw her glance my way. She joined the man and with lowered head spoke to him. He glanced sideways, then slid his arm around her waist, and the two turned along the street toward the cathedral.

I brought a book to the restaurant at which the tour had made reservations. The room was long and narrow, with windows glorious with light fronting the street. I was led to a back table set for one. After pointing to various mysterious items for the waiter, I read my book. At the tables around me the patrons spoke French. Words and phrases sometimes materialized, like a face in a dark crowd swept with a light, but mostly what I heard was a flow of inflections. It was like dining beside a waterfall. The couple entered talking in English, their voices pleased and open. They were greeted by the matron who led them into the room to a table beside a window. I held my gaze to the book. We were strangers. If the roles were reversed, would I not feel the strangeness of a stranger's sudden acknowledgement. I would.

I could hear nothing of the couple's conversation, but could see the woman's bright smile as she spoke. They were probably reviewing the day, anticipating what the morning would bring them tomorrow. She leaned on her hand and gazed along the street.

At four thirty, to the sound of birds outside the window, I woke. The sound burst in gushes, a sudden chatter and scuffle close at hand, the brush of sharp feet and wings against the ledge and glass, then a scraping rush and the chatter gathering in the distance. Light collected in grays and grew in intensity across the curtain. A breeze carried through the transept the occasional stutter of a car across the cobbles. Footsteps and voices, now loud and close at hand, gained frequency then urgency. I had no expectations for the day. And yet, lying there, I felt the passage of time as keenly as if it were blood pumping from an artery. I would presently rise and go down to the breakfast. I would separate my bicycle from those of the couple and follow the route laid out by the tour. The route had been carefully selected, the tour literature stated, for beauty and diversity. Yet, after it was over, what would I have, more than a passing sensation as after a heavy meal? Still, would I feel differently had I remained at home? No. But I had anticipated the tour with pleasure. And so far what it had not been was a pleasure.

At seven thirty, I was the second patron in the breakfast room. The first was an elderly English woman sitting at a table for four who, at every rustle, glanced over her shoulder. Soon, three elderly women joined her and they entered into a lively conversation about sore ankles and gardens back home. Breakfast consisted of coffee, baguettes, and jam. It wasn't difficult to eat quickly. I doubted that I would encounter the couple this early. But I was beginning to fear that I couldn't speak with them at all. Their faces, when we'd met on the street the day before, were hardly inviting. But we were doing the same tour together. We shared this much in common. And if I didn't speak to them, with whom then could I speak? The question troubled me.

The morning was cool and leached into an overcast as I rode. I had purchased new cycling clothes for the tour. This was my first chance to wear the jacket. It fitted nicely and was at once warm and cool. My legs were tight from the previous day's ride, but after the first few miles, the tightness had stretched itself out. The route proposed by the tour included a side visit to a thirteenth century cloister. The cloister was part of the tour, and I knew I should go. Still, when the turnoff approached, I continued straight. I knew it would be beautiful, and I had no inclination to see it.

The ride wound through a countryside of green, ripening wheat fields, and fields of sweet peas, both in flower and with fresh pods hanging like earrings from stems. The fields gave way to rolling pastures, across which herds of guernsey cows lay on their haunches at rest. Two near the fence lumbered up at my approach, then hurtled away, five or six paces, and stared at me. In other fields wide swaths of hay had been mown, rolled into bales and wrapped in black plastic. Small hamlets of five or six stone houses pressed up against the road, and from the barns a sudden wave of manure would catch me like a slap. I passed though villages with stone churches, their doors open to the squares, waited at lights as men and women carrying bread under arm crossed and entered news or butcher shops. My legs grew tired. I found I could not maintain the pace I had set in my training rides. As I made my way up an easy incline, a man past sixty, pedaled alongside, called good day, and steadily outpaced me.

Skipping the cloister proved to shorten the ride considerably. I arrived before noon at the next hotel. Was in fact so early that though the luggage lay in the lobby, my room was not prepared. From the cool expression of the hotel matron, I gathered my early arrival was neither usual nor appreciated. I should perhaps have stopped at the cloister after all, or entered some of the shops or churches I passed. This was no doubt what other riders did. I parked my bike in the garage, as the woman had directed, then entered the town to find lunch. A great château dominated the town, its crown and turrets rising above the treetops like a volcano jutting up from an island. After lunch, I visited the château. Cards detailing the items and functions of the rooms were handed out according to language, while the tour itself was conducted in French. Other tourists asked what seemed complicated questions, to which long and involved answers were provided.

It was after four when I returned to the hotel. The couple, I assumed, would have ventured out long before this. Yet, as I descended the street along the château, I found them making their way up the opposite side. The woman, her hand raised, examined the château as she walked. At my approach she lowered her hand and seemed to speak. The man said nothing, but turned and let his gaze follow after me for some distance.

Their luggage had been removed from the lobby. Mine, I dragged heavily to my room. I bathed and fell asleep. It was after eight when I woke. I had surely missed engaging the couple before they entered the dining room. How odd they must think me. I had wanted only to speak to them, and yet had behaved in ways that could only suggest the last thing in the world I wanted was to speak with them. But how could I have behaved otherwise? Could I have simply barged in and disrupted them? They were together and I was alone. And I was very afraid of burdening them.

The hotel restaurant lay off the lobby. Inside, French windows lined with flower boxes overlooked the park of the château. The couple sat at a table by the windows, staring quietly off into the corridors of trees. The hotel matron approached, and as I stepped forward, she motioned me out into the lobby, down a hallway through double doors, into a large room where groups of eight or ten sat around tables and talked over each other. She placed me beside a tall fish tank. I would have no opportunity to approach the couple tonight. And a strong sense of relief came over me as I watched the small circles of air rise through the tank.

The next morning I woke at five and listened to the trucks lumbering up the hill beside the château. The low, throaty grumble of their engines bore down heavily as they shifted into the grade. A gray light filed at the edges of the curtains, but gained no intensity as time passed. The morning must be overcast. A firm resistance from my legs met my effort to stand—down my thighs and into my calves a profound soreness radiated.

At 8:05 I sat in the breakfast room looking onto the street, sipping a coffee and eating a buttered baguette. The couple did not come to breakfast this early. They were probably still sleeping or in their room dressing. I let no images form around these thoughts. I finished the breakfast, left my luggage at the desk for delivery, and wheeled my bike away from the garage.

The sky was the color of concrete and as I pedaled away from the hotel, the weight of the sky seemed to settle onto me. At the base of the hill I dismounted, adjusted the seat and the straps of the backpack. The next destination was thirty two miles away. I remounted, pumped a block farther, stopped, and set the seat and straps back to their initial positions. I forced myself to the seat again. Half a mile on I stopped and shifted weight from the backpack into the bike's saddlebags. A mile farther, I systematically shifted as much weight from the pack as the saddlebags could hold, and still the pack remained leaden. The seat refused to maintain its setting. I marked the shaft with my pen, and after another mile, when I stopped to readjust it, I found it had not moved at all.

This was day three of a six day tour. What if I could not make it to the next hotel? And if I failed today what would happen with the rest of the tour?

A gray mist clung to the fields as I rode. Sweat soon soaked my clothes; the jacket, cold and sodden, restrained my arms and shoulders. The terrain grew hilly. Low, easy inclines became steep, abrupt climbs. I came to dread the breezy downward pitch, knowing it only ricochetted up into a long, relentless grade. From the summits, however, a vast sweep of landscape spread itself out from beneath the clouds. At the horizon's points, church towers in small villages strained upward. Between the villages, the fields dropped away into shadowy valleys where black rivers smoked with mist, like the scorches of lightning. A slate silence solidified over the countryside. Through the hamlets and villages the shutters and doors stood bolted to the street; the stone squares lay abandoned; the lights of shops glowed a jaundiced yellow. The houses, churches and barns seemed all to have gathered into themselves the harsh, cold, stillness of their stones.

I arrived in Tremblay after 1:00—the thirty two miles had taken over four hours. A short distance from town, the hotel lay up a silent drive that opened among trees onto a wide lot where two cars stood near the entrance.

Inside the lobby, a man perhaps thirty sat behind the counter. He stood, stretching thin wire glasses over his ears, combed his hair with his hand, and in French greeted me. At my reply, his voice shifted tone, and he asked in English if I was all right. My breathing was difficult, my face and hair damp with sweat. But I assured him I was.

"I'm happy to hear it," he said. He waited as I lowered my pack to the floor before asking my name.

"Of course. You're expected." He made a check in the book and again peered at me. "Are you sure you're all right?"

"I must not look it," I suggested.

"Well," he said, "it is warm outside." It was not the least warm. "Your bags are just here." He pointed over his shoulder with his pencil to the bags under the stairway.

My bags were alone. Where was the couple's luggage? When I'd arrived at hotels before them, their bags had always lain beside mine. Where were their bags? The question surged up in me—but what right had I to ask it? I was not associated with the couple. But if their bags had been lost, or missed in the transfer, shouldn't I alert the man? What would they do when they found no bags waiting for them? But a second thought began to gather inside me. What if they weren't coming?

The man straightened the ledger and seemed to adjust the papers on his desk. A young woman in a black skirt and white blouse entered the lobby from a back room. The man called and pointing to my bags directed her to take them to my room.

I must look dreadful, I thought. He thinks I can't carry my bags.

I showered and changed and walked the short distance to town for lunch, reasoning that, like me, the couple must have paid the full cost of the tour in advance. They wouldn't simply abandon it. The clerk must have had their bags taken to their room, or some other arrangement was made. They couldn't quit.

Tremblay consisted of a single stone church, closed for the afternoon, one pâtisserie over the windows of which a woman rolled the grates as I watched, and three bars, all fronting the church square. I peered through their windows and entered the most crowded one, thinking this might protect me from notice. I signed to the barman, and he stepped aside to the waitress, who glanced at me, looked into the dinning room, and nodded.

As I ate, I thought how natural it would be to speak with the couple here. We were virtually alone, and there was nothing to do. If they wanted, we could perhaps take a taxi together to Fougeres, a town nearby which the guidebook assured was a lovely medieval city. If money were a problem, I could offer to pay. I left the restaurant and returned to the hotel considerably easier in mind. But as I entered the lane, I fought to suppress a panic spreading through my limbs. What if they didn't come? And when I emerged from the drive, I saw that my bicycle alone stood at the entrance.

Inside the lobby, I found a squat, red-faced man bent over the ledger. Behind him, a woman in a stiff green dress jerked the leash of a small dog growling from behind her heels. I mounted the stairs to my room.

It was two thirty. I scanned the channels of the television, all in French, none the least interesting. I lay on the bed. From the hallway I heard the man and woman enter their room. The man's voice hard, impatient, the dog barking, the door jarred shut. The young couple were not coming. A kind of terror seeped into my blood. I couldn't remain in the hotel. I couldn't stay here alone. I would take a cab to Fougeres by myself. I rose and went down to the lobby. The man was not behind the desk, but there, open on the counter, lay the ledger. My name was written on the top line. Below it were the names of the man and woman who had just signed in. No other reservations were made. I put my hands in my pockets—where was the clerk? I clasped my arms across my chest. How could I get him here? I thrust my hands back to my pockets. The clerk now emerged from the back room. Stepping behind the counter, he turned the ledger and lowered it to the desk.

He placed the call, then cupped his hand to the receiver and said that a taxi to and from Fougeres would cost nearly a hundred dollars. It was now three o'clock. The trip might take an hour each way. If I wanted to eat dinner, I would need to be back no later than eight. I returned to my room.

Along the hall the dog's barking rose like a wail. The young couple was gone. If they were here now, I could speak with them. I didn't want anything except to speak to them. I lay back on the bed. They weren't coming. If I could speak to them, they would know they could trust me. They would see that just because I was alone I wasn't something monstrous. But they were not coming.

Hadn't I prepared for the trip months in advance, cycling and purchasing new clothes, buying film and guides? Hadn't I done all I could to prepare? And when it occurred that I would need to come alone or not come at all, hadn't I chosen to come? I had known what the trip would entail. Yet, when I spoke with others about it, I heard envy enter their voices. And I knew that their envy was for a trip I wouldn't have. I lay thinking of their envy, and smothered the urge to laugh.

But I could not return and tell them that the trip had failed. To admit that I had not had a good time was small and petty and selfish. I made myself get up, stood to windows that overlooked the empty lot, then sat and addressed my postcards, making a few simple statements about the countryside, the food, the stone churches and houses. I did not mention the young couple. Nor did I mention the terror I felt now that the couple was gone. And it seemed so natural a thing to do, that it was as if I had agreed in advance to misrepresent my experience. And as I wrote the cards, my terror eased, as if somehow misrepresenting my experience for others made it livable for me.

At seven o'clock, I dressed and went down to the dining room. The room opened down a hallway behind the front desk, expanded out to the width of the hotel, past tables and booths pressed up to a dance floor, then mounted a low stage and continued back through a mirror to the lighted doorway of the entrance. The room easily accommodated fifty. The hotel clerk, wearing the same exhausted shirt, led me to one of two tables set for dinner before the windows. A light rain had started to fall, and the sky was filled with the flutter of small birds.

"You were wise not to go to Fougeres." The clerk nodded to the windows. "You would now be wet and have gained no enjoyment at all." A casual politeness accented his tone, suggesting that I had carefully weighed my options and chosen well from among them. I couldn't tell if he were joking or not.

"I let myself rest, instead," I said, adopting his tone.

He left the menu and went to seat the old man and woman who now entered the dining room. The man wore a pale blue jacket over a pleated white shirt and crossed the floor as if a band were playing and the room filled with voices. He opened his jacket as he slid into his chair, his back to me. The woman followed in a cream-colored gown scalloped across the front in a way that accentuated the bones of her throat and shoulders. She led the dog on leash, and, sitting, tried to settle it at her feet by pushing its rump to the floor. The dog leapt around, barking, and I saw the man lean forward, and the woman suddenly stiffen. She let the dog wind its leash around her legs, and begin to whine loudly. She leaned forward, and through a tight smile whispered to the man in a way that with each word caused a shifting through his shoulders. She attended to the dog. But there was something oddly formal in their behavior, as if they were enacting a scene they had spent the afternoon preparing.

"You'll have the day off, tomorrow," the clerk said, when he returned to take my order. "If it's still raining, you can ride with me in the luggage van."

"Have you heard that it will rain?"

The old man, at my question, half turned in his seat and with a harsh laugh spoke to the clerk.

"He says it will pour all day," the clerk said.

"Then I will have the day off."

Given the difficulty of the morning's ride, I had not anticipated the next thirty-plus miles with willingness, let alone pleasure. But I felt a disappointment at the prospect of being released from it. Hadn't I come here to cycle through the countryside? Was this not what I had trained and paid for? I pressed my fingers into the stiff muscles of my thighs. But I did not need to decide tonight. And the thought left me free to enjoy the evening's meal. The clerk explained the courses and offered suggestions. There was a pleasure in speaking to him that was as cool and impersonal as the rain.

During the meal, the man and woman consumed three bottles of wine. As the man drank, his posture failed him and his sentences became long and slurred. The woman's voice assumed a sharp-edged clarity, like an overexposed photograph. I didn't understand them, but I knew what they said. They seemed to speak because proximity required it, as a physical necessity, and for no other reason. What if I had been wrong about the young couple? What if, after three days, they had burned each other up in their intimacy?

I went upstairs to my room. The time was nine o'clock. For the next forty minutes I scanned the channels looking for a weather report. Then it occurred to me that the report hardly mattered. The day would bring what it brought. And at nine forty-five, I slept.

The morning was overcast, but the pavements outside dry.

"No rain," the clerk said, stretching on his glasses. His hair and shirt suggested he had slept at the desk.

"And no day off."

"You could yet ride in the van," he said. "I must deliver the luggage, and the room is plenty for you and the bike."

I thanked him for his offer, and went in to the dining room. I ate my bread and jam and drank my coffee, sitting in the great room in silence.

At nine, I set out, cold but not uncomfortable in my jacket. The first hills were agony. Twice I dismounted and, stretching out my legs, walked the bike to the top. Yet, as I rode, I found I could maintain a steady, unhurried pace. What was the hurry anyway?

The clouds thinned and pulled apart, letting broken sunlight through. The day warmed, and along the village squares old women emerged carrying cloth-covered baskets, lowered themselves to benches and talked. I felt a perfect solitude riding through the squares, but it was not unpleasant. And as I rode, I knew with increasing certainty that I could complete the miles of the tour.

Near the halfway point of the day's ride I mounted a long hill and reaching the summit found in the distance the coast cut like veined marble into the horizon. A light breeze smelling of salt spread over me. And as I stood, my stomach seemed to draw slowly into a knot, my sight wavered, and to maintain my balance I had to lean forward into the arms of the handlebars. For two minutes, perhaps, I stood clutching the bars tightly, holding onto their arms. Then the knot unwound and my eyes cleared, and touching my sleeve to my face, I climbed to the seat and continued.

SUSAN WHEELER

IN SKY

The high that proved too high, the heroic for earth too hard,
The passion that left the ground to lose itself in sky....
Robert Browning

The girl is waiting in the room to be discovered.
The girl is attempting radiance.
The girl may be a boy, or vice versa.
The girl is anticipating the man's arrival, later.
The girl is anticipating the man's displeasure.
The girl is anticipating the man's disapproval.
The girl takes no guff.
The girl's mendacity has long been remarked upon.
The girl armors up with chic.
The girl carries the blooms, the veronicas, the perovskia.
The girl who may be a boy powders the smalt.

The girl fills the room like smoke.
The girl is a deer in the onrush of lamps; she sits on the planks of the pier.
The girl swings her feet above the surface of the water.

The girl presses out, inhales, still fills her seat not.
The seat is an ink room, not-girl, apprehension.
The girl is mottled with self, with indecision.
The girl's amethyst earrings window her eyes.
The girl twirls her cape before the bull.
She refuses her chest.
She refuses "alabaster."
She refuses your volupty at her expense.

The girl is the hole, the cutout.
The box she is punched from throngs with blue spirits.

The ground is blank as a plum, tank-deep.
O water, o silting of dust. Reticulate.
The room's tonnage sags.
The ground is figure to its own ground.
And she, blade of grass at the Battle at Troy.

The girl refuses the stadium seating.
The girl mixes lazule and vivianite.
The girl was or was not a mother; this is irrelevant.
The girl's skin shelters; her skin burns with self.
At the end of the pier, in the house light, she looks up.
Her shade engulfs her.
The girl's blueism offputs the man.

The Girl look't Blew. Blue funked. Cast indigo.
She yelled bloody blue; she talked a blue streak.
The girl blued her bluebacks on linnets and blue duns.
The girl was waiting to be overtaken.
The girl was cruising for a bruiser.
The girl tilted up at the ciel: blue-domer.
She struck into space like a bolt from the blue.
Azul ultramarino, when I confessed I repented, the girl said.
She was blue mouldy for the want of that drink.

The girl ardent was; ardent, wracked, and replete.
The girl took the *retablo* from the wall; in her hand its wings shone.
The girl watched, as she listened, the strung lights waver.
The girl's moment for radiance passed.
O she was stippled; O but her room was.
O that the treatment take hold and transform.

The girl swung a gun.
The girl jutted her chin fore.
The girl limped with her sidling and stalled.
She has a fast one; it's in a wheel rut, the girl and her blue ruin, gin and her car.
The girl has veined shoulders.
She passes wind.

The girl's form is landmined: flounces, the flesh.
The girl bats the red lock away from her ear.
The girl takes the synapse and invests it with scene (insensible sense).

The girl Rapunzel is (*NOT*). She disdains.

O discrete make me and blocked.
O scurry me forth on the slate patio, and applaud my every squeak.
O I am helpful like a shill (no groin).
Untransmutable plane with your shadowed door.
The room heats like a vise.

The girl splices the water like a seal or a grouper.
The girl's shell grows a rubbery skin.
The girl looks right back, planted.

The girl holds her thumb piano beneath our view.

She, the girl, regards the chimpanzee.
The chamber loses its ceiling and the stars prick through.

The girl breathes. Her sex bucks out of sight.

The girl, blushing: *O did you see me there? Did you?*

PENNY LANE

Beyond the walls of this house others will be nice to you.
They will not ridicule you every day.
And if you've something to say, they'll say okay.

I will put a nickel in the penny pot at Joe's;
I will make like Roxanne's saying something new.
And if I'm stuck with Lame C crew, I'll make do.

He's spinning, sponging and the man in the street—
He's sponging the worst off the man in the street—
The hawk's got a pigeon, and it's slamming its steak—
It wasn't my fault—
It wasn't my fault—

So for Pete's sake go make breakfast and then wake me up.
Wake Louise and me when you've seen J Z twice;
When it's ready everything is new, you'll make nice; you'll make do.

SUPPRESSION

He took the ham for his forerunner's failures;
"If you don't like the ham, get gone from the dinner,"
or so Rahm said in his usual white ham.
The ham index was up in the ham wave of summer.

One night in a dream, his ham-gun zapped Karzai,
then the High Explosive Anti-Tank missed,
and the oncoming came on: he woke in him water.
The ham index was up in the ham wave of summer.

If ham lightning happened to ignite the Gulf—
each gully, each inlet, beach piping him—
in the ham of the moment, no worse off he'd be.
The ham index was up in the ham wave of summer.

His tween wanted him-pants; his *teen* had the hims
for the himmest gone boy, benched, on the team.
"He's full of him air"—but this fell on deaf ears.
The ham index was up in the ham wave of summer.

You gauge the ham of our livers by the bitter in
your galls, he thought, his ham rising, then:
but wags we are, too. None were him stuff.
The ham index was up in the ham wave of summer.

'99: Mississippi Ham at Theresa's, south side.
'02: Reverend H. Ham at that joint off of Lincoln,
night the Rev was arrested for his packing ham.
The ham index was up in the ham wave of summer.

Notes sought now too, not Canned Ham but a
This Ham reprisal, storm of notes equal to this.
No surprise some folks get a ham on and tank.
The ham index was up, ham wave of summer.

Not he. He was ham resistant. He could strike
the tycoons while they were him; he could buoy those
broke by ham exhaustion on the border, by job loss,
ham rash, by him dogs in suits; he could take it hot,

the heat he could take, in the summer heat wave,
with the heat index high in that hot, hot July.

ELIZABETH WILLIS

NOTES FROM AND ON A LANDSCAPE: HELL, FIRE AND BRIMSTONE

Brimstone—or sulphur—is at the center of the discourse of infernal punishment and occult power.

It's the part of us that's subject to ignition. It is a kindler of rage.

When brimstone is used to set people on fire outside the gates of redemption, their suffering makes the exaltation of the righteous appear better than it is.

Some people are content to place their enemies in an imaginary torment, but there are also the very real histories of napalm, of lynching, of burning at the stake. The practice of tarring and feathering has had a vivid life on this continent.

Setting one's enemies on fire is a very old idea.

Perhaps this is why the setting of one's own body on fire has been viewed as the most extreme and symbolically precise voicing of outrage and resistance.

According to John Quincy's *Pharmacopoeia Officinalis* (1718): "Sulphur…is very soft and unctious, and the lightest part of Bodies next to Spirit."

Sulphur lozenges, soaps, ointments, and baths have been used to treat asthma, hemmorrhoids, and disorders of the skin.

You feel the side effects before you feel the cure.

Sulphur was said to fill the air when the righteous prayed for a witch.

Curious women and those who resorted to begging have been accused of witchcraft because they asked inappropriate questions or, like poets, muttered when they walked.

Where is there religion. There is always religion. (Gertrude Stein)

It wasn't until the 15th century that witches appeared on broomsticks and thus were linked irrevocably to domestic labor and disobedience.

All of Europe was threatened by the ingeniousness of this repurposing—the use of one tool to do something previously inconceivable.

Saint Joan was referred to as The Maid. Even after she led an army.

When she was on trial, her inquisitors pointed out that she had tried to escape and that God had not delivered her from her enemies. "A prisoner," she said, "has the right to attempt escape."

She said, "The voice is a light."

She said, "I can't recant."

She said, "Even fire won't change my mind."

Bertholt Brecht said he had nothing to say to those who did not already know that the world was on fire.

Last year more of the United States was burning than in any other year on record—7 million acres before the end of August. Kenya and Mongolia were on fire. Every state in Australia was on fire. The peat fires ignited during Siberia's 90-degree afternoons went underground last winter and resurfaced with the thaw.

How in *this* world can anyone be excluded from the discourse of fire?

Those of us who know that the world is on fire have ridden shotgun on the brooms of crones and degenerates, opium eaters and speakers in tongues, poets and tellers of fact, excommunicants and sodomites, insider artists and citizens of the outer dark, malcontents and depressives, urban farmers and dwellers in tents.

Like the Maid, we have the right to transform the disciplinary structures of our world with sulphurous language. To fight one fire with another.

+

Keeping in mind a history of the occult, I want to consider more broadly that which is occluded, hidden, overlooked.

Think for a moment about what obstructs vision. Our vision, as a species and as poets. What distracts us from looking more deeply. What ideological and imaginative barriers lead to an acceptance of the entrenched binaries of party politics, of gender, of race, of religion, of class, of technoculture. What interferes with wilder patterns of inquiry?

How invested are we, individually and collectively, in the concept of hell—or even in a hell-making device that forces certain individuals to pay for their crimes? And what kinds of progressive thinking does this block, as we live *among* each other's crimes, and in the case of global issues like climate change, pay for them collectively, albeit unevenly.

We—specifically and generally, as creatures and fellow-participants within larger systems—cannot afford for the network of resources that binds us together to be broken by actuarial science.

Reduce your carbon footprint and your mind will follow. (George Clinton)

It is not enough to recognize the systematic and willful destruction of "our" world, a place where the possessive pronoun can imply radically divergent value systems. Whatever we mean by the "world" is under constant revision from within and without. But recognizing the default settings of this place and time may be the beginning of claiming the right to revise our relation to various resources. Remapping any future requires us to seek out, consider, and re-value the perceptual apparatuses and experience of other species, living and dead. To see up close and differently. And at the same time to stand back far enough to see the disciplinary patterns and liberational pathways that are not immediately evident when we view this world as simply chaotic.

I'm thinking in particular of two obstructive concepts—or structuring beliefs—that are often treated as immutable.

The first is a paternalistic view of species relation. Although Darwin suggested—and Lorine Niedecker reminds us—that no species is inherently higher or lower than another, it has been taken as a given that humans are at the top of the evolutionary chain. Are we content to build a lonely planet on which we are the *de facto* arbiters of the future? What can we learn from the behavior and language patterns of other species; by observing how they survive—or don't survive—the death drive of capitalist expansion and human dominance?

Redwoods, for example, can be on fire for years without dying. A tree in California named Methusaleh is 4800 years old. There are trees in England that go back to the age of the druids. They can survive almost anything but a chainsaw.

If a 5000-year-old tree spoke would we understand what it said? Or would we calculate its potential effect on "housing starts"? (Ludwig Wittgenstein)

Redwoods are rhizomatic. The unit is the grove, not the tree.

This creature speaks so slowly, hardly anyone seems to notice.

What can be learned from the symbiotic world evolving hundreds of feet above us, entire ecosystems of plants and animals that coexist in redwood culture and that never touch the ground?

If we were to relinquish the current operating system of human supremacy, what could other species teach us about surviving as non-dominant entities?

The residual presence of a first-, second-, and third-world model of economic and cultural development is similarly problematic. Built on the assumption that a whitewashed version of western culture holds the duty, right, and privilege of shaping the political and environmental patterns of the rest of the "undeveloped" or "developing" world, it claims for the "developed" sector an unproblematically empathic relation to others, by which they always remain "other."

The American State Department has a lot to learn from the Somali refugees who have dry-farmed tiny gardens within overcrowded desert camps, and from communities that live off the grid of satellite communication. What if, instead of thinking that the world would be improved by cell reception and access to factory foods, we sought ways to un-develop, to consider differently the landscape that ATT forgot—or that didn't fit into Walmart's economy of scale?

What would the future sound like if the struggle to survive on limited resources, the necessity of balancing self-sufficiency and interdependency were distributed more broadly?

What is being said in the sensorial worlds beyond the reach of contemporary linguistics?

What are the sinkholes in Johannesberg and rural Pennsylvania saying to each other?

What does Fukushima mean on a planet whose surface is 71% ocean?

Can we spatially and temporally reorient the world map so that North America no longer appears in the upper left-center—the place on the page from which all else follows? Can we revise our relation to those who placed it there?

Our values shift according to our language. (William Carlos Williams)

By passing through a fiery word, one thing can be turned into another. A civil war, a coup, a revolution, a liberation, a takeover.

How willing are we to live by the consequences of our own thought?

How far will we allow poetry to take us?

+

At the institution where I teach, the library was recently "weeded" to make room for new acquisitions. Among the items withdrawn were books entitled: *Ideas are Weapons; Population and World Power; A Handy Guide for Beggars; What*

Are We For?; Liberalism Fights On; and *The Red Executive.*

I would like to speak in favor of the obsolete, the withdrawn, the hidden, the unread, and the cast off.

I would like to read *The Sorcery of Color* by W.E.B. DuBois, which was rejected by William Sloane, his editor at Henry Holt, in 1940, after which the manuscript was lost, though it eventually resurfaced in DuBois's papers at UMass Amherst.

What can we learn at the dump?

What can we learn from those who survive as gleaners?

The fact of global warming and other environmental realities push us out of boundaried identities and demand other forms of engagement and relation.

I think there is still a lot to learn from Occupy—about what structures can emerge from collective action and how they may be extended to include other commitments.

Poetry is a rival government always in opposition to its cruder replicas. (William Carlos Williams)

So much depends/ upon / the stone-cold generosity we have often been permitted to encounter in the wheelbarrow of discarded arts.

+

When "history" is used as a verb, it means to write, depict, narrate, or recount. When it first appeared in 5th-century Latin, *historiare* meant to seek by questioning.

The West has been witness to America writing itself, with the backhand of conquest, from right to left, east to west, clothed in a rhetoric as "natural" as the planet's turning.

The pen with which this country is historied is not mightier than its sword; it is with a sword that it learned to write.

Such power is both real and imaginary, as the mission of "real" power is to lay hold upon the imagination.

The Oregon Trail, the Lincoln Highway, the Trail of Tears, the Northwest Passage.

These lines too are written.

At what cost do we separate thought from feeling?

What acts of will and imagination remain in the uncombed weeds of the past, beyond the histories we have been conditioned to repeat?

Compare the populations of private prisons and college classrooms.

Do you begin to see a little what America is what American religion is what American war is. (Gertrude Stein)

In most western frontier towns the wooden churches have burned or collapsed, the general store has been leveled to make room for the poured concrete of a chain supermarket with its city block of parking spaces, the theatres have been converted into senior centers or have filled with pigeons before one agency or another shuts them down.

The AAA guide for Wyoming lists more jails as historical sites than any other category of tourist attraction.

Jails were made to last.

By what sulphurous art may poetry, the "true fiction," labor to take them down?

AMY WRIGHT

AGESTRATA

Beetle, the polished
metal acid trip mirror
of your exoskeleton
reflects your non-beetle
bug-eyed cousins
whose perception differs
markedly based on profit,
unseeing your green
getup's luminous beauty,
70s disco gypsy
otherworld holdover
come to show earthlings
how to shimmer, and shake
our pygidia, grove on
multiplicity's sunshine orchestra.

MICROGRAPHIA, OR, SOME PHYSIOLOGICAL OBSERVATIONS OF MINUTE BODIES MADE BY MAGNIFYING GLASSESWITH OBSERVATIONS AND INQUIRIES THEREUPON

Without Robert Hooke,
curious Charles II
might glimpse a flea
hop on a dog's
back to suck a drop,
or the paw scratch his
own hide off to find
the flick, but only
under magnification
might a scientist
witness the beast's *suit*
of sable Armour
shield that gambit
as it tucks foreleg A
(drawn and explained
to his Highness)
into B, and C
into D, later named
tibia, femur,
trochanter, coxa
by those who would
abrogate now common
knowledge to train
their sights on other
planets, while the flea
keeps stacking its springs
to launch unforeseeable
distances entrusted
to a similar idea
of progress.

LEPIDOPTERY

Grandfather, auto mechanic, lepidopterist
in the posture of upright fence, Tom
peers into oak groves.

Plain-clothed, no blaze-orange earflaps
outfit him for this encounter
with the annual emergence of buck moths,

in hunting season, though he bears a long-handled
butterfly net and permission from a local farmer
in lieu of a license or rifle.

After working all his life with his hands,
he knows where to hold the thorax
to relax these downy winders, keep their crushed

velvet scales perfect as a layer of baklava.
His blue Ford parked by the roadside,
what he wants before retirement

is to breed a female. He anticipates
with a fisherman's patience, sights the distance
for a falling leaf to come alive, beeline

behind him where a gravy-tailed egg-layer
calls, knows a fleck of planet dander will break free
from the hardwood, fly toward him,

waiting with a forked twig in a fastfood bag—
an Isadora Duncan comet on the horizon
will careen into his steady-widening orbit.

SPECIMENS, MOUNT 4

One may start from the fact that the true collector
detaches the object from its functional relations.
The Arcades Project

Dung Beetle

Egyptians say this
world is a digestive loop:
ingesters do best only if
they too filter waste from waste

Horned Scarab

Shiny horned devils
deflected Sir Charles
Darwin's clerical studies
with solvable mysteries

Mole Beetle

Hard-nosed, underground
gallery mavens weld wings
against oft-heralded heavens

Click Beetle

Ventral muscle contractors
who flex under pressure
teach us how to snap the catch,
right ourselves with a backflip

COLLAGE OF THIRTY DRAGONFLY SPECIES HEADSHOTS

Note the pseudopupils—from a pencil eraser
fleck to an ant's foreleg, pinpricks in the blue
foveal band indiscernible to untrained eyes,
nuclei-less whorl of locust grain on a dollhouse door,

where a petaltail scouts a swallowtail.
One might stumble hours inside closed buildings,
fall heat-of-the-day tired onto a lawn rattling with cicadas
where students glean meter and vie

for notice, reading Emily Dickinson, oblivious
to poetic distinctions between such moonstone lenses,
heavy-lidded opals, vitreous kyanites—
beauty rare as larimars, inside which trillions

of genetic modifications uplift clypei, incline
prothoraxes by micrometers slight as pupils sliding
toward beloved crushes, or one fingered engagement
ring rising higher than another's angle.

These all-eye heads are cool, scanned
before they lose refrigeration's stupor,
fly into the bright background where one Susan
shines extra ultraviolet among a field of black-eyed strangers.

INSECT TIME

Consult a termite queen
before she scratches
off her nuptial flight wings
and after, when she sweats fat
inside her earthen capsule
where she once nestled
with her king, nymphs in love
with solitude. Who counts
seconds when every third
she lays another quarter billionth
egg, grows translucent.
Colony whirr fills the cathedral
mound above her, an insistent
dispenser whose stillness
releases everything that is
not it in a static procession
of white, like bubbles drawn
around captioned thought.

LAURA E. WRIGHT

WHICH SECRETS SHOULD I TELL AND WHICH STORIES SHOULD I LET BURN?

…ung mountain belts and modern island associated with the highly seismic and c belts adjacent to consuming plate mar— his association occurs at continent/ocean ries (e.g., the Andes), in island arcs n oceans (the New Hebrides), and where mental collision has occurred (the…

PRELUDE, I

Which secrets should I tell and which stories should I let burn? Passion, mostly, makes me cry, makes my hands prick and my body yearn. But it does not change my mind.
Faces. Faces do not make me change my mind. Water does not make me change my mind. Deliberation does not make me change my mind.

The graffiti I knew, the map of our lives, was painted over, white. The walls still looked like spaghetti. The commentary was erased, but it was not erased if I still remember. I still remember. She turned around to look at him. How do you know? Be you drunken. I wish I could tell you. All the things. I am greedy, as you will later see.
Which secrets should I tell first? The ones that make me burn. This, then, is where to begin. Burning.

PRELUDE, II

The sky was *that* blue. Ella was saying *you got pajamas* and the sky was going along with all that. I was driving west, toward the mountains, but that's not where this begins. Things break; this is predictable. The shape of the pieces is not.

The first piece is the shape of everything I will not say, everything I promise not to reveal. The face in the desert that, even when I begged for advice, gave none. So I will not tell your name.

I am always headed west; the sky is always that blue; I am always crying about someone else's lost love. I am always losing you.

LOVE LOST

Love, not Paradise. Why tell the real story? What does Prometheus have to do with this? (Prometheus Bound was such a compelling title. But Percy Bysshe Shelley was an asshole. At sixteen, I fell in and out of love with both Shelley and Napoléon. I fell into desire. I am falling still.)
But not paradise because if there were such a place, it would have been destroyed. The ecstatic is not accessed by repeating the word "ecstatic." Pause. A blank space in the shape of what would have been. My children, for instance, would be older than yours. But mine, unlike yours, do not exist. Their temperament, then, is irrelevant.

Begin. A thousand beginnings, each of which is, at the outset, clearheaded and sober. A thousand heroines all of whom, it turns out, like to have sex. "Like" is not strong enough and "a thousand" is a vast underestimate. This is just the beginning. This is an introduction to the temperate zone.

The next line comes from the song or maybe from the kid you pass while walking the dogs, the kid screaming "I'm gonna go pee." And then. This is not what you would have chosen. It is also not what you would have imagined or expected. Perhaps you expected subtlety. Silly you. We talk about the weather as if it were a disobedient child. The weather is, in fact, a disobedient child. But it doesn't pee on the sidewalk.

But back to the beginning, that is, the burning words. I put the words in my coat pocket for later, pieces of pages that were all that was left:

This story begins with words falling on my head, not so much words as pieces of pages, pieces of words, and with David (David Henderson) telling me this is important, this is a story I should tell. I'm not sure which story is "the" story. Pieces of pages, all that's left.

I put the whistle of the southbound train in my pocket, too. But I don't give that away. Extreme fire behavior, they say now, is the "new normal." Does that mean I'm not lucky to have seen it all?

If I can't be accurate, I guess I'll be heartbroken. Pieces of pages rain down on me. All I can hear is the roar of fire, and I know now that fire is a she. She is ferocious.

Fight fire with fire. Fight fire with water, which increases in volume by 1,600 times at standard temperature and pressure when it turns to steam. But what is water, other than a reflection? Water is bigger, slower, and stronger than any of us. In the end we fight fire with water. But in the beginning we can't fight water, we can only get out of the way.

In the middle there is wind. Wind forcing us to keep driving, me falling asleep. (*Detour: S yelling at me to stay awake at first, the same Crystal Method tracks playing over and over because we were both too tired or too frustrated to do anything about it, or maybe because he couldn't hear and I no longer cared*). Detour: wind awakening the fire the next morning and once she is awake the rest of us had better be too.

Interruption: this fleeting, flooding, this feeding. Fire is omniverous. Let anything get hot enough and it will burn. Unless it is water, which increases in volume by 1,600 times at standard pressure when it turns to steam. Unless it is water, which carries us all away.

Fire, like the metaphorical heart, goes in all directions. All directions at once. Water follows a path of least resistance, gravity bound, ever downward. Fire consumes, while water washes away or erodes. Neither discriminates.

If I can't be accurate, I guess I'll be heartbroken. There are holes. Holes in all directions, holes in the real heart which as you know is driven by electrical conduction. There is that tell-tale violence in each of us which compels us to repeat, our breath, our genes. We are a copy of a message forgotten long ago by its sender, an arc of charged particles. We are both attracted and repelled; we are an admixture of opposing forces that results in holes. Even the holes have broken hearts. Even these continue to twitch and pump; valves open and close.

LOVE LOST, PART II

Because I said I would begin with the words falling. But that's not where it began. The words fell in the middle. The beginning was disputed, and was not what I photographed. But the beginning was near. The beginning is documented elsewhere [see: Fourmile Fire 2010]. Then we were on standby and the wind was so strong we could barely stand outside, more like surf the road, and the engine door blew open so hard it broke, and we drove around the rest of the day and the night with it held half closed with webbing and a carabiner. Someone asked later, so I might as well say now, yes, the wind really did break the engine door. And we waited.

"Fiercen" is not a word, but it should be: to grow fiercer.

We drove in. The truck was yellow and the apocalypse was now. We couldn't see. There was a deck; we used a saw; we pulled hose; we put hose back; we drove. We drove away quickly; we returned. Fire came over the ridge, against the wind or at least that's how it appeared. Somewhere in there the words fell. I put them in my pocket for later. I should have shared them with H, who was there when the words fell. But I am greedy and I want to keep all the words for myself. H is real and could also be called D. H prefers bourbon. I want to keep the bourbon too. I'll leave out all the rest for now, including how R was at the station that day, and another fire where I had to hitchhike and change out of my skirt.

Detour: I can mispronounce all your names with the best of them. You can't stop me now. Now. Now. Know. No.

What had I learned? Identify and move pokey things before placing. It's not, they say, rocket surgery. Slow is smooth and smooth is fast. What did I learn?

We drove in. The horses all got out. Smoke in every direction from every direction and I couldn't picture how to turn toward the source, though I should have been able to. Smoke thicker than blood, thicker than you or me. The flames didn't lick, they poured. Mostly we couldn't see and the door flapped slightly where it wouldn't close all the way. I forgot my camera and my glasses and my food. I cried when the Red Cross showed up and gave me the last veggie burger. I swore I'd do better next time.

(There was a next time. There was less to do and more food. I napped in the hose bed and daydreamed about someone to nap there with me. My helmet was crooked. There was ice (snow), water (creek) and fire. I remembered to look up. There was a next time. I changed out of my skirt by the side of the road. I got a ride by showing my radio, by begging, by explaining. The truth? We threw some wood around; we found someone's vibrator; we acted the part; we sat in lawn chairs and watched the air show. I made it out in time for a belated birthday dinner. I had to call about the dogs. We moved the woodpile quickly, knowing someone would need to move it back again, piece by piece. We waited. The fire smoldered. Remember, fire is a she.)

We drove in; the words fell. I kept the words but I'm giving them back now. We drove in; we drove out; down the steep escape route road [Lickskillet, if you have the map], we drove back in. Lots of us. We moved some water. The words had already fallen.

INTERLUDE

Because this doesn't make much sense, does it, if you weren't there? You weren't there. There was a fire. You can look it up. After several years of preparing for fires there I was, in the middle of a fire, exhausted before it even began, eyes open wide. One thing I realized was this: those who don't return did nothing more wrong than anyone else who goes in. That's the way she goes. Fire is a she. She is ferocious. Those of us who go home did nothing more right. The words fell. The right words. We went home that day. "Everyone goes home." Except those who don't. Because she is capricious. There is nothing to lose. There is everything to lose. She always wins. Wins what?

LOVE, FOUND?

The words fell on my head or fell into my pocket. I set them aside for later. Who is the main character here, the words or the fire? This last hurrah.

BAD DEBTS EXPENSE

unts eceivable wance for Bad Debts rchandise Inventory uipment owance for Depreciation nts Payable Control Investment er Drawing eaning Service Income Accessories Sales Income Sale Ret. & Allow.-Cl. Serv. ales Returns & Allow.-Access. rchandise Purchases urchases Returns & Allow. lary Expense t Expense Supplies Used Bad Debts Expense preciation Expense iscellaneous Expense otals t Profit for the Month

dise Inventory vice Income Sales In

e adjusting entries have be fle same bala eet

POSTLUDE

I would like to erase much of what comes next. Erase, not burn, because burning leaves a trace. In fact, I would prefer to dissolve.

Oh, well, sadness…you know? Burning leaves a trace. Here is what comes next:

The house hums with laundry, dishes, heat, passing cars. Sugar. Click. Sometimes I admit to myself how much I hate you. Sometimes I delight in having been so very wrong.

KIRSTIN HOTELLING ZONA

IF THEY SUCCEED IN LOVING*

the distance between them
they will reach into each others' lungs and inhale

the smell of pooled blood
in their palms.

When the blood dries, their children will pry
then lift small bowls to the light,
delight in patterns

cast in relief by the pressure of each parent's hold.

The children's task: place the bowls
on the sills of the house by the shore.

Arrange them by season.

Tree pollen, salt, insect wings, dust.

*The title of this poem as well as its first line are from a letter by Ranier Maria Rilke to his wife, Lou Andreas-Salomé, to whom he was married for 35 years.

SO WE THANK THE GODS BY DANCING ON GRAVITY'S FLOOR

Because dancing's for the devil
and devils are hot

Because hotness is a matter
of degree and degrees are defined
as set changes measured
against a given scale

Because scales trill skin-teeth hungry for weight

Because weight is what you feel
borne by the ball of one foot
as you're poised to pivot
for the dip into your lover's arms

(by gradient pressure within one's body parts)

Because parts create wholes and holes can be filled

And filling requires fitting
into something you touch

Because touch does not make you
small but stickies the skin for attachment

Because attachment is the milk
of subsistence and subsistence is the slurp of care

Because caring for and taking care are not ethical abstractions

Because abstractions join concepts
by contraction

Because contractions spew babies
and vowels and red magma

And magma is lava once it flows
through the puncture

(vesuvian mama stoking the rupture)

Because ruptures interrupt and interruptions are rude

Because rudeness can be shrewdness—
a refusal of erasure

BIOS

WILLIAM ALLEGREZZA edits Moria Books and teaches at Indiana University Northwest. He has previously published many poetry books, including *In the Weaver's Valley* (2006), *Ladders in July* (2007), *Fragile Replacements* (2007), *Collective Instant* (2008), *Aquinas and the Mississippi* (with Garin Cycholl), *Covering Over* (2006), and *Densities, Apparitions* (2014); three anthologies, seven chapbooks, including *Sonoluminescence* (2007), co-written with Simone Muench, and *Filament Sense* (2008); and many poetry reviews, articles, and poems.

ROBERT ARCHAMBEAU's books include the studies *Laureates and Heretics* (2010) and *The Poet Resigns* (2013) as well as the poetry collections *Citation Suite* (1997), *Home and Variations* (2004), and *Slight Return* (2011). He is the editor of *Letters of Blood and Other Works in English* (2011) by Göran Printz-Påhlson and *Word Play Place* (1998), and coeditor with Davis Schneiderman and Steve Tomasula of *The &NOW Awards* (2009). He teaches at Lake Forest College.

CHARLES BERNSTEIN is the author of *Recalculating* (2013), *Attack of the Difficult Poems* (2011), and *All the Whiskey in Heaven* (2010). He is Donald T. Regan Professor of English and Comparative Literature at the University of Pennsylvania, where he is codirector of PennSound.

R. M. BERRY is professor of English at Florida State University. His books include the novel *Frank* (2005), the fiction anthology *Forms at War* (2009) and the critical anthology, *Fiction's Present* (2007), coedited with Jeffrey R. Di Leo. His criticism has appeared in *New Literary History*, *Philosophy and Literature*, *symploke*, and *The Oxford Handbook of Philosophy and Literature*.

BARRY BLINDERMAN is a curator of contemporary art, educator, and essayist on art from the 1980s to the present. He has been the director of University Galleries of Illinois State University, Normal, since 1987. From 1980-87, he directed Semaphore Gallery in SoHo and Semaphore *EAST* in the East Village. He is also a musician and songwriter whose duo Blinderman & Freeman released the CD *Music for the Sunrise* in 2014.

JUNIOR BURKE is a novelist, dramatist, and lyricist. His novel *Something Gorgeous* (2005) was hailed for its invention by the UK's *Historical Novels Review.* His most recent musical productions, *Mythos* and *One October Midnight*, were staged in 2013. His songs have been widely performed and recorded and have received critical acclaim in the *New York Times*, the *Chicago Tribune*, the *Wall Street Journal*, and music publications including *Billboard*, *Dirty Linen*, *No Depression,* and *Downbeat.*

DON BYRD taught at a large public university for forty years. For the first twenty-five of those years, he published extensively. Then he decided to figure out what he was doing. He continued to write but published rarely. "Between a Shit and a Sweat" is a new departure. He now lives in Brooklyn.

MAXINE CHERNOFF chairs the Department of Creative Writing at San Francisco State University and edits the journal *New American Writing* with Paul Hoover. She was cotranslator with Paul Hoover of *Selected Poems of Friedrich Hölderlin*, which won the 2009 PEN USA Translation Prize and was a 2013 NEA Fellow in Poetry. In 2013 she was a Visiting Professor at University of Exter in England. She is the author of fourteen books of poetry and six books of fiction, one of which was a NYT Notable Book. She lives in the Bay Area.

ANDREI CODRESCU is a poet born in Sibiu, Transylvania, Romania, who resides in the Arkansas Ozarks and New Orleans. He founded the journal *Exquisite Corpse,* and wrote *The Posthuman Dada Guide* (2009). He won the Peabody Award for his film Road Scholar and the ACLU Freedom of Speech Award for "Talking too Loud" on NPR.

JACK COLLOM. Born Chicago 1931, grew up in nearby Western Springs. Woods and birds. Moved to Colorado, studied Forestry. USAF four years, factory, GI Bill English degrees. Freelance poetry teacher forty years. Longtime Naropa U. adjunct. Books on kids' writings. Twenty-five books of own poetry. NEA awards, FCA award. Seeks to match nature's variety with variety of ways to think/talk about it. Married to writer Jennifer Heath. Father of four.

MEL COYLE is from Chicago and other places where the corn grows. She received her MFA from Louisiana State University and is part of a duo that runs the online literary gallery: TENDERLOIN and the Cold Cuts Poetry Reading Series. Currently, she teaches high school English in New Orleans.

RICARDO CORTEZ CRUZ, a beast blowing up during the creation of a new black avant-garde aesthetic, is the author of *Straight Outta Compton* and *Five Days of Bleeding*, novels short and funky. He has stitched together a third black body of (s)language—"Premature Autopsies." His autobiographic short fiction, including that on Trayvon Martin, has appeared in numerous journals and anthologies. Cruz—reviewed by the *Nation*, the *Source* music magazine, *High Times*, etc.—teaches English at Illinois State University.

BRENT CUNNINGHAM is a writer, publisher, and visual artist living in Oakland, California. He has published two books of poetry, *Bird & Forest* (2005) and *Journey to the Sun* (2012). He currently works as the Operations Director at Small Press Distribution in Berkeley. He and Neil Alger are the cofounders of Hooke Press, a chapbook press dedicated to publishing short runs of poetry, criticism, theory, writing and ephemera. He has been working on a novel since at least the Clinton administration.

GARIN CYCHOLL's recent work includes *Horse Country* (2014), a collection of shorter poems that reconsiders the iconography of the horse in American culture, as well as a screenplay adaptation of Walker Percy's novel, *Lancelot*. Since 2002, he has been a member of Chicago's Jimmy Wynn Ensemble.

DEBRA DI BLASI is founding publisher of Jaded Ibis Productions and Jaded Ibis Press, and author of *The Jirí Chronicles* (2007), *Drought* (1997), *What the Body Requires* (2009), and *Prayers of an Accidental Nature* (1999). Awards include a James C. McCormick Fellowship in Fiction, AAUW Thorpe Menn Literary Excellence Award, and *DIAGRAM* Innovative Fiction Contest Prize. Her fiction is included in leading anthologies of innovative writing and has been adapted to film, radio, theatre, and audio in the U.S. and abroad.

JOHN DOMINI's recent books include a selection of essays and criticism, *The Sea God's Herb*, and the short fiction collection, *MOVIEOLA!* (2015). *A Tomb on the Periphery* (2008), the second installment of his Naples trilogy, was a finalist for Gival Press's 2005 Novel Award. *The Color Inside a Melon*, the final installment, is forthcoming in 2016. Domini has received numerous accolades, including an NEA Fellowship.

JOHANNA DRUCKER is the Breslauer Professor of Bibliographical Studies at UCLA and has published widely on topics related to aesthetics, visual poetry, and digital humanities. In addition to her academic work, Drucker has produced artists books and projects that are the subject of a travelling retrospective, *Druckworks*, Her recent titles include *Stochastic Poetics* (2012), *What Is* (2013), *Diagrammatic Writing* (2014), and *Graphesis* (2014).

MARK DUCHARME is the author of *The Unfinished* (2013). Other print titles include *Answer* (2011), *The Sensory Cabinet* (2007), *Infinity Subsections* (2004), and *Cosmopolitan Tremble (2002). The Found Titles Project* (2009) was published electronically. His work has appeared widely in journals, and has recently been included in *Water, Water Everywhere* (2014), edited by Jennifer Heath, and is forthcoming in *Poets for Living Waters* (2015), edited by Heidi Lynn Staples and Amy King.

BRIAN EVENSON is the author of a dozen books of fiction, most recently the story collection *Windeye* (2012) and the novel *Immobility* (2012), both of which were finalists for a Shirley Jackson Award. He is the recipient of three O. Henry Prizes as well as an NEA fellowship. His work has been translated into French, Italian, Spanish, Japanese and Slovenian. He lives and works in Valencia, CA where he teaches at CalArts.

THALIA FIELD's most recent works include *Bird Lovers, Backyard* (2010) and *A Prank of Georges* (2010). Her novel "Experimental Animals (A Reality Fiction)" is forthcoming from Solid Objects, and her next collaboration with Abigail Lang "Leave to Remain" is on its way!

PATRICIA FOSTER is the author of the memoir *All the Lost Girls* (2000), and a book of essays, *Just beneath My Skin* (2004). She is the editor of *Minding the Body* (1995); and *Sister to Sister* (1996); coeditor of *The Healing Circle* (1998) with Mary Swander and *Understanding the Essay* (2012) with Jeff Porter. She has published over fifty essays and stories in literary magazines. Ten of her essays have been named Notable Essays in the *Best American Essays*. She is a professor in the MFA Program in Nonfiction at the University of Iowa. She has also taught writing in France, Australia, Italy, Czech Republic, and Spain.

TONYA M. FOSTER is a New Orleans native living in Harlem and author of *A Swarm of Bees in High Court* (2015). Her work has been published in *Callaloo*, *Tripwire*, *MiPOESIAS*, the *Hat*, *Lungfull*, and elsewhere. A recipient of various awards, she is writing a dissertation and often thinking about home.

JOANNA FUHRMAN is the author of five books of poetry, most recently *Pageant* (2009) and *The Year of Yellow Butterflies* (2015). She teaches poetry writing at Rutgers and in private workshops.

FRED GARDAPHE is Distinguished Professor of English and Italian American studies at Queens College, CUNY and the John D. Calandra Italian American Institute. His books include *Italian Signs, American Streets* (1996), *Dagoes Read* (1997), *Moustache Pete is Dead!* (1997), *Leaving Little Italy* (2003), and *From Wiseguys to Wise Men* (2006). He is cofounding coeditor of *VIA: Voices in Italian Americana* and editor of the *Italian/American Culture* series from SUNY Press.

GEOFFREY GATZA is an award-winning editor, publisher and poet. He was named by the Huffington Post as one of the Top 200 Advocates for American Poetry (2013). He is the author of *Apollo* (2013), *Secrets of My Prison House* (2010), *Kenmore* (2008) and *HouseCat Kung Fu* (2009). He is the editor and Publisher of the small press BlazeVOX. He lives in Kenmore, NY with his girlfriend and two beloved cats.

GABRIEL GUDDING's books include *Literature for Nonhumans* (2015), *Rhode Island Notebook* (2007), and *A Defense of Poetry* (2002). His essays and poems have appeared in *Harper's Magazine*, the *Nation*, *Journal of the History of Ideas*, *Great American Prose Poems*, *Best American Poetry 2010*, and the *&Now Awards*. His translations from Spanish appear in the *Oxford Book of Latin American Poetry*, *Poems for the Millennium, Volume Three*, and the *Whole Island*. His work has been translated into French, Spanish, Portuguese, Danish, and Vietnamese.

DAVID HAMILTON is in retirement after years enough teaching at the University of Iowa. He has new essays out in *december* and *Chaucer Review*, a poem in *Midwestern Gothic*, and works on more. Books to date are *Deep River* (2014), recently reprinted by the University of Missouri Press, and a volume of poems, *Ossabaw* (2006), from Salt Publications in the UK.

ROBERTO HARRISON is the author of three collections of poetry: *Counter Daemons* (2006), *Os* (2006), and *bicycle* (2015), as well as many chapbooks, including *Bridge of the World* (2011). With Andrew Levy he published and edited *Crayon* magazine from 1997 to 2008. He currently publishes and edits the Bronze Skull Press chapbook series. He lives and works in Milwaukee with his wife, the poet Brenda Cárdenas.

ELIZABETH HATMAKER is the author of *Girl in Two Pieces* (2010). Her poetry is featured in *Life As We Show It* (2009), *ACM*, *Bird Dog*, *Epoch*, *MiPOesias*, *Mandorla*, *Mississippi Review*, *Mirage #4/Period(ical)*, and *Projector Magazine*. She teaches writing, cultural studies, film, and urban education at Illinois State University in Normal, Illinois.

QUINTUS HAVIS is a southern author currently located in Georgia, with work published in *theNewerYork* and *Heart*. His poetry album "The Sea Will Kill Us All" is due out next year. Currently, Quintus is daydreaming about you, wondering if you're thinking of him right now, and if that connects the two of you on a spiritual level. He certainly hopes so.

GREG HEWETT is the author of *darkacre* (2010), *The Eros Conspiracy* (2006), *Red Suburb* (2002), and *To Collect the Flesh* (1996)—poetry collections that have received a Publishing Triangle Award, and have been finalists for two Minnesota Book Award nominations and a Lambda Book Award. His fifth book, *Blindsight*, is forthcoming from Coffee House Press. He is Professor of English at Carleton College in Northfield, Minnesota.

LILY HOANG is the author of four books, including *Changing* (2008), recipient of a PEN Open Books Award. With Joshua Marie Wilkinson, she edited the anthology *The Force of What's Possible* (2014). She teaches in the MFA program at New Mexico State University, where she is Associate Department Head and Prose Editor for Puerto del Sol.

PAUL HOOVER is the author of fifteen poetry books, most recently *Desolation: Souvenir* (2012), *Sonnet 56* (2009), *Edge and Fold* (2006), and *Poems in Spanish* (2005). He has also published *Fables of Representation* (2004). Professor of Creative Writing at San Francisco State University, he is editor of the anthology, *Postmodern American Poetry* ([1994] 2013) and coeditor, with Maxine Chernoff, of the literary magazine *New American Writing*.

TIM HUNT's publications include the collections *Fault Lines* (2009) and *The Tao of Twang* (2014); and the chapbooks *Lake County Diamond* (1986), *Redneck Yoga* (2010), and *Thirteen Ways of Talking to a Black Bird* (2013). Awards include the Chester H. Jones National Poetry Prize and two Pushcart Prize nominations. His academic work includes *The Collected Poetry of Robinson Jeffers* (1988, 2000) and two critical studies of Jack Kerouac. Originally from northern California, he and his wife, Susan, live in Normal, Illinois.

KENT JOHNSON has most recently published a book of fictional criticism, *A Question Mark above the Sun* (2012), and a long-poem chapbook, *Homage to Villon* (2014), and *The Black Herald of Madrid* (2014), a translation and annotation of César Vallejo's only known interview.

PIERRE JORIS is the author of some fifty volumes, including poetry and essays. His most recent books are *Barzakh (Poems 2000-2012)* (2014); *A Voice Full of Cities* (2014), a collection of Robert Kelly's essays, coedited with Peter Cockelbergh; *The University of California Book of North African Literature* (2013; volume four in the *Poems for the Millennium* series); and a collection of Celan's later poetry, *Breathturn into Timestead* (2014).

MICHAEL JOYCE's eleven books include seven novels, including *Disappearance* (2012), *Twentieth Century Man* (2014), and *Foucault, in Winter, in the Linnaeus Garden* (2015). He is also the author of a book-length sequence of poems, *Paris Views* (2012), a mixed collection of media essays and short fiction, *Going the Distance* (2013), and two collections of essays on digital media, *Othermindedness* (2000) and *Of Two Minds* (2001).

GEORGE KALAMARAS, Indiana Poet Laureate, is the author of fourteen poetry collections, seven of which are full-length, including *The Mining Camps of the Mouth*, winner of the New Michigan Press/*DIAGRAM* Chapbook Contest (2012), *Kingdom of Throat-Stuck Luck*, winner of the Elixir Press Poetry Award (2011), and *The Theory and Function of Mangoes*, winner of the Four Way Books Intro Prize in Poetry (2000). He is Professor of English at Indiana University-Purdue University Fort Wayne, where he has taught since 1990.

BHANU KAPIL is a poet of earth memory. Her poetry is briefly trapped in books. Most recently, in 2014, she performed multiple street actions in New Delhi, combining public ritual and non-violent protest against gender/sexual violence as part of a memorial cycle for Jyoti Singh Pandey (Nirbhaya). Her most recent work is *Ban en Banlieue* (2015). Bhanu teaches creative writing through the monster, architecture, and philosophies of time at Naropa University in Colorado. She maintains a widely read blog intended to cheer up anyone who reads it: Was Jack Kerouac a Punjabi?

STEVE KATZ started with *Exaggeratuons of Peter Prince* in 1968, won the America Award in Fiction with *Swanny's Ways* in 1991. Many books of fiction & poetry came between. Screenplays. Small films. *Antonello's Lion* (2004) is a novel. Then he published *Kissssss* (2007), a book of short works. *Time's Wallet* , a selection of his "memoirrhoids," arrived in 2010 followed by *The Compleat Memorrhoids* (2013), a total memoir in shattered form.

KEVIN KILLIAN, one of the original "New Narrative" writers, has written three novels, *Shy* (1989), *Arctic Summer* (1997), and *Spreadeagle* (2012), a book of memoirs, and three books of stories. He has also written three books of poetry, *Argento Series* (2001), *Action Kylie* (2008), and *Tweaky Village* (2014).

DAVID LAZAR's books include essays: *Occasional Desire* (2013) and *The Body of Brooklyn* (2005); prose poetry: *Powder Town* (2008); and edited nonfiction anthologies: *Truth in Nonfiction* (2008), and *Essaying the Essay* (2014). He is the founding editor of Hotel Amerika, in its fourteenth year, and is a professor at Columbian College Chicago.

JOSEPH LEASE's critically acclaimed books of poetry include *Testify* (2011) and *Broken World* (2007). Lease's poems "'Broken World' (For James Assatly)" and "Send My Roots Rain" were selected for *Postmodern American Poetry*. "'Broken World' (For James Assatly)" was also selected for *The Best American Poetry 2002*. The Academy of American Poets published Lease's poem "True Faith" on poets.org, and e-mailed the poem to 70,000 subscribers.

FRANK LENTRICCHIA was raised in Utica, New York, to working-class, first-generation, Italian-American parents. A chaired professor of literature at Duke University, he is the author of several highly acclaimed and often controversial critical studies; novels including *Johnny Critelli and The Knifemen* (1996), *The Accidental Pallbearer* (2012), *The Morelli Thing* (2015); and a memoir, *The Edge of Night* (1994).

ANDREW LEVY's recent titles include *Don't Forget to Breathe* (2012), *Nothing Is in Here* (2011), and *Cracking Up* (2010). *Memories of My Father* was published in a private edition by Innerer Klang. With Roberto Harrison he published and edited *Crayon* magazine from 1997 to 2008. Levy is a contributor to the President of the United Hearts' *The Big Melt* (2007), author of *Ashoka* (2002), *Paper Head Last Lyrics* (2000), *Values Chauffeur You* (1991), and other titles.

TOM LUTZ is the founder and Editor in Chief of *Los Angeles Review of Books*. His books—*Doing Nothing, Loungers, Slackers, and Bums in America* (2007), *Crying* (1999), *Cosmopolitan Vistas* (2004), *These Colored' United States*, ed. (1996), and *American Nervousness, 1903* (1981)—have been translated into twelve languages and have appeared on *NYT* and *LAT* bestseller lists. He teaches in the departments of Creative Writing, Media & Cultural Studies, and English at University of California, Riverside.

JODY MCAULIFFE is a director, writer, and translator who has directed new plays at theaters across the United States, including the Mark Taper Forum, where she was a National Endowment for the Arts directing fellow. An award-winning professor of theater studies and Slavic and Eurasian studies, she is the author of three earlier works, *Plays, Movies, and Critics* (1994), *My Lovely Suicides* (2007), and the memoir *The Mythical Bill* (2013), and is the coauthor with Frank Lentricchia of *Crimes of Art + Terror* (2003).

MICHAEL MEJIA's novel *Forgetfulness* (2005) was published by FC2, and his fiction and nonfiction have appeared in many journals and anthologies. A recipient of grants from the NEA and the Ludwig Vogelstein Foundation, he is cofounding editor of Ninebark Press and editor of *Western Humanities Review*. He teaches creative writing at the University of Utah.

MIRANDA MELLIS is the author of *The Quarry* (2013); *The Spokes* (2012); *None of This Is Real* (2012); *Materialisms* (2009); and *The Revisionist* (2007). She teaches at Evergreen State College and edits *The Encyclopedia Project*, the final volume of which is in production.

LAURA MORIARTY's recent books include *The Fugitive Notebook* (2014), *Who That Divines* (2014), *A Tonalist* (2010), *A Semblance* (2007), and the novel *Ultravioleta* (2006). She is Deputy Director of Small Press Distribution and is currently helping out at the Bay Area Public School at the Omni Commons in Oakland where she and Zoe Tuck just completed a class in Vampire Poetics.

LAURA MULLEN is the author of eight books: *Complicated Grief* (2015), *Enduring Freedom* (2012), *The Surface* (1991), *After I Was Dead, Subject* (1999, 2008), *Dark Archive* (2011), *The Tales of Horror* (1999), and *Murmur* (2006). Recognitions for her poetry include Ironwood's Stanford Prize, a National Endowment for the Arts Fellowship, and a Rona Jaffe Award. She is a frequent visitor at the Summer Writing Program at Naropa. Mullen is the McElveen Professor in English at LSU and the Director of Creative Writing.

SHEILA E. MURPHY has been published widely in the United States, Australia, England, and other countries. She received the Gertrude Stein Award from Green Integer Press for *Letters to Unfinished J.* (2003). Her most recent published books are the visual poetry collaborations *Yes It Is* (2014) with John M. Bennett and *2 Juries + 2 Storeys = 4 Stories Toujours* (2013) with K. S. Ernst. en.wikipedia.org/wiki/Sheila_Murphy

A. L. NIELSEN's most recent book of poetry is *A Brand New Beggar* (2013). Previous books include *Mantic Semantic* (2011), *Vext* (1998), *Mixage* (2006), *Stepping Razor* (1997), *Evacuation Routes* (1992) and *Heat Strings* (1985). *Tray* is forthcoming from Make New Press. Nielsen is the George and Kelly Professor of American Literature at Penn State University, and Visiting Professor at Central China Normal University. With Lauri Ramey he is the coeditor of the anthologies *Every Goodbye Ain't Gone* (2006) and *What I Say* (2015).

LANCE OLSEN is author of more than 20 books of and about innovative writing, including, most recently, the novel based on Robert Smithson's earthwork the Spiral Jetty, *Theories of Forgetting* (2014); *How to Unfeel the Dead* (2014); and *[[there.]]* (2014), a trash-diary meditation on the confluence of travel, curiosity, and aesthetic/existential experimentation. He teaches experimental narrative theory and practice at the University of Utah.

MAUREEN OWEN is the author of eleven books of poetry, most recently *Edges of Water* (2013). Her title *Erosion's Pull* (2006) was a finalist for the Colorado Book Award and the Balcones Poetry Prize. Her collection *American Rush* (1998) was a finalist for the LA Times Book Prize and her work *AE (Amelia Earhart)* (1984) was a recipient of the prestigious Before Columbus American Book Award. She has served on the faculty of Naropa University's low-residency MFA Creative Writing Program.

MICHELLE NAKA PIERCE is the author of eight titles, including *Continuous Frieze Bordering Red* (2012), awarded the Poets Out Loud Editor's Prize, and *She, A Blueprint* (2011). She is the editor of *Something on Paper*, the online poetics/multimedia journal. Pierce is professor and dean of the Jack Kerouac School of Disembodied Poetics at Naropa University. Born in Japan, she currently lives in Colorado with the poet Chris Pusateri.

PATRICK PRITCHETT is Visiting Assistant Professor in English at Amherst College. His academic work focuses on poetry, disaster, and the messianic. Among his many publications are essays on Ezra Pound, George Oppen, Lorine Niedecker, Ronald Johnson, Rachel Blau DuPlessis, Fanny Howe, Michael Palmer, and John Taggart. His books of poetry include *Burn* (2005), *Gnostic Frequencies* (2011), and *Song X* (2014).

CHRIS PUSATERI is the author of several books of poetry, most recently *Common Time* (2012), which was shortlisted for the Colorado Book Award. A librarian by trade, he lives in Denver with his partner, the poet Michelle Naka Pierce.

JED RASULA teaches at the University of Georgia, and is the author of *Destruction Was My Beatrice* (2015) and *History of a Shiver* (2015). Other scholarly books include *The American Poetry Wax Museum* (1996) and *This Compost* (2002). Rasula has also coedited two anthologies, *Imagining Language* (1998) and *Burning City* (2012), and published two poetry titles, *Tabula Rasula* (1986) and *Hot Wax, Or, Psyche's Drip* (2007).

MARTHE REED is the author of five books: *Nights Reading* (2014), p*leth*, with j/j hastain (2013), *(em)bodied bliss* (2013), Gaze (2010) and *Tender Box, A Wunderkammer* (2007). She has published six chapbooks; *thrown* (2015), text by j/j hastain with Reed's collages, won the 2013 Smoking Glue Gun chapbook contest and will appear in Spring 2015. She is publisher of Black Radish and Nous-zot Press chapbooks.

MATTHEW ROBERSON is the author of three novels, *1998.6* (2002), *Impotent* (2009), and *List* (2014), and the editor of a critical book, *Musing the Mosaic* (2003). His short fiction has appeared in journals such as *Fourteen Hills*, *Fiction International*, and *Western Humanities Review*. He teaches at Central Michigan University in Mount Pleasant, Michigan.

LASANTHA RODRIGO earned his PhD in English studies (creative writing focus) from Illinois State University. Originally from Sri Lanka, he draws from trauma theory, queer theory, postcolonial theory, critical race theory, and disability studies in his creative endeavors.

JOHN RUSSELL has published several stories in magazines and anthologies. The story that appears here is from a work-in-progress, "Where Have All the Girls Gone?"

SELAH SATERSTROM is the author of the novels *Slab* (2015), *The Meat and Spirit Plan* (2007), and *The Pink Institution* (2004). Along with HR Hegnauer, she curates Madame Harriet Presents: an occasional performance series. She is the Director of Creative Writing at the University of Denver.

DAVIS SCHNEIDERMAN's recent novels include the DEAD/BOOKS trilogy (Jaded Ibis), including the blank novel *Blank* (2011), the plagiarized novel *[Sic]* (2013), and the ink-smeared novel *Ink* (forthcoming); along with the novel *Drain* (2010). He coedited the collections *Retaking the Universe* (2004, 2014), *The Exquisite Corpse* (2009); and *The &NOW AWARDS* (vol. 1, 2009 and vol. 2, 2013). He is Associate Dean of the Faculty and Director of the Center for Chicago Programs, as well as Professor of English and Director of Lake Forest College Press/ &NOW Books at Lake Forest College.

SUSAN M. SCHULTZ is a poet, critic, editor, professor, and baseball fan. Recent books of poetry and poetic prose include *Dementia Blog* (2008), *Memory Cards* (2011), and *"She's Welcome to Her Disease" Dementia Blog [Volume Two]* (2013). She's the author of *A Poetics of Impasse in Modern and Contemporary American Poetry* (2005) and the editor of *The Tribe of John* (2014). She founded Tinfish Press in 1995.

MARK SCROGGINS is the author of three books of poetry—*Anarchy* (2003), *Torture Garden* (2011), and *Red Arcadia* (2012)—a biography, *The Poem of a Life* (2007), a critical study, *Louis Zukofsky and the Poetry of Knowledge* (1998), and many essays and reviews.

STEPHEN SPOTTE, a marine scientist and native West Virginian, is author or coauthor of eighty scientific papers on marine biology, ocean chemistry and engineering, and aquaculture. His eighteen books include three volumes of fiction, the memoirs *The Smoking Horse* (2010) and *My Watery Self* (2015), and a work of cultural theory. His technical books are widely read, and his popular articles about the sea have appeared in *National Wildlife*, *Explorers Journal*, and other national magazines. Spotte is affiliated with Mote Marine Laboratory, Sarasota, Florida.

STEPHANIE STRICKLAND's most recent digital works include *House of Trust* and *Vniverse*, both with Ian Hatcher in 2014; her most recent books include *V : Wave Tercets / Losing L'una* (2014), *Dragon Logic* (2013), and *Zone : Zero* (2008). In 2015 she was included in *Pushcart Prize XXXIX: Best of the Small Presses.*

COLE SWENSEN is the author of fifteen collections of poetry and a volume of critical essays. Her most recent, *Gravesend* (2012), was a finalist for the Los Angeles Times Book Prize. Her work has been supported by a Guggenheim Fellowship and a Creative Capital grant, among others. The founding editor of La Presse Poetry and coeditor of *American Hybrid: A Norton Anthology of New Poetry* (2009), she teaches at Brown University.

JODY SWILKY is an Ellis and Nelle Levitt distinguished professor of English at Drake University. He has published a chapbook of poems, *A City of Fences* (1977), and his poems have appeared in many journals, including *Yale Review*, *Georgia Review*, *Ohio Review*, *The Missouri Review*, and *North American Review.* He has received grants for his writing and documentary filmmaking from The National Endowment for the Humanities, Humanities Iowa, and Iowa Arts Council.

CATHERINE TAYLOR is the author of *Apart* (2012), a mixed-genre memoir and political history that combines prose, poetry, cultural theory, and found texts and photography from South African archives. Her first book, *Giving Birth* (2002), won the Lamaze International Birth Advocate Award. Taylor is a Founding Editor of Essay Press, which focuses on innovative book-length essays. She received her PhD from Duke University and teaches at Ithaca College. She is the Codirector, along with photographer Nicholas Muellner, of the Image-Text-Ithaca Workshop and Symposium, imagetextithaca.com.

STEVE TOMASULA is the author of the novels *The Book of Portraiture* (2006); *VAS* (2004), the novel of the biotech revolution; *IN & OZ* (2005, 2012); and the new media novel *TOC* (2009), which received the Mary Shelly Award for Outstanding Fictional Work, and has just been released as an app for iPad. He is also the author of a collection of short fiction *Once Human* (2014).

ANNE WALDMAN, deemed a "countercultural giant" by *Publisher's Weekly* is a poet, performer, professor, editor, cultural activist and cofounder with Allen Ginsberg of the Jack Kerouac School of Disembodied Poetics at Naropa University. Her over forty books of poetry, include *Manatee/Humanity* (2009), the feminist epic *The Iovis Trilogy* (2011) which won the 2012 PEN Center USA Award for Poetry, *Gossamurmur* (2013) and *Jaguar Harmonics* (2014). She has collaborated with many artists on stage and CDs, and coedited with Laura Wright *CROSS WORLDS* (2014). She is a Guggenheim fellow for 2013-2014 and has performed her poetry all over the world.

MARK WALLACE is the author and editor of more than fifteen books and chapbooks of poetry, fiction, and essays. Most recently he has published a book-length prose poem, *Notes from the Center on Public Policy* (2013), and a novel, *The Quarry and The Lot* (2011). He lives in San Diego, California and teaches at California State University San Marcos.

MARK WEISS is the editor (with Harry Polkinhorn) of the anthology of Baja California poetry, *Across the Line / Al otro lado* (2002), and the anthology of Cuban poetry, *The Whole Island* (2009). He has translated several books of Latin American poetry, among them, José Kozer's *Stet* (2006). His tenth poetry title is *As Luck Would Have It* (2015). He lives at the edge of Manhattan's only forest.

ROSS WHEELER is a writer and a photographer. He earned an MFA from the University of Iowa and a PhD in English from SUNY Binghamton. He lives in New York City and is currently the director fo the Queens of Macaulay Honors College.

SUSAN WHEELER is the author of one novel, *Record Palace* (2005), and six books of poetry, most recently *Meme* (2012), which was shortlisted for the National Book Award in Poetry. Recipient of Guggenheim and New York Foundation for the Arts fellowships, she was awarded the Witter Bynner Prize for Poetry from the American Academy of Arts & Letters and teaches at Princeton University. Widely translated, her poems have appeared in many editions of *The Best American Poetry* and in journals ranging from the *New Yorker* to *Talisman.*

ELIZABETH WILLIS is the author of *Alive* (2015). Her other books of poetry are *Address* (2011), *Meteoric Flowers* (2006), *Turneresque* (2003), *The Human Abstract* (1995), and *Second Law* (1993). Her critical work includes editing the collection of essays on Lorine Niedecker's writings, *Radical Vernacular* (2008). She teaches at Wesleyan University and was a 2013 Guggenheim fellow in poetry.

AMY WRIGHT is Nonfiction Editor of Zone 3 Press and the author of five chapbooks. She received a Peter Taylor fellowship for the *Kenyon Review* Writers' Workshop, an Individual Artists Fellowship from the Tennessee Arts Commission, and a fellowship for the VCCA. Her work appears in a number of journals, including *Brevity*, *Drunken Boat*, *Kenyon Review*, *McSweeney's Internet Tendency*, and *Tupelo Quarterly*, which are linked online at awrightawright.com.

LAURA E. WRIGHT is or has been a poet, translator, musician, firefighter, and librarian. She is the author of *Part of the Design* (2005) as well as various chapbooks. With Anne Waldman she has coedited two anthologies, *Beats at Naropa* (2009) and *Cross Worlds* (2014), both of which comprise work primarily transcribed from the Naropa Audio Archives.

KIRSTIN HOTELLING ZONA's most recent collection of poems, *Drift* (2011), was a semi-finalist in the Finishing Line Press Open Book Contest. Kirstin is the editor of SRPR (*Spoon River Poetry Review*), as well as the author of a book of criticism: *Marianne Moore, Elizabeth Bishop, and May Swenson: The Feminist Poetics of Self-Restraint* (2002). She is Cohost of *Poetry Radio* on WGLT, a local NPR affiliate, and Associate Professor of English at Illinois State University.

CREDITS

William Allegrezza: "if the disbelieving eyes could see," first published in *LIGHTNING'D*. © 2013 by William Allegrezza. Used by permission. "consider our direction misdirection." First published in *Otoliths*. © 2012 by William Allegrezza. Used by permission. "conform" and "the dance," from *Portlight*. © by William Allegrezza. Used by permission. "from *STILL. WALK*." from *STILL. WALK*. © by William Allegrezza. Used by permission.

Charles Bernstein, "The Lie of Art" from *The Battersea Review*, #2 March 2013. "High Tide at Race Point" from poets.org / The Academy of American Poets Poem-A-Day, Oct. 15, 2012.

Maxine Chernoff, "Fossil," "Saved," "Sleep," "Ballad," and "The Work of the Poem," from *The Work of the Poem in Free Versen, Saved in Lungfull*. © 2014 by Maxine Chernoff.

Jack Collom, "Passage" and "Oil," from *Second Nature*. © by Jack Collom. Used by permission of Instance Press.

Garin Cychol, "Prairied," from *Atticus Review*. © 2013 by Garin Cycholl.

John Domini, "Closing Credits Fun & Counterforce," from *Movieola*. © 2015 by John Domini. Used by permission of Dzanc Books.

Fred Gardaphe, "Italian Ices," from *Almanacco*. © 1992 by Fred Gardaphe.

Thalia Field, "Sweat," "Land at Church City," "Envelope Bag," and "Softness" originally appeared in *Incarnate: Story Material*; New Directions Press, 2004.

Gabriel Gudding, "Writing Literature to Benefit Nonhuman: On the Failures of Ecological Writing." Parts of this essay appeared in *Matter: A Journal of Political Poetry and Commentary.* © 2013 by Gabriel Gudding.

Tim Hunt, "A Truck Stop in Kansas," from *Thirteen Ways of Talking to a Blackbird* (2013).

Kent Johnson, "Into the Heat-Forged Air," from *Homage to the Last Avant-Garde.* © Kent Johnson. Used by permission.

George Kalamaras, "Letter to Don from Gunbarrel," from *Map Points.* © 2014 by George Kalamaras. Used by permission. "On the Brink," originally appeared in *Tupelo Quarterly.* © 2013 by George Kalamaras. Used by permission. "Symposium on the Body's Left Side," originally appeared in *ACTION, YES.* © 2009 by George Kalamaras. Used by permission.

Steve Katz, "Blues Borrowed and Broken," "Improvements," "What Has Been Done," and "For Ed Dorn" first appeared in n*ot enough night* (2010).

David Lazar, "Death, Death, Death, Death, Death," was originally published in *Seattle Review.* © 2009 by David Lazar. Used by permission.

Frank Lentricchia, "Part III: Still Life," from *The Italian Actress*, reprinted by permission of the State University of New York Press. © 2009 by State University of New York. All rights reserved.

Andrew Levy, "Brighter than any map ever seen," "Speak Up for Yourself," and, "My Father said it could Happen Here," from *Memories of My Father.* © 2008 by Andrew Levy. Used by permission of Innerer Klang.

Jody McAuliffe, "Bozo's Circus," from *The Mythical Bill: A Neurological Memoir.* © 2013 by Jody McAuliffe. Used by permission of University of Iowa Press.

Sheila E. Murphy, "Adagio," from *Pocket Litter* (2014).

Michelle Naka Pierce, excerpt from *Continuous Frieze Red.* © 2012 by Michelle Naka Pierce. Used by permission of Fordham University Press.

Chris Pusateri, "from *The Liberties,*" from *OR: A Literary Tabloid.* © 2009. Used by permission of Otis College of Art & Design.

Marthe Reed, "Awakening," first appeared in *Fell Swoop.* © 2012 by Marthe Reed. "Plaquemines Aquifer Report," first appeared in *Marsh Hawk Review.* © 2014 by Marthe Reed.

Matthew Roberson, "This Placed," from *Contrary Magazine.* © 2010 by Matthew Roberson. Used by permission.

Selah Saterstrom, "On Writing from the Exclusion Zone, Part 1: The Line," from *DREGINALD.* © 2014 by Selah Saterstom. Used by permission.

Susan Schultz, "Meditation on Meditation," and "Meditation on My Mother's Ashes," from Tinfisheditor.blogspot.com. © by Susan Schultz.

Mark Scroggins, "The Heights and the Grange" from *The Cultural Society* (2012), "Force Feed, Force Field" and "The Roué" from *The Cultural Society* (2013), and "Post-tropical" from *Cloud Rodeo* (2013).

Stephanie Strickland, "ALGORITHM," "MEASURABLE pleasures," "THE SAME interaction the same charge and enormous," "UNTIL recently considered not writing," and "BRIGITTA the Healer" were first published in *Dragon Logic* (2013) and are used by permission of Ahsahta Press.

Cole Swensen, "Sinclair" and "Debord," first appeared in *Prelude.* © 2014 by Frank Guan. Used by permission.

Jody Swilky, "Animation," from the *Georgia Review.* © 1978 by Jody Swilky. Used by permission. "A Small Gathering," from the *Georgia Review.* © 1980 by Jody Swilky. Used by permission. "Tenants," from the *Yale Review.* © 1983 by Jody Swilky. Used by permission. "Carnations," from the *Greensboro Review.* © 1994 by Jody Swilky. Used by permission.

Steve Tomasula, "Mem," from *Rampike.* © 2011 by Steve Tomasula. Used by permission.

Mark Weiss, "Different Stories" was originally published in *Poetry Salzburg Review* No. 15 (2009). The three poems appearing here are included in *As Luck Would Have It* (2015).

Susan Wheeler, "In Sky," originally appeared in the *Boston Review* © 2002 by Susan Wheeler. Used by permission. "Penny Lane," from *Vanitas*. © 2008 by Susan Wheeler. Used by permission. "Suppression," from *Times Literary Supplement*. © 2010 by Susan Wheeler. Used by permission.

Amy Wright, "of Minute Bodies Made by Magnifying Glasses with Observations and Inquiries thereupon," first published in *Kenyon Review*. © 2014 by Amy Wright. Used by permission. "*Agestrata*," from *POOL: A Journal of Poetry*. © 2014 by Amy Wright. Used by permission. "*Lepidoptery*" previously appeared in the environmental ezine *Canary*. © 2014 by Amy Wright. Used by permission. "Specimens, Mount 4," from *CALYX*. © 2014 by Amy Wright. Used by permission. "Collage of Thirty Dragonfly Species Headshots," from *Salamander*. © 2014 by Amy Wright. Used by permission. "Insect Time," originally appeared in *Ohio Edit*. © 2014 by Amy Wright. Used by permission.

EDITOR BIOS

CAITLIN M. ALVAREZ is the author of *True or False: __Break __Mend __Live* (2014). Her work has appeared in *Frontiers: A Journal of Women Studies* (2014), *The Reservist* (2013), and *Coal City Review* (2009). She served as a guest coeditor for *PoetsArtists* magazine (2013). She teaches writing in Peoria, Illinois.

KASS FLEISHER's most recent publications are *Talking Out of School: Memoir of an Educated* Woman (2008) and the novel Dead *Woman Hollow* (2012). She is the founding publisher of Steerage Press and teaches writing and women's literature in Normal, Illinois.

Made in the USA
San Bernardino, CA
19 July 2018